Russia's Economic Transformation in the 1990s

Edited by
Anders Åslund

CW01551833

PINTER

London and Washington

PINTER
A Cassell Imprint
Wellington House, 124 Strand, London WC2R 0BB, England
PO Box 605, Herndon, Virginia 20172, USA

First published 1997
© Anders Åslund and the contributors 1997

British Library Cataloguing in Publication Data
A catalogue record for this book is available from the British Library
ISBN 1 85567 461 0 (Hardback)
     1 85567 462 9 (Paperback)

Library of Congress Cataloging-in-Publication Data
Russia's economic transformation in the 1990s/edited by Anders
     Åslund.
          p.   cm.
     Selection of papers presented at four conferences held in June each year from
1991 till 1994 in Stockholm, at the Institute of East European Economics,
Stockholm School of Economics.
     Includes bibliographical references and index.
     ISBN 1-85567-461-0. — ISBN 1-85567-462-9 (pbk.)
     1. Russia (Federation)—Economic conditions—1991—   2. Russia
(Federation)—Economic policy—1991—   I. Åslund, Anders, 1946—
HC340. 12.R878   1997
338.947'09'049—dc21   97-19559
                                                                              CIP

Typeset by BookEns Ltd. Royston, Herts.
Printed and bound in Great Britain by Bookcraft (Bath) Ltd.

Contents

List of Figures

List of Tables

Russia and its Neighbouring Countries

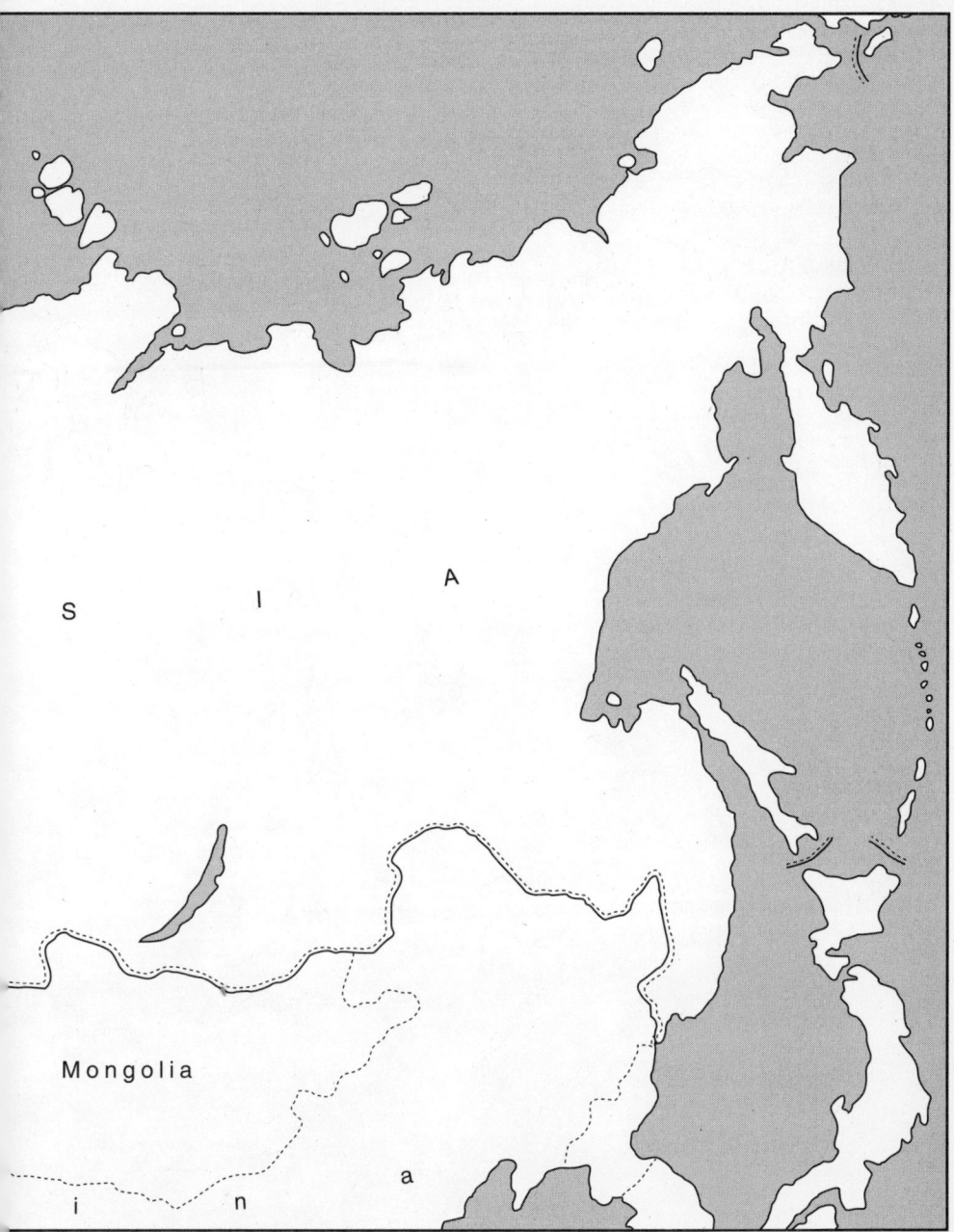

S   I   A

Mongolia

i   n   a

K identifies the Kalingrad Region which is part of (but physically separated from) Russia, and N likewise Nakhichevan which is part of Azerbaijan. The twelve countries identified by numbers are: **1** Estonia; **2** Latvia; **3** Lithuania; **4** Moldova; **5** Georgia; **6** Armenia; **7** Azerbaijan; **8** Tajikistan; **9** Kyrgyzstan; **10** Czech Republic; **11** Slovakia; **12** Hungary.

Introduction

At the end of 1991, when the Soviet Union still existed, President Yeltsin formed a Russian government designed to pursue radical economic reform. A veritable change of economic system was launched in January 1992, and Russia was transformed into a market economy. However, in comparison with reforms in several other post-Communist countries, those in Russia hardly qualify as radical.[1]

This book is a collection of papers on the Russian economic transformation written from 1991 until 1994, and it offers a unique inside perspective of the reform process. All the papers are written by people, who were deeply involved in the economic reforms, either as senior Russian policy-makers or as foreign advisers to the Russian government, and the articles were written at the height of the reform. They reflect what the chief reformers and their advisers knew and thought, while they were attempting a radical transformation of Russia. The contributors advocate radical reform, mostly supporting the government, but sometimes criticizing it for not being sufficiently radical.

The origin of this volume is a series of four conferences held in June each year from 1991 till 1994 in Stockholm, at the Stockholm Institute of East European Economics at the Stockholm School of Economics. At the time, I was the director of that Institute. This was a rare and important exercise in co-operation between Russian and Western economists favouring radical post-Communist reform in Russia. Each of the conferences resulted in a conference volume, edited by me and in one case co-edited with Richard Layard.

The first conference was held in June 1991, when the Soviet Union was plunging into a profound economic crisis. The meeting was characterized by a strong feeling among both Russian and Western participants that things could not go on like that much longer (Åslund, 1992). Most of the participants saw not only an horrendous economic crisis, but also an opportunity to make a fundamental break to a free market economy. The seemingly successful Polish radical reform dominated the discussion on what to do. Most also thought that the Soviet Union was over, and that we had to look to Russia for the desired radical reforms.

In June 1992, the attempt at radical economic reform had been made, but at our conference the mood was pretty sombre (Åslund and Layard, 1993).

1

The participants realized that the reform had not become as radical as virtually all of us had hoped for, and it seemed to be unravelling. Privatization had not really started, while the stabilization attempt was still fledgling, and liberalization had stopped far short of our expectations.

The April 1993 referendum offered a happy surprise with popular support not only for President Yeltsin but also for radical economic reform. In parallel, the mass privatization was making great strides. The June 1993 conference was therefore held in a cheerful spirit, but our optimism did not prove sustainable (Åslund, 1994). 1993 was a year of fluctuating policies, though also of considerable achievements. Subsidized credits, the rouble zone and import subsidies were eliminated

In 1994, it appeared once again as if financial stabilization was around the corner. However, the undoing of the stabilization attempt was already under way, as some participants argued (Åslund, 1995). The fall of 1994 saw no financial stabilization, but an exchange rate crisis, labelled 'Black Tuesday' (11 October). Only in 1995, a regular financial stabilization finally took hold, and inflation was brought under control in 1996.

These conferences attracted contributions from a great many Russian economists and policy-makers: Anatoly Chubais, Boris Fedorov, Aleksandr Shokhin, Yevgeny Yasin, Petr Aven, Maxim Boycko, Sergei Vasiliev, Sergei Aleksashenko, Vladimir Kosmarsky, Andrei Kazmin, Aleksei Mozhin, Vitaly Naishul, Andrei Vavilov, Leonid Grigoriev, Andrei Illarionov, Grigori Khanin, Aleksandr Bim, Aleksei Ulyukaev, Irina Boeva, Tatiana Dolgopiatova. Western contributors were notably: Jeffrey Sachs, Richard Layard, Marek Dabrowski, Andrei Shleifer, Stanley Fischer, Charles Wyplosz, Peter Boone, Ardo Hansson, Simon Johnson, Jacek Rostowski, Stuart Brown, Pekka Sutela, Brigitte Granville, Judith Shapiro, and Jaques Delpla. Many others participated, including Rudiger Dornbusch, Michael Bruno, Ronald McKinnon, John Flemming and Olivier Blanchard.

This volume represents an attempt to select the best and most cited articles. It focuses on the main contributors, but it also reflects an attempt to balance the selection in several regards. There are approximately as many Russian as Western contributors, and different themes are somewhat balanced. All the volumes are represented, though not with equal weight. I have tried to avoid several contributions by the same authors, though two authors do recur.

Many papers had to be excluded because they were dated, for instance, containing detailed predictions or prescriptions specified with numbers or dated statistics. Naturally, this approach leads to a bias towards reflective or historical papers. Since the papers largely represented a radical reform consensus from the outset, no balancing by views has been necessary.

Unlike many a Soviet editor of historical works, my ambition has been to provide the reader with the naked truth in original. Therefore, I have abstained from re-editing the articles, apart from correcting a few minor typographical errors, cutting a couple of appendices and a few tables to save space.

This volume contains eleven chapters, and it is divided into four parts. The first two chapters discuss preconditions of the reform. The second part contains three chapters about liberalization and privatization. Four chapters on macro-economic stabilization comprise the third part, and the last part consists of two chapters providing a social evaluation of the transition. Only one chapter has been taken from the conference in 1991, while four derive from the 1992 conference, two from the 1993 conference, and four from the 1994 conference.

The first chapter in this volume is my own 'Critique of Soviet Reform Plans', written in 1991. I think it is worthwhile to refresh the reader's memory about the state of the economic thinking in Russia just before the reforms. My chapter is a critique of the most significant Soviet reform plans. It draws lessons from the transition process in East–Central Europe. A major point in this chapter is that democracy is of vital importance for successful systemic change in formerly socialist countries. Moreover, surprisingly, many problems stemmed from intellectual inability to conceptualize a market economy. Typical flaws were an unfounded belief in gradual transition, implying both slow price liberalization and a gradual reduction of the budget deficit, while the socialist economists had excessive confidence in the capabilities of the state apparatus and failed to comprehend the high costs of transition.

Sergei A. Vasiliev was the author of 'Social, Political and Institutional Aspects', which also deals with preconditions for reform. It was written in 1992. At the time, Sergei Vasiliev was the head of the Russian government's Centre for Economic Reform — an in-house think-tank, and he is presently Deputy Minister of Economy. In this chapter, Vasiliev goes through social, political and economic intricacies. His conclusion is that, on the one hand, the preconditions for building a market economy are meagre in Russia. On the other hand, he sees no other solution than a market economy. Hence, he sees persistent contradictions that will lead to a long-lasting crisis in Russia. In particular, he doubts that macro-economic stabilization can be successful before substantial institutional changes have been undertaken, including the development of democratic institutions, privatization and a market infra-structure, which inevitably requires some time. Today, this chapter stands out as particularly prophetic.

In the part on liberalization and privatization, Marek Dabrowski has written the first chapter, 'The First Half-Year of Russian Transformation', also from 1992. Dabrowski was and remains a Professor of Economics working at the Centre for Social and Economic Research in Warsaw. He was First Deputy Minister of Finance during the radical reforms in Poland in 1989 and 1990. He remained a Polish MP and worked as an economic adviser to the Russian reform government. Dabrowski provides a broad assessment of the first half-year of the Russian transformation, comparing intentions with outcome. His general assessment is pretty pessimistic. Both liberalization and macro-economic stabilization had been half-hearted. Already the concept of the reform was not sufficiently comprehensive and radical, and the outcome had been considerably worse. Dabrowski emphasizes that the initial conditions were so difficult that the problems were rather understandable, but more lessons should have been drawn from the Polish experience.

Petr O. Aven discusses 'Problems in Foreign Trade Regulation in the

Russian Economic Reform' in a paper from 1993. He recounts his experiences as Minister of Foreign Economic Relations of Russia from November 1991 until December 1992. Aven is now President of Alfa Bank. He offers a forceful account of all the problems he faced. He draws rather diverse conclusions, sometimes defending the slow deregulation of Russian foreign trade, but his main lesson is that 'any obstacle to economic activity ... will be circumvented in Russia, and therefore, this country has to be more liberal than any other'.

Anatoly Chubais and Maria Vishnevskaya have contributed the chapter on privatization, 'Main Issues of Privatization in Russia', written in 1992. Chubais was Minister of Privatization from November 1991 till November 1994, as well as Deputy Prime Minister. At present, Chubais is the head of President Yeltsin's administration. Vishnevskaya is his wife and formerly his co-researcher. In this early chapter, they draw up the main features of the Russian privatization programme. The reader will by struck be the consistency in the government's privatization policies. This degree of correlation between a government programme, legislation and its implementation is rare in Russia. Today, we can see that Chubais knew what he wanted to do, and he did it.

The 1992 chapter by Jeffrey Sachs and David Lipton is called 'Remaining Steps to a Market-Based Monetary System'. At the time, both were economic advisers to the Russian government. Jeffrey Sachs is a Professor of Economics at Harvard University, and David Lipton was a Fellow at the World Institute for Development Economics Research. Today, he is Assistant Secretary of the US Treasury. Their chapter is a thorough analysis of the peculiarities of the Russian monetary arrangements just after Communism. Their view is: 'The monetary problems facing Russia are perhaps the most complex in world history.' They also suggest comprehensive solutions. Their chapter offers an outline of a whole new monetary system for Russia, but the key issue was to clarify the rouble area and its monetary regime. Much of what Sachs and Lipton proposed at the time has later been adopted, but not all. During the delay, Russia saw far too high inflation. (Two prescriptive technical appendices have been omitted.)

The most shocking failure in the transition to a market economy in the former Soviet Union was the maintenance of the rouble zone, in which several central banks issued the same currency without coordination, until late 1993. Brigitte Granville is a Senior Research Fellow at the Royal Institute of International Affairs in London, and has worked for a long time as an economic consultant in Moscow with the Russian government. In her chapter, 'Farewell, Rouble Zone', she tries to explain how such a situation could arise and analyses its effects. Granville reviews the arguments against the preservation of the rouble zone. A major consequence was a large outflow of financial resources from Russia to the other former Soviet republics. The overall result was high inflation in the whole rouble zone. Granville outlines the various stages of the dissolution of the rouble zone. However necessary it was, the dissolution was so poorly prepared and undertaken that two-thirds of the fifteen former Soviet republics ended up with hyperinflation. Still, the introduction of separate, increasingly convertible currencies provides a base both for domestic stabilization and revived trade between the former Soviet republics.

From December 1992 until January 1994, Boris G. Fedorov was Minister of Finance and Deputy Prime Minister of Russia. At present, Fedorov is a Deputy of the State Duma, chairman of the political party 'Forward Russia', and chairman of the United Financial Group, a Moscow investment bank. In his article 'Macro-economic Policy and Stabilization in Russia', he draws lessons from his time as Minister of Finance and reviews the state of affairs in the middle of 1994. He emphasized the lack of real macro-economic policy and called for a proper macro-economic stabilization. Very accurately, Fedorov foresaw rising inflation during the second half of 1994 because of this lack of macro-economic policy and government rigour. He argued that without full stabilization, production would continue to fall, while bankruptcies and unemployment would increase moderately, as indeed was the case.

Considering his great intellectual contribution to the Russian transformation and debate, it appears appropriate to let Jeffrey D. Sachs sum up 'Why Russia Has Failed to Stabilize'. This paper was written in late 1994 when Sachs no longer advised the Russian government. His fundamental argument is that despite all the uproar over 'shock therapy' in Russia, this did not really happen. He outlines what a true shock therapy should have entailed, but he observes that only at the end of 1994 had these elements formed the agenda of negotiations between the IMF and the Russian government, although all these measures could have been undertaken in 1992. The economic and technical preconditions for a real macro-economic stabilization have been established, but only gradually. In the meantime, public opinion has turned against reform, and most reformers have fallen out of government. Sachs' key question is how much economic mismanagement can Russian politics bear. We may add that the answer from the presidential elections in the summer of 1996 is: more than hardly anybody could have imagined.

The fourth and last part of the book contains two chapters with a social evaluation of the reforms. In a paper from 1993, Andrei Illarionov, Richard Layard and Peter Orszag assess 'The Conditions of Life'. At the time, Andrei Illarionov was chief economic adviser to Prime Minister Viktor Chernomyrdin, and now he is Director of the Institute of Economic Analysis in Moscow. Richard Layard is Professor of Economics at the London School of Economics and has been advising the Russian government continuously since November 1991. Peter Orszag and Andrea Richter (contributor to the next paper) worked with Professor Layard in Moscow and later on as staff economists at the Council of Economic Advisors of the US Government. Admirably, the authors go through and interpret all kinds of relevant statistics and put them in perspective. They found a substantial decline in average consumption, but a small reduction in food consumption. Social inequality as well as regional inequality had risen, as is generally perceived. The authors found that large families were worst hit by poverty, since child allowances had lagged behind other social transfers. Yet, unemployment remained low.

In the final chapter, Richard Layard and Andrea Richter reflect on 'Labour Market Adjustment: The Russian Way'. Their observations are rather controversial. Throughout the initial transition period in Russia, various bodies issued patently exaggerated forecasts of unemployment. In reality, actual Russian unemployment has stayed low by international standards. In this carefully argued paper, Layard and Richter go through all the plentiful statistical evidence at hand on Russian unemployment. They guide us through a web of seemingly contradictory numbers, and they manage to show lucidly and convincingly that actual unemployment in early 1994 was almost 6 per cent – in sharp contrast to the overstated numbers provided by the International Labor Organization in Geneva. Moreover, they established that the Russian labour market was characterized by a very high mobility. They found amazingly flexible real wages and few lay-offs. The problem in Russia appears to be less a problem of unemployment than of low wages of the working poor.

The two last chapters contain many tables and a great deal of statistics. Even if some official statistics used have been revised, the changes have been minor. I have preferred not to alter the statistics to show the picture as it appeared at the time of this analysis. A few appendices and figures of minor relevance have been excluded to save space.

I have added a brief epilogue to set the events discussed in this book in some perspective.

Acknowledgements are due to all the many participants in these conferences, as well as the staff of the Stockholm Institute of East European Economics, who helped organize this large project. The advisory project for the Russian government that Jeffrey Sachs and I ran was financed by the Ford Foundation and the government of Sweden. I am particularly grateful to Frances Pinter, who enthusiastically published the original four volumes arising from these conferences.

Anders Åslund
Carnegie Endowment for International Peace
Washington, DC
November 1996

Notes

1. In Åslund, et al., 1996, p. 219, we define 'radical reform' by two criteria – the degree of financial stabilization and the degree of liberalization. Both measures are made ex-post and no ex-ante. By our definition, Russia's reform did not qualify as radical, while the reforms in Poland, Czechoslovakia, Albania, Estonia and Latvia did.

References

Åslund, A. (ed.) (1992) The Post-Soviet Economy: Soviet and Western Perspectives, Pinter, London.
Åslund, A. (ed.) (1994) Economic Transformation in Russia, Pinter, London.
Åslund, A. (ed.) (1995) Russian Economic Reform at Risk, Pinter, London.

Åslund, A. and Layard, R. (eds) (1993) *Changing the Economic System in Russia*, Pinter, London.
Åslund, A., Boone, P. and Johnson, S. (1996) 'How to Stabilize: Lessons from Post-Communist Countries', *Brookings Papers on Economic Activity*, **26** (1), 217–313.

Part 1
Preconditions

1 A Critique of Soviet Reform Plans

Anders Åslund

First published in 1992

The Soviet government, the republican governments and Soviet economists are preoccupied with writing reform plans. Since the 'Ablakin Plan' was published in October 1989 (*Ekonomicheskaya gazeta*, No. 43, 1989), a large number of reform plans, partial or comprehensive, have been drawn up and many have been published. The purpose of this paper is not to discuss them in detail, but rather to bring out the major weaknesses of the most important programmes. I shall focus on the programmes, that is their declared intentions, leaving the implementation aside.

The choice of which programmes to focus upon is clear-cut. First of all, the current union government programme stands out as a guideline. Its present form is the draft of Prime Minister Valentin Pavlov's 'Anti-crisis Programme' ('Programma deistvii', 1991), which was presented to the USSR Supreme Soviet on 22 April 1991 (*Izvestiya*, 23 April 1991), though it was explicitly introduced as a further elaboration of the 'Basic Guidelines on Economic Stabilization and Transition to a Market Economy' ('Osnovnye', 1990), which in turn were presented as President Mikhail Gorbachev's programme and adopted by the USSR Supreme Soviet on 19 October 1990. The natural contrast to the government programme remains the 500-day or Shatalin Programme of August 1990 (*Perekhod*, 1990). I shall also pay some attention to the rather short programme of the RSFSR government which was adopted on 12 May 1991 by the RSFSR Supreme Soviet. In many ways, it is a sequel to the 500-day programme, but there are significant differences and it is clearly designed for the RSFSR, omitting concerns unique to the Union.[1]

My intention is to contrast these programmes with the mainstream of the Western and East European literature on systemic change in socialist economies. All of a sudden, a substantial literature of this kind has emerged. On a number of points a broad consensus prevails among Western and East European economists.[2] First, 'the transition must be achieved rapidly if it is to stand a chance of success' (Dornbusch, 1991, Summary). Second, the transition must imply a comprehensive switch to a fully-fledged market

11

economy with a strict macro-economic stabilization policy, together with a comprehensive domestic and external liberalization. The domestic liberalization should comprise the freedom of entrepreneurship, production, sales, purchases and pricing. Foreign trade needs to be liberalized which requires a unified exchange rate. Differences remain on whether the exchange rate should remain floating or be fixed in order to serve as an anchor for the stabilization (Lipton and Sachs, 1990a; Blanchard *et al.*, 1991).[3] Some issues, notably privatization, are still subject to extensive dispute, and no obvious road to success has emerged so far.[4] Moreover, the details of the future society with all its institutions are far from elaboration.

Given these assumptions, what are the major shortcomings of the principal reform programmes that have emerged in the USSR to date? I have tried to select the most crucial issues, by scrutinizing the key elements in a systemic change, starting with political preconditions, and continuing with intellectual comprehension, stabilization, liberalization and overall issues, though admittedly my choice must be considered subjective. I shall focus entirely on the initial stage of systemic change and avoid problems that become evident later on, such as structural changes and ensuing unemployment, as well as the vital but controversial issue of the means of privatization.[5] Thus I pinpoint nine factors that appear to me to be the major stumbling-blocks for the switch to a new economic system in the short term:

1. neglect of democracy;
2. relations between the centre and the republics;
3. inability to conceptualize a market economy;
4. unfounded belief in gradual transition;
5. the budget deficit;
6. gradual price liberalization;
7. faith in import substitution;
8. excessive confidence in the capabilities of the state apparatus;
9. failure to understand the costs of transition.

As is evident from these formulations, I focus on the instruments of actions rather than the consequences of action or non-action (such as inflation or shortages).

Neglect of Democracy

An outstanding lesson from East–Central Europe is that no comprehensive economic change was possible before democratization. With characteristic vagueness, President Gorbachev evaded this point when declaring his commitment in Oslo: 'to stabilize the democratic process on the basis of broad social contract and a new state constitution of our Union as a true, free and voluntary federation' (*Izvestiya*, 7 June 1991). As opinion polls show, the bitter truth is that Gorbachev is highly unpopular in his own country and would lose a democratic election. The lesson the Soviet Nomenklatura seems to have drawn from the revolutions of 1989 in East–Central Europe is that any roundtable agreement or coalition government will quickly put an end to their days in power. Therefore, they are extremely reluctant to accept any real democratization. Since the Shatalin Programme, after all, was drafted with Gorbachev's consent, it is naturally coy about the importance of democratizing the political system. Many economic programmes tend to forego this point as a purely political matter.

Nor do truly democratic sentiments run particularly deep among Soviet economists. There is a widespread belief among the Soviet intelligentsia that workers and peasants are not 'mature enough' for democracy. In early 1991, it had become commonplace within a large part of the Communist Party establishment to speak of South Korea, Taiwan, Singapore, Spain under General Franco and Chile under General Pinochet as suitable models for 'a gradual transition to a market economy'.[6] However, this reasoning is seriously flawed. None of these states had a command economy or a Communist establishment to begin with; they had predominantly private ownership and a market economy. There the issue was the need to deregulate and liberalize the economy.

Why is democracy so important for the change of economic system in a formerly socialist state? First, it is a question of credibility. Nobody can be less credible as a marketeer and privatizer than a party that was created in order to abolish the market economy and confiscate private property. Second, legitimacy is vital, because the change of system will inevitably be very costly. Thus it is important to offer the population a leadership it can trust and support. Otherwise, mass discontent leading to serious social unrest is likely. Third, it is a question of interests. The Communist establishment represents all the vested interests of the old system. It is implausible that the Communist Party of the Soviet Union (CPSU) can succeed in breaking these vested interests, and even if it could, it would be much more difficult for it than for any other party in power. Fourth, economics must gain superiority over politics. Enterprise directors are more accustomed to listening to political demands than to economic ones, because they were politically appointed. Even if they are told to pursue economic objectives, they are wise enough to know that in the end they will be judged by their political loyalty.

In practice, the consequences of these limitations were well clarified by the abortive attempts by General Jaruzelski to undertake authoritarian reforms in Poland from 1982.[7] Rather than turning to capitalist dictatorships in a wishful manner, the Soviets should focus on the experiences of Poland, to which Egor Gaidar (1990, 1991) in particular has given appropriate attention. Poland has long been the politically and economically most complex Communist country after the USSR: it was the largest European Communist country and its level of economic development and economic structure were reasonably similar to those of the USSR. Their cultural affinity is significant, although both Poles and Russians prefer to deny that.

Thus, the evidence suggests that capitalist countries can enjoy good economic development for a long period under dictatorship, though only at an intermediary level of economic development. However, for Communist countries, democratization seems to be an absolute condition for a successful change of economic system. This is something few Soviet economists seem to realize.

One frequent line of argument is that the Soviet military and policy apparatus are so strong that no systemic change can be carried out against their wishes. This argument can be countered in several ways. The military may be co-opted, persuaded or defeated. Still, the eventual outcome in all three cases should be democratization, though it seems plausible that time is needed to cajole the military in one way or the other.

Powers Must be Delimited Between the Centre and the Republics

There must be a clear division of powers between the union and the republics. In a series of draft union treaties the centre has gone ever further in the devolution of powers to the republics, but the problem is that no functioning agreement has been reached to date. This is hardly because of any lack of understanding, but merely a result of a prolonged political struggle over power between the centre and the republics.

One effect of this dispute has been the 'war of laws' which implies that there is no agreement on jurisdiction between the republics and the centre. As a result, nobody can know which law applies – if any. More frequently than not, there are two conflicting laws on vital economic issues that apply in the same territory. Without law, there can be no property rights and without these there can be no real economic stabilization or development.

Another consequence of disagreements between the centre, the republics and the local organs is that tax revenues are dwindling. Since all three levels claim the right to collect the same taxes, it has frequently become possible not to pay to any level. Significantly, the union budget received only 40 per cent of anticipated revenues during the first quarter of 1991. The rest, it seems, was not absorbed by other organs, but simply not collected (*Ekonomika i zhizn'*, No. 21, 1991, p. 1).

Obviously, no economic order can be introduced before the basic issue of jurisdiction is resolved at least provisionally. Most of the points raised in favour of democratization are also valid here. The government of whatever territorial unit we discuss must be considered legitimate by the vast majority of the population concerned, if it is to be possible to undertake a far-reaching economic change.

Inability to Conceptualize a Market Economy

Even reasonably knowledgeable Soviet reformers have great difficulty understanding what a market economy actually entails. It seems that travelling abroad is necessary but not sufficient to give reformers such insights. The preamble of the Shatalin Programme presents a relief in this regard. It clearly sets out the right of man to property, to economic activity, and to free consumer choice and the right of enterprises to the freedom of economic activity. However, it also grants citizens the right to 'just prices', increasing incomes and social guarantees, implying that many prices should remain regulated (*Perekhod*, 1990, pp. 5–12). While the basic principles of the Shatalin Programme are essentially market-oriented, substantial state intervention is envisaged when details are discussed. One of the worst lapses occurs in the section on social guarantees and wages, where a far-reaching regulation of wages is outlined, and a guaranteed minimum income superseding the average per capita income is suggested (ibid., pp. 100–6). Admittedly, these regulations are contradicted by the ensuing section on the labour market, but it is this inconsistency in thinking that is the problem. Similarly, after having declared that peasants should have the right to claim their share of the land and to leave a state or collective farm, the Shatalin Programme suggests that the resources for the next few years are only sufficient for 150–180,000 peasant farms, implying that peasant farms are to be both formed and equipped by the state (ibid., pp. 172–4).

In the government programme, a proper concept of a market economy is noticeably absent. The 'Basic Guidelines' restate a number of principles from the Shatalin Programme, though they are somewhat diluted: maximum freedom for economic activity, full responsibility of economic organizations, competition among producers, free price formation, refutation of the state to participate directly in economic activities (with exceptions) and an open economy ('Osnovnye', 1990, p. 1). However, the basic economic rights are connected with enterprises rather than individuals, and the rights of individuals and private enterprise are not specified. Evidently, the reason for this confusion is political or ideological, but regardless of the cause, such foggy language impedes the proliferation of an understanding of the market.

Still, the situation has improved. The most lucid and advanced legal document on the rights of entrepreneurship to date is the 'Law on the General Basis of Entrepreneurship of Citizens in the USSR', adopted by the USSR Supreme Soviet on 2 April 1991. For the first time, private (*chastnoe*) enterprise as well as hired labour were legally recognized without any particular limitations. Moreover, this law heralded the principles of 'equality between all forms of ownership, the freedom to dispose of ownership and the choice of sphere of activity' (*Izvestiya*, 10 April 1991). Thus, freedom of private enterprise has been legislated in the USSR.

Even so, President Gorbachev and the CPSU are only prepared to embrace private ownership in very limited forms.[8] Pavlov's 'Anti-crisis Programme' simply bypasses basic principles and is characterized by an extraordinary confusion between principles pertaining to a market and a command economy. Gorbachev made a typical statement on the principles of the reformed economy in Oslo: 'the intensification of economic reform in the direction of the creation of a mixed market economy based on a new system of ownership relations' (*Izvestiya*, 7 June 1991).

It is difficult enough to conceive of a market economy if you try, but Gorbachev and the Soviet government insist on confusing the principles by talking of a 'mixed' economy rather than embracing private enterprise. Similarly, the frequent references to the unique nature of Russia, implying that private enterprise is alien to the nation, further undermine attempts to move in the direction of a market economy.

A clear declaration of the need for guaranteed property rights of private ownership and a free market, followed by all legal and preferably constitutional guarantees, is required if a change of system is to gain credibility. The government must prove its commitment to capitalism. In short, capitalism has to be declared and to become a basis of the new rule, as it was in the East—Central European countries before they launched a true shift to a new economic system.

An Unfounded Belief in Gradual Transition

In the USSR, there is a nearly universal belief in the necessity of gradualism in the transition to a market economy. Indeed, this . was the outstanding shortcoming of the Shatalin Programme. Although it favoured a swift transition to a market economy over 500 days, it suggested that various measures should be introduced at different times, mostly without providing any grounds for the sequencing; nor was it possible to discern any economic logic in the proposed timing of events. On the contrary, both prior experiences of stabilization and systemic changes elsewhere, notably in Poland, and the dominant current of economic theory suggest that a swift and comprehensive change, comprising as many simultaneous measures as possible, is most likely to minimize the social costs of transition (Blanchard *et al.*, 1991). Naturally, the transition will last for years and be muddled by political upsets, but the aim should be to see it through as quickly and consistently as possible.

One ground for the Soviet appreciation of gradualism is common sense. The cost of transition appears to be less if the change occurs in small steps. This belief is partly inspired by lingering notions of central planning. It is far too common to aspire to plan oneself out of the old system rather than to formulate a general strategy.

Another argument for gradualism, primarily used by former Deputy Prime Minister Leonid Abalkin, is that the Bolsheviks had pursued fast changes and that it would be wrong to do the same as they had done in reverse. This is an untenable argument. Current decision-makers should not avoid policies simply because they are reminiscent of the Bolsheviks. Obviously, the needs of any particular situation must be considered on their own merits.

In fact, gradualism is probably preferred simply because it is the ordinary way of administration — taking one decision after the other without considering any coordination. Furthermore, the Russian mentality is widely perceived as conservative and resistant to change. If any alteration is required, it had better be gradual. These sentiments are reinforced by all members of the old establishment who want a minimum of change. Progressive proponents of gradualism would be well advised to scrutinize the actual reasons for gradualism seen by conservatives and draw their own conclusions.

A refreshing exception is the RSFSR programme for economic stabilization and transition to a market economy. It states in all clarity: 'There is one conclusion: a gradual transition from a planned to a market economy is impossible.' However, by the next page, it has lapsed into a contradiction: 'To move gradually to a market mechanism of price formation' ('Programma Pravitel'stva', 1991, pp. 2–3).

The Budget Deficit Must be Eliminated

A major conclusion of the general stabilization theory is that when inflationary expectations are high, it is vital to pursue policies which reduce them drastically. One such standard device is to eliminate the budget deficit. It could also be argued that in former Communist countries, it would be preferable to have a certain budget surplus, as few instruments of a monetary policy exist or can function at the outset. The Shatalin Programme, though somewhat ambiguous, was basically in favour of a swift elimination of the budget deficit (*Perekhod*, 1990, pp. 44, 86–8). Still, it made the elimination of the budget deficit a top priority, together with control of the money supply.

The Soviet government, on the contrary, has continuously stated that it would be irresponsible to cut the budget deficit so much as to harm social programmes (*Pravitel'stvennaya*, 1990). Considering that the actual decline in the national income in 1991 was feared to be between 15 and 20 per cent (*Pravitel'stvennaya*, 1990, p. 6), this argument sounds nothing but populist. Such a fall in the national income would have a far greater social impact than social benefits amounting to several per cent of the GNP. The real reason was probably that it is very difficult to cut expenditures, especially for a weak government representing the vested interests of the old system.

Consequently, raising social benefits appeared politically more important than reducing the budget deficit. Thus the budget deficit was allowed to rise to possibly 20 per cent of the GNP, because social programmes and subsidies that have been considered politically necessary have grown extraordinarily (Åslund, 1991c). Typically, the anti-crisis programme suggests that the union and the republics should elaborate 'extraordinary budgets' without suggesting any target for the budget deficits ('Programma deistvii', 1991). A clear target must be formulated; and it must be above most other considerations, if any stabilization is to take place.

All sides seemed anxious not to cut defence expenditures significantly. The Shatalin group wanted to reduce defence expenditures by a mere 10 per cent and the government by about 7 per cent (Åslund, 1991b, pp. 214–15). Apparently, both sides were so afraid of the military–industrial complex that they did not dare to demand the necessary cuts from the exaggerated defence budget.[9] Hardly any disbursements seem as superfluous as the huge defence expenditures. The USSR wanted to maintain virtually the same level, although its defence commitment for Eastern Europe had been abandoned; much of its armaments production would go straight to scrap, because of the disarmament agreements; no apparent threat to Soviet territory was at hand.

The budget deficit must essentially be reduced through massive cuts, because in the transition to a market economy, traditional state revenues are bound to fall (McKinnon, 1990, p. 133). The profit tax rate has fallen to 35 per cent of enterprise taxes, while it used to amount to 55–60 per cent; turnover tax revenues have been very high and cannot be maintained at such a level when prices become deregulated and much of trade becomes privatized; the foreign trade tax revenues must fall with the liberalization of trade.

The first response of reformers has been to call for higher taxation for individuals. Thus, Grigorii Yavlinskii proposed taxation on individual property, higher land tax rates and gift taxes and individual tax declarations on a quarterly basis in March 1990 (Yavlinskii, 1990, p. 32). This response approaches the issue from the wrong direction. Instead, reformers must realize that the country will have to make do with small state revenues in the transition period for a number of good reasons. First, the state budget has traditionally been far too large, with expenditures amounting to slightly over 50 per cent of GNP. Second, the state apparatus is in no shape to handle large sums of money efficiently. It is better for the efficiency of the society as a whole that the money stays with the citizens. Third, it is vital to avoid the Soviet economy developing into a mafia economy and the best method of prevention is a maximum of liberalization: the fewer limitations there are, the fewer the opportunities to extort bribes. Fourth, since unemployment is likely to rise sharply in the wake of systemic change, it is important to stimulate supply and the creation of private viable jobs as much as possible. Therefore, taxes and tax regulations limiting supplies should be kept at a minimum. Fifth, it will take a long time to develop a tax-revenue administration in any case. Sixth, for a market economy with such a relatively low level of economic development, it would seem normal to have a tax burden of some 30 per cent of the GNP to judge by the experiences of successful market economies around the world.

Price Liberalization Should be Comprehensive

The current Soviet price structure is utterly distorted in all aspects. Any partial alteration will only lead to new distortions, which in turn will cause distortions in the real economy. If prices on only some goods are set free, substitutes will be exposed to an exaggerated demand. Since the original price structure is highly distorted, considerable shifts in relative prices will occur whenever some prices are liberalized. Repetitive sharp swings in relative prices are highly disruptive, both to enterprises and to macro-economic stability. The domestic price structure has no relation to relative prices on the world market, obstructing any liberalization of foreign trade before virtually full-price liberalization. The extraordinary degree of distortions of relative prices is a strong argument for a greater extent of free prices than is mostly the case in mature market economies. As long as a new free-price structure has not been established, no enterprise can know what its true costs are — which is a perennial argument against any bankruptcy. Potential investors will be dissuaded if there is no way of knowing or guessing future prices and costs.

Even so, every programme under consideration is in favour of a gradual liberalization of prices and justifies this with social considerations. A typically slippery formulation is to be found in the anti-crisis programme: 'to pursue a gradual reduction in the sphere of administrative regulations, with the intention of completing the transition to *primarily* free price formation by 1 October 1992' (my emphasis; 'Programma deistvii', 1991). The confusion on this point in the RSFSR Programme has already been cited. The Shatalin Programme was most gradualist on prices (*Perekhod*, 1990, pp. 93–8). Economists and politicians are giving in to popular pressures on the price issue, since the population at large seems to believe that the gradual liberalization of prices will bring about fewer social costs.

A Lasting Belief in Import Substitution

Currently, there is little understanding for protectionism in economic theory; and where it exists it is limited to particular cases, preparing for an outward-oriented economic strategy (Sachs, 1989, p. 16). There is hardly any defence left for import substitution: that is, the importation of capital goods for the domestic production behind high customs walls, but it remains the Soviet attitude. The traditional Soviet system was highly protectionist and a mercantilist attitude to foreign trade seems to have survived. It is widely considered preferable to allow foreign investment and to import equipment than to liberalize foreign trade. The anti-crisis programme calls for 'measures to develop import-substituting production and technology' (Programma deistvii, 1991) even though it also calls for the introduction of internal convertibility. Effectively, it wants to maintain extensive quotas and tariffs.

Although the Shatalin Programme advocates economic openness in words, the foreign-trade regime that it outlines is surprisingly similar to the government programme. Although the concept of import substitution is not used, the programme insists on the 'necessity of strict state regulation' of foreign trade, while the attitude to foreign investment is rather more positive (*Perekhod*, 1990, pp. 124–31).

Presumably, this dislike of free trade is a combination of the Soviet tradition of isolation and the huge size of the country. Foreign trade is also perceived as a speculative source of high private incomes and the black-market exchange rate is rightly considered to undervalue the rouble grossly. However, these arguments are essentially of a political and populist nature. With its high degree of monopolization and distorted relative prices, the USSR is in great need of outside competition to bring about a swift improvement.

Excessive Confidence in the Capabilities of the State Apparatus

The steady stream of demands directed to the state illustrates how weak a notion people have of what a market economy is about. The government programmes in particular are full of specific requests to the state apparatus.

Typically, the government is supposed to 'pursue an active policy to develop entrepreneurship' ('Programma deistvii', 1991) while it would be more appropriate to demand liberalization instead. All kinds of specific state actions are proposed, primarily in the fields of social and structural policy.

Not only would it be inappropriate for the state to undertake all kinds of activities, it would be impossible. The state apparatus has long been both overextended and overstrained and it has been severely reduced during perestroika — by about half its employees at central levels. It is also demoralized because bureaucrats and the old *Nomenklatura* are incessantly criticized in the media. Nor do civil servants know what to do in the new system, not least since the legal system is patchy and rudimentary. Their salaries tend to be fixed and thus decline in a time of inflation. The change of system requires completely new abilities and different state organizations.

The conclusion is that the Soviet Union should adopt much more liberal conditions than usually exist in the West. Demands on the state should be reduced to a bare minimum — to the essential issues, such as law and order, basic state institutions, providing fiscal and monetary balance, an infrastructure and a social safety net. State revenues should be reduced accordingly, which will happen more or less automatically. Naturally, this will imply that a pretty wild capitalism will develop, reminiscent of Charles Dickens' Britain in the 1840s or a wild west economy. But currently the most likely alternatives seem to be lasting misery or a mafia economy worse than in southern Italy, which would provide far more limited benefits.

Failure to Comprehend the High Costs of Transition

Two important lessons may be drawn from the initial transition in East– Central Europe. First, the previous level of economic development has turned out to be very low indeed, as only few had understood. Second, great structural changes are required, involving huge social costs, although it is an open question how large these costs will be (Lipton and Sachs, 1990a).

Regardless of how big each of these factors will be, the country will experience a shock. In order to make it acceptable, the people must be prepared psychologically. The Polish and Czechoslovak governments did a great deal to inform their populations about the imminent severe hardships. Hence, their populations accepted the consequences with surprising calm. The East Germans, on the contrary, have felt cheated, since the impending grand future suggested to them turned out to be more distant.

In the last few years, populism has prevailed in Soviet politics. It has resulted in a reluctance to allow price rises and decisions to expand social programmes without any real source of financing. Although the current anticrisis programme expresses great worry over the economic situation, it fails to clarify the severity of the economic situation, in particular since it contains virtually no figures. Thus the government is stuck in populism. It needs a source of legitimacy to overcome this tendency.

Poland offers an illuminating example of how fast the necessary transition can be. The Polish roundtable agreement of April 1989 was highly populist, because the Communists were still in power and the democratic opposition just added up its demands. However, in October 1989, one month after the non-Communist government had taken office, it presented a programme which possessed all the clarity one could ask for, spelling out all the harsh measures that were necessary for an economic recovery and systemic change (*Rzeczpospolita*, 12 October 1989).

Conclusions: Political Reform is a Precondition for Systemic Change

The concerns I have focused upon may be divided into two groups of problems, political and intellectual, though some issues involve both aspects. Unequivocally political matters are the neglect of democracy, the conflict between the centre and the republics, the lenience towards the budget deficit and the hesitance about price liberalization. In fact, they may be grouped into two main problems: the democratization of the Soviet Union and the new federal structure − and partial dissolution − of the Soviet Union. These are clearly the crucial initial issues to solve − at least provisionally − before a true systemic change can be unleashed.

Yet, surprisingly, many problems are primarily caused by a lack of intellectual comprehension: policy-makers do not understand what a market economy is; they believe in a gradual transition, in import substitution and in the bountiful capability of the state apparatus. They fail to realize just how economically backward their country really is. Also, the policy-makers' inability to recognize the economic importance of democracy is to a great extent an intellectual deficiency. On the one hand, this may arouse optimism, because none of these issues are all that difficult to understand. On the other hand, it makes plain how scarce economic knowledge and market-oriented thinking are in the USSR. Even if these foremost issues are being solved, there are a great many others below the surface which are bound to cause trouble as soon as any detailed economic programme is implemented.

A long-term problem is the shortage of all kinds of skills specific to a market economy. Initially, the lack of general conceptualization may be the predominant problem, but later on the poor knowledge of ordinary legal and auditing practices and management and marketing skills will become major stumbling-blocks.

It may seem strange that I have not called any economic issues difficult, but the reason rests in the very definition of our query − to investigate what factors within the commonly agreed economic framework hamper the initiation of systemic change. Privatization, inflation, unemployment and structural changes are later worries. It is also apparent that a great many ideas have already been tested and the lessons learned in East−Central Europe. The USSR stands to benefit from these lessons. Its leaders should look realistically into the Polish drama rather than wishfully at the East Asian fairy-tale. It is at least as important to learn from other people's mistakes as from their successes.

Hopefully, these observations have also cast some light on the role of President Gorbachev. To judge from his behaviour and statements during

1990, he has been steadfast on three issues. First, he has avoided arranging any democratic election involving himself, thus skipping true democratization, since he realized that he would lose. Second, he has been dragging his feet on the union issue and it remains uncertain how far he has actually travelled. Third, he has insisted on 'the socialist choice' and resisted mass privatization. As I have argued above, all these positions must be abandoned, if true change of the economic system is to take place. Gorbachev may shift his position on these issues as on so many prior points, but he has already maintained this stand for so long that his credibility is limited.

The parallel with General Jaruzelski seems apt. He could stay on only as President with limited powers (and not as party leader) and for a short period. Admittedly, Jaruzelski did not block the systemic changes, but he was a much weaker personality than Gorbachev.

This reasoning leads us to focus upon democratization as the most crucial precondition to systemic change, while there are also strong arguments in favour of a solution of the union–republic relationship as a vital precondition. It should be comparatively easier to find economic leaders who realize what is necessary; and an economic programme can easily be adopted from the Polish experiences. Therefore, the two political preconditions seem decisive, though they in turn are naturally influenced by economic and social developments.

Notes

1. For a discussion of the government programme of September 1990 (*Pravitel'stvennaya*, 1990), the 500-day programme, the Aganbegyan compromise (Aganbegyan, 1990) and the President's programme ('Osnovnye' 1990) see Hewett (1990/91), Åslund (1991bc), EC (1990) or IMF *et al.* (1991). The anti-crisis programme has been discussed in Bush (1991).
2. See Kornai (1990), Lipton and Sachs (1990a), Dornbusch (1991), EC (1990), IMF *et al.* (1990) or Blanchard *et al.* (1991). For a more universal argument for rapid change, see Olson (1982). I share the essence of these views, as should be evident from the rest of this paper.
3. There are still people who argue for gradualism. However, the arguments are not very convincing. One group led by John Kenneth Galbraith (1990) has simply failed to realize the depth of the crisis. Another argument forwarded by Mathias Dewatripont and Gérard Roland (1991) assumes the knowledge of costs, which means implicitly the existence of relevant prices and statistics, and that the very stability of society is not in danger. Their argument seems to be valid for structural changes in a stable Western economy but not for the transition process. A third group simply refuses to accept the cost of transition and thinks that it will be less if the transition is protracted – an argument for which the mainstream finds no evidence.
4. For a discussion, see Grosfeld (1990), Hare and Grosfeld (1991), Lipton and Sachs (1990b) and Åslund (1991a).
5. I have discussed these issues in Åslund (1991d).
6. Arkadii Volskii, Chairman of the Scientific-Industrial Union has mentioned Japan, South Korea and Taiwan (*Ekonomika i zhizn'*, No. 11, March 1991, p. 6). Kazakhstan's President Nursultan Nazarbaev has embraced Singapore, South

Korea and the Asian dragons in general (*Izvestiya*, 11 May 1991), while the first party secretary of Moscow, Yurii Prokof'ev has gone furthest, naming Spain under Franco and Chile under Pinochet (*The Financial Times*, 6 February 1991).
7. Philip Hanson (1991, p. 311) arrives at the same conclusion with somewhat different arguments.
8. Gorbachev's worst statements are to be found in *Pravda*, 1 and 2 December 1990, where he declared that he would never accept the private ownership of land.
9 I have been informed that there was a secret part of the Shatalin plan, suggesting larger defence cuts, but if it exists, it seems more significant to me that it has remained both secret and neglected.

References

Aganbegyan, A.G. (1990) 'Programma stabilizatsii ekonomiki i perekhoda k rynku (proekt)', mimeo., 11 September.
Åslund, A. (1991a) 'Principles of Privatisation for Formerly Socialist Countries', Stockholm Institute of Soviet and East European Economics, Working Paper No. 18.
Åslund, A. (1991b) *Gorbachev's Struggle for Economic Reform*, 2nd ed., Pinter, London.
Åslund, A. (1991c) 'Gorbachev, *Perestroyka*, and Economic Crisis', *Problems of Communism*, 40, No. 1, January–April, pp. 18–41.
Åslund, A. (1991d) 'Four Key Reforms: the East European Experiment Phase II', *The American Enterprise*, 2, No. 4, July–August, pp. 48–55.
Blanchard, O., Dornbusch, R., Krugman, P., Layard R. and Summers, L. (1991) *Reform in Eastern Europe*, MIT Press, London.
Bush, K. (1991) 'Pavlov's Anticrisis Program', *Report on the USSR*, Radio Liberty, 17 May, pp. 1–6.
Commission of the European Communities (1990) 'Stabilization, Liberalization and Devolution: Assessment of the Economic Situation and Reform Process in the Soviet Union', *European Economy*, No. 45, December.
Dewatripont, M. and Roland, G. (1991) 'The Virtues of Gradualism and Legitimacy in the Transition to a Market Economy', CEPR Discussion Paper No. 538, London.
Dornbusch, R. (1991) 'Priorities of Economic Reform in Eastern Europe and the Soviet Union', CEPR Occasional Paper No. 5, London.
Gaidar, E.T. (1990) 'Trudnyi vybor', *Kommunist*, 67, No. 2, January, pp. 23–34.
Gaidar, E.T. (1991) 'V nachale novoi fazy', *Kommunist*, 68, No. 2, January, pp. 8–19.
Galbraith, J.K. (1990) 'The Rush to Capitalism', *The New York Review of Books*, 25 October, pp. 51–2.
Grosfeld, I. (1990) 'Prospects for Privatization in Poland', *European Economy*, No. 43, March, pp. 139–50.
Hanson, P. (1990) 'Property Rights in the New Phase of Reforms', *Soviet Economy*, 6, No. 2, pp. 95–124.
Hanson, P. (1991) 'Soviet Economic Reform: Perestroika or "Catastroika"?', *World Policy Journal*, 8, No. 2, Spring, pp. 289–318.
Hare, P. and Grosfeld, I. (1991) 'Privatization in Hungary, Poland and Czechoslovakia', CEPR Discussion Paper No. 544, London.
Hewett, E.A. (1989) 'Perestroika — "Plus": The Abalkin Reforms', *PlanEcon Report*, 1 December.
Hewett, E.A. (1990/91) 'The New Soviet Plan', *Foreign Affairs*, 69, No. 5, Winter, pp. 146–67.
IMF, IBRD, OECD and EBRD (1990) *The Economy of the USSR Summary and Recommendations*, Washington, DC, 19 December.

IMF, IBRD, OECD and EBRD (1991) A *Study of the Soviet Economy*, Vol. 1, Paris.

Kornai, J. (1990) *The Road to a Free Economy*, Norton, New York.

Lipton, D. and Sachs, J. (1990a) 'Creating a Market in Eastern Europe: The Case of Poland', *Brokkings Papers on Economic Activity*, No. 1, pp. 75–147.

Lipton, D. and Sachs, J. (1990b) 'Privatization in Eastern Europe: The Case of Poland', *Brookings Papers on Economic Activity*, No. 2, pp. 293–341.

McKinnon, R.I. (1990) 'Stabilising the Ruble', *Communist Economies*, 2, No. 2, pp. 131–42.

Olson, M. (1982) *The Rise and Decline of Nations*, Yale UP, London.

'Osnovnye napravleniya po stabilizatsioi narodnogo khozyaistva i perekhodu k rynochnoi ekonomike' (1990) *Pravda*, 18 October, pp. 1–4.

Perekhod k rynku. Kontseptsiya i Programma (1990) Moscow, August (the programme of the Shatalin group).

Pravitel'stvennaya programma formirovaniya struktury i mekhanizma reguliruemoi rynochnoi ekonomiki. Proekt (1990) Moscow, September (the government programme).

'Programma deistvii Kabineta Ministrov SSSR po vyvodu ekonomiki iz krizisa (proekt)', (1991) *Delovoi mir*, 16–17 April (the government anti-crisis programme).

'Programma Pravitel'stva RSFSR po Stabilizatsii ekonomiki i perekhodu k rynochnym otnosheniyam' (1991) mimeo., Moscow, May (the RSFSR government programme).

Sachs, J.D. (1989) (ed.), *Developing Country Debt and the World Economy*, University of Chicago Press, Chicago.

Yavlinskii, G.A. (1990) 'Program of Economic Reform: Popular Support, Stabilization, Restructuring', in Aven, P.O., Shatalin, S.S. and Schmidt-Beck, F. (eds.), 'Economic Reform and Integration', proceedings of 1-3 March, IIASA, CP-90-004, pp. 27–38.

2 Economic Reform in Russia: Social, Political, and Institutional Aspects

Sergei A. Vasiliev

First published in 1993

When analysing the course of economic reforms in Russia, observers often draw parallels with transformations in this field, in Eastern Europe and Latin America. However, they sometimes overlook a specific feature of Russia's transition period, namely that the transition in Russia involves more than a stabilization and deregulation of the economy. It also constitutes a change of its basic elements, setting in motion a different mechanism.

In Russia, where Communist ideology and practice evolved as a result of the country's own historical development, the model of the centrally planned economy has been rather firmly rooted. The economic transition has been much easier for Eastern Europe and the Baltic countries, since socialism was transplanted into these countries, and was always perceived as an alien system, kept alive by force. Accordingly, most people there were mentally prepared for a return to a market economy. Indeed, the swift transition to a market economy demonstrated by these countries is a result of concentrated efforts by both their governments and society.

Meanwhile, the countries where Communism developed as an organic ideology (Yugoslavia, China, and Cuba) have to traverse a long and tortuous path to market economy and democracy. In 1989–1991, many analysts assumed that the people in Russia (the Soviet Union) would not accept radical reforms, with liberalized and rising prices as their first stage. Their assumption was that after price liberalization, mass public protest would prompt the government to mount social expenditures to an extent that would soon lead to hyperinflation.

Reality proved to be different in practically every aspect. The multiple price rises following liberalization in January 1992 did not provoke any upsurge in social protest either in the form of strikes or in any other action, whether organized or spontaneous. Yet, the process of change itself develops extremely slowly, which to a large degree is due to social inertia and institutional barriers to reforms. Thus, if we are to gain a clear view of the prospects for reforms, it is important to identify the social, political and institutional factors that will aid or impede economic reforms in Russia.

Long-Term Social Factors

Certain features of the Russian national character have commonly been regarded as serious impediments to increasing the role of the market in Russia. Indeed, traits such as the communal spirit (as opposed to individualism), contempt for commerce as an occupation, mistrust of the rich, especially of the newly-rich, and a grudge against prosperous neighbours have a long history. They impeded the development of capitalism in the nineteenth century and played a certain role in the socialist revolution. Naturally, they became even more emphasized in the post-revolutionary period.

No less important is the traditional Russian attitude of the individual towards power and law. For a Russian, power is always more authoritative than law. The lack of grass-roots initiative has been compensated by subordination to the initiative of the boss. Law was seen as just a nuisance in everyday life. While the boss's instructions or orders might occasionally be ignored, laws were never observed. Lodging a complaint with the powers-that-be, that is, the boss, the chief, or the superior administrator, was the most natural way of upholding one's rights in Russia. Turning to the court of law was condemned as petty solicitation.

The lack of respect for property rights and terms of contract arises from the same source. Over the centuries, the overwhelming majority of Russia's population had practically no property, and whatever it had could be removed any time by the arbitrary order of the authorities. Nor could contractual law develop, since the right of property is at its core.

For this reason the early Russian capitalist market was plagued by broken commitments. Business hinged on what we call common law and moral obligations, what playwright A.N. Ostrovsky termed 'the merchant's word of honour'. Of course, this 'word of honour' evaporated in the 70 years of socialism. And yet, the financial and industrial groups emerging today are very often based on kinship or friendship. Amid these vaguely defined patterns of property and contractual relations, bribes seem quite a natural instrument. They are still considered justified in pursuing private economic interests, but they also impose a burden on the economy, particularly the private sector, with additional non-productive costs.

On the other hand, there are also cultural and historical factors facilitating the implementation of economic reforms, for instance, the absence of xenophobia in business relations, and a public consciousness that treats Western businessmen as more experienced and practical than the local ones.

Achievements of Socialism

These specific social features of Russia changed little over the socialist period, but there were some radical shifts in social structure, which most experts tend to overlook. These shifts, however, are highly important for Russia's readiness to accept a market economy today.

The transition to capitalism, to a market economy, in earlier times always occurred in the environment of the traditional stratification of society with a predominantly rural population. Social mobility was very low. The transition process and the development of market relations were accompanied by revolutionary changes in at least two spheres. Traditional societies were broken down and stratification barriers between estates collapsed. Second, the process of urbanization swept the countries in transition, prompting huge masses of people to change their habitual way of life in the course of just one or two generations. Both these factors played a highly destabilizing role in the transition period and set the stage for various extremist trends and deviations in the ensuing development.

Russia today is in an exceptionally favourable position in this respect. The urbanization process is practically completed, society has achieved an advantageous homogeneity, and the geographical mobility of the population is high. Altogether, this creates favourable conditions for the development of a market economy, and contract-based relations between individuals.

Russian society is also much more homogeneous than the advanced Western societies, because its horizontal links are extremely slim and scanty. This is the heritage of the administrative command system under which all links in society were structured vertically and whatever horizontal links that spontaneously appeared were quickly suppressed. The abolition of the command mechanism has brought about the destruction of these traditional vertical structures. New horizontal structures are taking shape, albeit rather slowly. On the whole, this situation is highly favourable for market reforms.

Current Social Dynamics

Apart from the long-term factors that have a bearing on the course of economic reforms, recent changes have altered the dynamics of social forces and social expectations of the population in various ways. The process of polarization of forces was nearing a peak in 1991, when the country was fraught with a destructive social outburst. Expectations grew that new conspiracies and coups would erupt and bring at least some clarity to the economic and political situation, stop the disintegration process, and break the vicious circle of populism, which had a strong impact on government policy both in the Union as a whole and in the Russian Federation. At the same time, it was evident that extremist actions could not solve the practical tasks facing the country, but only destabilize the situation, possibly giving rise to armed conflicts between various groups of the population.

For the economy, the political developments in 1991 contributed to an accelerated production slump and hyperinflation was set in motion. Various

28   SERGEI A. VASILIEV

sociological surveys showed that pessimistic attitudes predominated among
the public, and there was no serious hope for any real shifts in economic
policy.

When the Russian president rejected his previous populist ideology he
created a fundamentally new situation and resolutely turned towards real
(however painful) socio-economic change, creating a fundamentally new
situation. His turn offered a way out of the standard logic of revolutionary
crisis, which usually entails a social explosion and dictatorship following the
polarization of social forces. Instead, a radical change of system in Russia
could be implemented with smoother, peaceful political methods.

This, however, was in itself laden with socio-political dangers. To pursue
economic stabilization, and in particular a radical reform of a liberal type,
amid a profound crisis, inevitably aggravates the social situation and entails
considerable expenses for almost all strata of the population. The question
that naturally arose was whether the people were prepared to go through
such a reform despite the considerable cost, and thus whether the reform
would work.

Historical experience and common sense indicate that economic stabilization and subsequent reforms produce the best results in a society that has
been recently hit by social upheavals, high unemployment, and hyperinflation. In these conditions, the people's expectations are lower, and the bulk of
the population are prepared to pay a high price for the restoration of
economic stability.

In this respect, the situation in the country in early 1992 was rather
ambiguous. Although no explosive effect was evident, social attitudes were
blunted by fatigue, the people were no longer responsive to slogans calling
for violence, war, or confrontation of classes. The popularity of the president
who led the government of unpopular reforms was still rather high. There
were no indications of a 'revolution of expectations'. Hopes for an economic
miracle were practically exhausted, and nearly two-thirds of the population
did not believe the crisis could be overcome without declining standards of
living. But the potential threat of mass discontent remains an essential
element in the country's political life, and must be reckoned with the
economic stabilization.

This threat has not materialized. Price liberalization and the first
stabilization measures caused no open social conflict. On the contrary, the
first stage of economic reforms were met with fairly high acceptance of the
liberalization and stabilization policies. As indicated in Tables 2.1 and 2.2,
public opinion polls conducted regularly from November 1991 to march
1992 in four major cities recorded practically unchanging attitudes to free
prices.

In some places (e.g. St Petersburg) the share of supporters of price
liberalization increased significantly in this period. In parallel, citizens grew
more aware of their own responsibility for their own well-being, implying
their acceptance of economic liberalization.

At the same time, the next stage of reforms is likely to bring about a
considerable realignment of socio-political forces. Certain conclusions can be
drawn from the experience of both industrialized and developing countries.

Table 2.1 Attitudes to free prices, 1991–1992. The table shows the share of respondents answering 'yes' to the question: 'Will the introduction of free prices help overcome the economic crisis?'

City of poll	1991 November	1992 January	February	March
St Petersburg	32%	28%	35%	45%
Moscow	30%	30%	33%	29%
Kemerovo	–	–	23%	19%
Samara	–	–	–	19%

Table 2.2 Attitudes towards price liberalization in St Petersburg, 1991–1992

		1991	1992 January	February	March
% supporting price	Yes	32	28	35	45
liberalization	No	25	33	22	16
% admitting	Yes	19	17	20	27
responsibility for	No	56	63	56	50
their own well-being					

In a reform aiming at the stabilization and deregulation of an economy, anti-inflationary measures face the least resistance. Indeed, inflation affects the interests of the entire society, while stabilization may be tackled at the macro-economic level.

On the other hand, deregulation measures, which form the strategic continuation of the stabilization programme, will encounter stiff resistance from various social groups, whose privileged status they undermine. Such privileges are all kinds of subsidies, credits on easy terms, and customs preferences. Each of these privileges incurs a certain cost on society as a whole, but the popular perception is that the cost in each particular case is insignificant compared with the lucrative benefits the group in question derives. A strong pressure group therefore tends to gather around each of the privileges to obstruct its repeal. During Russia's fast transition to a market economy, new pressure groups and corresponding political structures have not taken shape, while the old pressure groups are more or less demoralized at present.

Survey of Political Forces in Russia

Russia's political parties are small numerically and poorly organized. The parties' real political clout in an election will presumably depend on the strength of their candidates' appeal to the voters rather than on the party's organizational potential. The experience of the election campaigns in 1989 and 1990 indicates that so far it is the personality of the candidate, not the

programme, that matters to voters in Russia. The introduction of propor-
tional representation would accelerate the formation of parties, but it will not
change the situation radically or swiftly.

Trade unions and associations of businessmen and industrialists are also
only in their nascent stage. The traditional pro-Communist trade unions,
though retaining part of their property, financial resources and — formally —
their members, are absolutely incapable of exerting any influence among the
workers. Independent unions, though energetic and led by more intelligent
people, are still small and locked in competition with one another. There is
nothing similar to Poland's Solidarity in Russia as yet.

The situation is about the same in the entrepreneurial community. The
proportion of businessmen who belong to associations is quite small, and their
various organizations, as in the case of trade unions, compete in just about
every sphere of activity. Many businessmen are merely formal members rather
than active ones. This is not to say that entrepreneurs exert no influence on
the government, quite the contrary. However, entrepreneurs prefer to deal
with the government on an individual basis, soliciting specific privileges for
their enterprises. Of course, to a certain extent this devalues some reform
measures, but poses no immediate threat to the principal course.

Considering the status of trade unions and business associations, the
creation of a tripartite commission appears a mistake by the government,
since in this commission the government has to interact with two other
parties, the unions and business associations, which represent practically
nobody. The government's obligations are real, while those of its partners are
fictitious. In addition, since 90 per cent of Russia's economy is state-owned,
employers and hired labour are in no conflict with each other, and
consequently, the government does not have the role of moderator. In fact,
it is the other way round — the unions and employers are in conflict with the
government.

However weak the cohesion of workers and entrepreneurs, there are
already indications that the situation is changing. The state employees who
were hit hardest by the price liberalization (medical workers, teachers and
transport workers) staged well-organized strikes and managed to gain
considerable wage increases. Thus, soon the government might no longer be
able to ignore organized entrepreneurs and workers. Therefore it has to make
the best of the time left to draft and enact rules and procedures for the
interaction with the leading interest groups in society, in order to minimize
the scope for non-constructive pressure.

Since parties, trade unions, and entrepreneurial interest groups are only
loosely identified, we should instead look to the representative bodies of
power elected three years ago, and to a lesser extent, to the presidency, as
major possible sources of resistance to reform.

The Power Structure

The most essential element in Russia's political life today is the split of power
structures, cutting society practically from top to bottom. The split is most

pronounced in the upper echelons of power. The conflict between the executive branch and the legislature is certainly not of a personal nature and cannot be overcome by a mere reshuffling of posts.

The Congress of People's Deputies of Russia and the Supreme Soviet (Parliament) were formed on a non-party basis with candidates running as individuals. These bodies do not have close links with political parties, business associations, or trade unions. Deputies have poor ties to their electorate, since most of them stand no chance of being re-elected. The best organized groups in the Supreme Soviet, managers of collective farms and the old party cadres, are openly opposed to reforms.

In principle, the corps of deputies, connected as it is with the interests of pressure groups, cannot support harsh unpopular decisions. Given the absence of any clear stratification in post-Soviet society and the extreme weakness of political parties, parliamentary groups and individual deputies often come out as advocates of rather narrow interests that they purport are national concerns.

The government can interact with the Parliament through individual contacts with vacillating centrist deputies, who after all constitute a majority in Parliament, though their vacillation implies political instability. Another option would be to dissolve the Parliament and re-draft the Constitution; while this would provide for short-term stability, it would subvert the legitimacy of the government's further actions in pursuing economic reforms.

Before the presidential office was formed in Russia, the mechanism of parliamentary democracy itself (apart from the old Communist structures) blocked any decisive economic transformations. The institution of the presidency arose as a new legitimate branch of power, it provided an alternative to the Parliament of equal legislative weight, and it is capable of pursuing a sufficiently independent political course. These constitutional measures opened the way for reforms, but they also provide a basis for inevitable political crises in the future. This is the political price that has to be paid for a democratic, non-violent path of economic reforms.

The Presidency exerts a rather contradictory influence on the course of reforms. On the one hand, the concentration of power in the hands of the president and the additional powers to implement economic reforms that have been granted to him by the Congress eliminate delays in the adoption of legislative acts. This accelerates the process of reform. On the other hand, this concentration of power makes the president's apparatus a very attractive place for sundry lobbyists, and the solution of various issues may be decided not only by the knowledge and experiences, but also by their biases and personal connections of presidential advisers. Such personal factors have led to the adoption of many decisions on specific privileges for certain enterprises and regions.

At the first stage of reforms, one distinction of the executive branch is the degree of ideological thrust in its policy, especially in matters of principle. This is a necessary condition, if profound reforms are to be implemented, while political pragmatism, which is normally justified, becomes extremely dangerous. But it has proved difficult to follow this principle. The list of compromises the reforms suffered in the first months of 1992 is sizeable, though it did not surpass the critical limits.

Another feature of the reform government was that it lacked both a political profile of its own and any visible and reliable social constituency. Since its measures were unpopular in all social strata, the government simply could not have such a base. Instead the reform team has to be prepared for continual political manoeuvring. Yet there is not much leeway for such manoeuvring for the reasons mentioned above.

At a practical level, the government has to choose all the time between alternative alliances with influential forces in order to achieve a constructive interaction and political stability, so that it can pursue its policies. This has been possible so far, because of a balance of powerful groups, support for the government and the support of the president. But the events during the 6th Congress of Russia in April 1992 demonstrated that the government has to turn into a political force in its own right, but this does not necessarily mean any orientation to a specific social group.

The Relationship Between Politics and the Economy

Political life today is characterized by a low degree of social and political activism among the population. We can see indications of this in the constantly declining turnout of voters in local elections, the lack of mass support for practically all political parties and movements, and the absence of mass actions on socio-political issues. Sociological surveys invariably demonstrate that rallies, both of democratic and Communist orientation are dominated by pensioners and white-collar workers. Russian businessmen and industrialists are showing scant interest in political life. Exceptions to this rule are rare, and can be explained by personal traits.

The relationship between politics and the economy and their impact on the country has changed greatly since the reform government was formed in November 1991. Before, the economy was hostage to a political struggle, and it was used as a pawn in the fight for power. For instance, production slumps were provoked by strikes and local separatism, while duels over taxation and price between Russia and the USSR took place. The situation began to change in late 1991. Economic decline was getting out of control, assuming its own inertia and inner logic. Meanwhile, the depth of the crisis and the fall of living standards were brought out by the government's measures to liberalize the economy, to make inflation an overt process and to raise public awareness of the depression and prospects of unemployment. As a result, the population began to pay much more attention to the economic aspects of politics. Any government that wants to hold on to power must be able to convince the president and the people that it is best suited to grapple with the present economic problems. In short, the economy will become the field for decisive political battles in the foreseeable future.

If we look at the effect of social factors on the formation of reform policy, we can see that theorists and practitioners alike have suffered from a profound delusion. Their delusion has consisted of a belief that a correct policy must be based on a balance of the interests and demands of various social groups. Thus, a rational policy should emerge as a combination of the interests of all social groups, and the main objective of politicians should be to 'expand the social basis for reforms'. This approach may be justified in a stationary society or when the balance of various forces ensures a steady development of society. However, neither is applicable to a society in crisis. The present crisis of Russian society is of systematic nature. It was the 'normal' functioning of social relations in the old system that led the country into steady decline; and it was the principle of political consensus of the Brezhnev era that was conserving the traditional system and slowly pushing the country into a crisis.

The reforms have not arisen out of the daily interests of any particular group of people, let alone social groups, but rather from society's awareness of being in an impasse. In fact the reform runs counter to the daily interests of most of the population, disrupting established patterns of production and consumption. This explains the unstable, contradictory position of reformist governments. A society vexed with crisis tends to entrust its destiny democratically to a charismatic leader and a group of reformers, because it believes in their programme and sees no other way.

Hence the government does not endeavour to maximize its popularity, but it is important that its active opponents are not too numerous at the critical political moments. In any case, public sentiment during a crisis cannot serve as an indicator of whether the course of reform is correct or not.

Social Prospects of the Reforms: The Relationship between the Executive and the Legislative Branches

The chance of the preservation of a strong legislative branch in Russia appears slim for the foreseeable future. The deterioration of the economic situation and the social hardships brought about by the economic reform have been accompanied by a reinforcement of authoritarian principles in the exercise of political power. The situation is compounded, first, by the absence of consensus in society and in Parliament, and second, by the need to bolster state authority so that important political decisions can be adopted quickly.

But concentration of power and strong state authority do not imply the centralization of power, as power is concentrated in the hands of the leader and delegated down the entire administrative chain. How Russian state authority will be legitimized in the future will largely be clarified within a year. In the presence of two bearers of legitimate power, the Parliament and the president, there is a legal way to concentrate the entire authority in the hands of the president. The procedures for the formation of a government will be one of the crucial issues for the nature of a new political regime. In a democratic order, the weakening of Parliament and consolidation of strong state power will be accompanied by increasingly frequent messages from the head of state to the nation and regular referendums.

A simple dissolution of Parliament can hardly be expected. Parliament may stay put, turning in practice into a politically obedient body, sharply criticizing executive power but supporting it in time of need. Then, the president will have a wider choice of means for exerting pressure on Parliament than if new elections were to be held on a multi-party basis. He can issue covert threats to organize a referendum, or to discuss the adoption of a new constitution in order to put pressure on Parliament. In such a situation, Parliament is likely to turn into a committee lobbying for the interests of rather small and socially unrepresentative pressure groups.

Direct dissolution of Parliament would be dangerous, since it might enhance political instability and undermine the legitimacy of presidential power in the eyes of part of the population, and especially in the regional administration.

The consolidation of presidential power, with the establishment of strong legitimate state authority, should be copied at the local level. Local executive structures should grow more powerful, while regional councils should lose clout, regardless of their political colour.

But if strong state power fails to gain hold, with Parliament sticking to its guns and the president unable to get hold of the legislative structures, the result will not be the preservation of democracy and plurality. Instead the worsening economic crisis will increase the chances of illegitimate authoritarian rule being established.

Meanwhile, an aggravation of the economic crisis will be practically inevitable, as legislators will actively intervene politically in the functioning of the economy. At present, parliamentary groups do not adequately reflect the balance of forces in society. Therefore, a broad consensus in Parliament does not necessarily mean that a decision enjoys genuine majority support in society. The reason is that a considerable proportion of parliamentarians confuse their narrow factional interests with national and strategic aims. This is not strange, since industrial managers predominate among the legislators. As a result, their decisions tend to block radical reforms. All of this has the effect of discrediting those very institutes of democratic power, which makes the task of eliminating them so much easier for a 'third force'.

Social Prospects of the Reforms: Government and Society

The strengthening of state power in the implementation of economic reforms would give a greater scope of action for the president in forming the government and its structures. The government would become more dependent on the president, while the constitutional system remains intact.

Undoubtedly, the political stability of the reform course depends on the consolidation of state power. However, as Parliament's role weakens, the president–government relationship may be endangered, if the head of state no longer considers himself bound by earlier obligations to the government. Therefore it will be critically important for the government's ability to implement reforms, how the president will deal with well-organized pressure groups, such as the security and law and order agencies, while pressure from Parliament will be less significant as well as pressure groups formed by traditional rivals, such as the military–industrial complex and the agricultural industries, or entrepreneurs and trade unions. In principle, the government does have the leverage to prevent the formation of such blocs, but these issue must constantly be kept in mind.

The government's effective tool here may be to differentiate the granting of credits — and later — tax privileges. A large number of unpredictable factors influence the prospects of the reform. One important issue is that the government develops a more definite and well-established image. Essential features of the image of the present government should be: constant active moves, even if rather painful; a resolute rejection of any populist bent, and readiness to opt for unpopular measures, including allowing a growth of unemployment; a reduction of inflation; the saturation of the market, whatever the prices of the goods; and caution with regard to large-scale privatization. A large part of the population is aware that considerable hardships are an inevitable cost of overcoming the crisis but they must be convinced that the measures are effective, so that they sense that they can see the light at the end of the tunnel.

As in January, in the middle of 1992, the question will again arise whether the effectiveness of the liberalization policy should be measured by the amount of goods available in the shops. It is not only a question of inflation on the consumer market. First, the convertibility of the rouble and the liberalization of foreign trade must be tackled. So far this has been a weak point in the reform programme, but now it is possible to take decisive reform steps in this sphere. Second, the harvest will have important consequences. presumably deliveries of farm produce to the market will suffer from complications. Russian grain prices have moved closer to the world level and producers have reoriented themselves to free sales instead of the state, but because of inflationary expectations less grain will probably be available for sales. Meat supplies will be even more complicated, since production costs are increasing and production is declining. The situation will be worse if the Russian farm sector encounters foreign competition in the autumn of 1992. Imports of consumer goods will stimulate agricultural sales, while the influx of food will create dangerous competition on the home market.

However, the consumer market will probably become reasonably balanced in the course of 1992, which is highly important for the image and stability of the reform government. If the market receives first a certain minimum of goods thanks to the liberalization of prices and at a second stage more goods because of the liberalization of foreign trade, the main focus of social and political discontent will soon be the problems of stagnant production and unemployment. At present, the only plausible source of production growth is foreign investments. Therefore it will become an essential policy issue to attract foreign investment and make sure that they are used efficiently. However, before economic recovery starts, negative attitudes will grow among the population, causing a period of instability and unpredictability. If this period lasts for more than a few months, severe economic disruption is all too likely and it will pose a serious threat to the reform.

The Regional Dimension

The disintegration of the vertical power structures of the former Soviet Union prompted various regions of Russia to demand autonomy. Centralized authority within Russia has been greatly undermined. The traditional form of administration, which was based on the party's control and ultimately on fear and coercion, has disappeared, while a new, civilized interaction between power and society, based on the principle of law, has not yet taken shape. As a result, local government, which is located closer to the population has retained much more of its power than the central government.

Today Russia is often compared with the USSR, and many expect that Russia will disintegrate into a number of independent states. Separatist trends do exist, but in themselves they present little threat even in the long term. There are several factors that influence inter-regional relations. One important factor is the deepening economic crisis. The struggle for survival amid the severe crisis brings people's primary values and links to the foreground, such as ethnic and territorial identities. Growing economies are usually more inclined towards integration. But it is yet to be proven that integration helps to overcome a profound crisis.

Second, this is a case of the disintegration of a huge unitary state which in its present form is poorly adjusted to a market economy. A search is under way for the most effective political and economic territorial structure for market economy and democracy. In the near future attention should be concentrated on the issues of administrative and territorial structures, on the one hand, and the improvement of the federal system of government, on the other.

Economic difficulties will soon cease to dominate as a cause of regional discord, if the reform policies continue. Economic stabilization is impeding disintegration and promotes the formation of a national market. Neither ethnic nor political problems are so sharp that they will bring about a final disintegration of Russia. The dominating Russian nation does not suffer from any regional splits in its cultural roots or political links.

In order to curb the process of disintegration, a constitutional restructuring of Russia's territories would be advisable. No uniform federal pattern can be applied as current local developments are so varied. In contrast to the USSR, the present central government of Russia can conclude separate agreements with territorial governments concerning their scope of authority in its own right. The status of territories and ethnic formations may gradually change, eventually reaching a confederative level, which would not be very dramatic, if it is only caused by the geographic peculiarities of Russia.

Consequently, in order to ensure the success of the reforms as a whole, the central government will have to make significant concessions to regional elites. Deregulation of the economy means a shrinking of the sphere of political influence. In this regard the interests of the central and local governments diverge radically, as the local politicians want to retain power. The only way out is to transform local political elites into managerial personnel. This process has already gained speed: former party bosses are moving into recently founded commercial establishments, carrying parts of the state property with them.

This administrative privatization should be treated with a measure of caution. What would be even more dangerous is the fusion of new commercial establishments with new bodies of power, through which these new businessmen could gain privileges, such as monopoly rights. The emerging regional monopolies are highly resilient: they use their extra-ordinary profits to retain their monopoly position by political pressure and bribery of officials. This kind of monopoly presents one of the most grave threats to the reforms, since it blocks any local transformations.

Conclusion

This analysis indicates that while Russia's historical and cultural traditions are unfavourable for the development of a market economy, a number of prerequisites for market development, such as urbanization and social homogeneity have appeared in recent times. The collapse of the vertical links that were characteristic of the Communist society created an institutional vacuum in the wake of the transformation, but the weakness of democratic institutions makes the government vulnerable to pressure groups.

This contradictory state of affairs does not offer great hope for a speedy end to Russia's crisis. Institutional changes will apparently go ahead, albeit slowly. At the same time, the stabilization policy will come up against considerable difficulties. If democratic institutions are maintained, frequent changes of cabinets are inevitable, and at least some of them will opt for populist policies. In the near future, Russia's economy will probably face a sequence of stabilization and periods of high inflation, while the depression will continue. Only gradually can successful privatization and the develop-ment of the market infrastructure set the stage for long-term stabilization as the basis for future non-inflationary economic growth.

Part II
Liberalization and Privatization

3 The First Half-Year of Russian Transformation

Marek Dabrowski

First published in 1993

In the beginning of November 1991, the new Russian government started its policy of radical economic reforms. Its declared aims were the transformation from a planned to a market economy and macro-economic stabilization. This chapter will examine the first half-year of the Russian transformation. I shall discuss the economic and political conditions at the outset, the different possible approaches to reform that were available, the results of the first stage of the reform process, the situation in spring 1992, and possible scenarios for the future. Having the advantage of being an active participant in the Polish transformation process,[1] I shall analyse the Russian course of events from the point of view of the Polish experience. Therefore I shall try to compare the initial conditions in Russia with those in Poland, and, formulate a few lessons Russia can take from Poland's experience and finally show how the current Polish debate can be illuminated by the Russian experience.

Economic Conditions at the Outset of Reform

The economic conditions in which the Russian transformation was to begin in the autumn of 1991 were extremely difficult. The economy of the former USSR and of the Russian Federation was in the deep disintegration typical of most post-Communist countries in Central and Eastern Europe. In such an economy the central planning system has already ceased to work as a mechanism of micro-economic discipline and macro-economic coordination. Nor has a new market mechanism yet assumed this role. We have the typical syndrome of a non-planned, non-market economy, without sufficient micro-economic motivation or the means to achieve elementary macro-economic equilibrium. Moreover, the government is weak in the sense that it does not have political support, and it is prepared to buy temporary social peace in exchange for inflationary money. This scenario is not unique to the former USSR in 1989–91. It was also evident in Poland in 1987–89, in Romania after the collapse of Nicolae Ceausescu's dictatorship, in Bulgaria, and in Albania. Only East Germany, Hungary, and Czechoslovakia were able to avoid macro-economic chaos in the transition period.

The last two years of the former USSR were marked by a constant decline in output and an uncontrolled increase of the monetary overhang. In the past the money supply in the Soviet economy (as in other countries with traditional command economy) was permanently excessive by standards of a normal market economy. For example, in 1981–85 the average annual rate of growth of the money supply (M2, measured as cash, plus current and deposit accounts) amounted to 7.5 per cent (IMF *et al.*, 1990, p. 49).

This excessive supply of money combined with predominantly fixed prices contributed to the repressed inflation and forced savings, which seem to be a quite normal phenomenon in a traditional command economy. In the former USSR, however, the level of repressed inflation was probably traditionally higher than in some other socialist countries like the GDR, Czechoslovakia and Hungary. The monetary overhang was mitigated to some extent by the internal (or commodity) inconvertibility of the rouble, especially in the enterprise sphere, because of the thorough rationing system with administrative allocation of material resources and investment goods, as well as rigid monitoring of different kinds of expenditures (such as the wage fund, investment money, etc.) of state-owned enterprises (McKinnon, 1991).

In the second half of the 1980s the monetary disequilibrium started to worsen gradually. The traditional discipline of the central plan began to crumble because of the partial political and economic liberalization of the perestroika period. the money supply also increased. According to IMF estimates, the M2 annual rate of growth was 8.5 per cent in 1986, 14.7 per cent in 1987, 14.1 per cent in 1988, 14.8 per cent in 1989, and 15.3 per cent in 1990 (IMF *et al.*, 1990, p. 49). The rising fiscal deficit was the main reason for this monetary expansion. It amounted to 2.4 per cent of the GDP in 1985, 6.2 per cent in 1986, 8.4 per cent in 1987, 9.2 per cent in 1988, and 8.5 per cent in 1989 (IMF *et al.*, 1990, p. 10).

At the same time, partial economic liberalization increased the level of internal convertibility of the rouble (by giving enterprises more flexibility in using their financial assets), thus increasing money velocity. This is also a standard effect of the deregulation of the traditional socialist economic system (McKinnon, 1991).

The second half of the 1980s was also a time of significant deterioration of external balances. Current account balance in convertible currencies had been positive until 1988 (US$2.3 bn in 1986, US$6.7 bn in 1987 and US$1.6 bn in 1988), but decreased radically in 1989 (US$3.8 bn) and in 1990 (US$10.7bn) (IMF *et al.*, 1990, p. 10). Consequently, the gross external debt rose from US$28.9 bn in 1985 to US$54.0 bn in 1989 (ibid., p. 50). These developments were connected both with the growing level of internal macroeconomic disequilibrium (budget deficit and monetary expansion) and with the sharply worsening terms of trade, especially on the oil market (ibid., 1990, p. 50). Declining oil export revenues and oil profits, resulting from a steady decrease in oil production, also contributed to fiscal difficulties since oil exports had been a significant source of budget revenue.

The level of repressed inflation continued to increase because of monetary expansion, increasing money in circulation, and the continuing price controls. Until the beginning of 1991 the official consumer price index (CPI) was rather stable. The CPI in state retail trade rose by 2.4 per cent in 1989 and 5.2 per cent in 1990.

The retail price increase in cooperative trade was recorded as 0.5 per cent in 1989 and 5.2 per cent in 1990. The same indicators for the kolkhoz market were 7.4 per cent in 1989 and 34.3 per cent in 1990 (IMF, 1992, Table 11). These figures illustrate indirectly the increasing level of repressed inflation and forced savings. Carlo Cottarelli and Mario I. Blejer considered that

at the end of 1990 the amount of wealth accumulated in monetary form by Soviet households as a result of forced savings was around 170–190 billion rubles, close to 20 percent of GDP and around one third of the existing financial assets. (Cottarelli and Blejer, 1991).

After 1 April 1991, and the price reform of Valentin Pavlov,[2] inflation started to have a more open form. The average price level in state retail trade was 89.5 per cent higher in 1991 than in 1990, and the state retail price index rose by 146.1 per cent from December 1990 to December 1991. The consolidated retail price index rose by 152.1 per cent, and the kolkhoz market price index by 281.2 per cent (IMF, 1992, Table 11). Inflation (and later hyperinflation) in the second half of 1991 showed up partly in the form of open price increases, partly in the form of rising market shortages.

The rising budget deficit, financed exclusively by credit from the USSR State Bank (Gosbank) was a key cause of hyperinflation in 1991. According to IMF estimates, the total budget deficit of the Russian Federation in 1991 (including the consequences of taking responsibility for the former all-union budget) reached a level of 31 per cent of GDP (IMF, 1992, p. 13). The sources of this huge fiscal deficit were ever-increasing state subsidies to support administratively controlled prices, the decrease of output, and poor tax discipline.

This weakening of the financial discipline at the micro level brought about the fast growth of the nominal and 'real' wages in the second half of 1991. In the last quarter of 1991 the 'real' wage in industry was 33 per cent higher than its average level in 1990 (IMF, 1992, p. 11).[3] This contributed to the significant decrease in the real profits of enterprises.

In the years of perestroika, the economic growth of the USSR and the Russian Federation was lower than in the preceding decades and was gradually decreasing. The net material product (NMP) of Russia increased only by 2.4 per cent in 1986, 0.7 per cent in 1987, 4.5 per cent in 1988, and 1.9 per cent in 1989. In 1990 the NMP started to decrease: by 3.6 per cent in 1990 and by 11.0 per cent in 1991 (preliminary estimates, see IMF, 1992, Table 4). In the same period, gross industrial output grew by 4.5 per cent in 1986, 3.5 per cent in 1987, 3.8 per cent in 1988, 1.4 per cent in 1989, and fell by 0.1 per cent in 1990 and 8.0 per cent in 1991 (ibid., Table 5).

The main reasons for the 1990–91 recession were the crisis of the central planning system, the motivational crisis in state-owned enterprises, the disintegration of trade relations between Eastern European countries after the collapse of CMEA, as well as the gradual weakening of trade links between former USSR republics. After the political dictatorship and terror were gradually dismantled under perestroika, the system of central planning lost its capacity to mobilize resources for economic growth. For example, the rate of investment decreased in the second half of the 1980s. Also lost was the ability to guarantee elementary macro-economic balance and micro-economic discipline. The deep recession in the former USSR supports the hypothesis that a deep fall in output is unavoidable in post-Communist economies even before the start of a real stabilization and liberalization.

Russia's Starting-Point: Similarities and Differences with Poland in 1989

Many Russian politicians and economists as well as foreign observers and advisers tend to view market reforms in Russia as an imitation of Balcerowicz's programme in Poland. One of the aims of this chapter is to examine this popular view. I shall try to answer two questions: is Russia really following the Polish way, and can Russia copy the Polish experience? Let us look at how Gaidar's starting-point was similar to that of Balcerowicz. The main economic similarity seems be the deep macro-economic disequilibrium (Poland in 1989 and the USSR in 1991) which had almost the same source in both countries. However, the extent of the budget deficit and monetary imbalance in the former USSR at the end of 1991 was worse than in Poland in September 1989. The major difference is the level of 'marketization' of both economies. In 1989 the Polish economy had already seen eight years of semi-market reforms. These reforms were not effective from a macro- or micro-economic point of view. They nevertheless created portions of a market infrastructure and prepared the Polish society for the new rules of the game. At this time, Poland already showed the strong beginnings of a private sector. This was evident even outside of agriculture, which in 1989 made up 28 per cent of GDP. (Polish agriculture was never collectivized.) Russia and the other CIS states have no significant capitalist traditions. On the contrary, for 60 years they have lived under a rigid planning system. This is an important difference from Poland and other Central and Eastern European countries.

Turning to the political aspects, both the Mazowiecki government in Poland and Boris Yeltsin's cabinet in Russia were the first non-Communist, democratic organs of executive power in these countries. The revolutionary atmosphere after the collapse of the *coup d'etat* in Russia in August 1991 was not unlike the political atmosphere in Poland after the 'Solidarity' victory in the June 1989 general elections.

Tadeusz Mazowiecki's government received nearly the full support of all serious political parties and movements in Poland. His cabinet was able to create national unity around the programme of economic and political reform, partly by virtue of Solidarity's political position and influence. This atmosphere lived on until the summer of 1990 when the 'War at the Top' and the presidential election campaign started to dissolve the post-Solidarity political camp.

In Russia, strong political and intellectual opposition against market-oriented reforms appeared at the very beginning, and has been stronger than in Poland. The Yeltsin—Gaidar government has met strong resistance to its programme both in the Supreme Soviet and in the Congress of People's Deputies.

The new Russian government also inherited a powerful industrial and agricultural bureaucracy from the old command system. In Poland this bureaucracy gradually lost political influence during the semi-market reforms in the 1980s. Thus the number of industrial ministries in Poland had been decreased to 3 in 1981, and to one Ministry of Industry in 1987. Traditional industrial trusts (ob'edinenie) were abolished in 1982 and replaced primarily by voluntary associations, and sometimes by compulsory ones. But even these were phased out from 1987 to the first half of 1989. After eight years of partial labour-management in state-owned enterprises, the state and party bureaucracy were no longer capable of interfering in the day-to-day activities of enterprises to the same extent as earlier. During these eight years economic actors had the opportunity to gain a certain market mentality. When Balcerowicz's programme was put into action at the end of 1989, resistance from the old apparatus was no longer the main political barrier to reform. Nevertheless, it still existed, and it created constant interventionist pressure (Dabrowski, 1992a).

In Russia this anti-reform lobby is considerably stronger than it was in Poland in 1989. The process of concentration of many industrial ministries in Russia really got started in the autumn of 1991 when the 'reform' cabinet was nominated. Even after this, and after the dissolution of the all-union government, the number of different sectoral ministries and committees remains higher than in Poland, Czechoslovakia or Hungary. Some ministries such as the Ministry of the Economy, Ministry of Trade, and Ministry of Foreign Economic Cooperation are heavily involved in protecting the structures and instruments inherited from the previous system. At the end of May and the beginning of June 1992, three rather conservative (in the Russian sense) representatives were appointed to positions as new industrial Deputy Prime Ministers, creating a fear that the anti-reform lobby would gain hold inside government.

Different branch structures such as trusts, concerns, and associations still survive, and they provide an organizational base for various lobbies, which are very active in the Russian parliament. The military—industrial complex seems to be the most influential lobby on this scene. Old staff in the state administration also continue to play an important role.

The Yeltsin—Gaidar government has also met with difficulties that Poland luckily did not have. First, the political crisis of the former Soviet Union and the problem of cooperation between the former Soviet republics have seriously hampered macro-economic policy-making in the first half-year of the Russian transition. Until the beginning of 1992 nobody knew who was responsible for the monetary and fiscal policy on the former USSR territory.

Neither the 'nationalization' of the former USSR Gosbank by Russia nor the decision to grant to the Central Bank of Russia the role of a central monetary authority over the rouble area have solved all these problems. Up to mid-June 1992 the coordination of the monetary, fiscal, trade and custom policies inside the rouble area has been too loose to guarantee a stable macro-economic policy and effective market transformation.

This political situation has created a very strange monetary system – a monetary union of fifteen independent states with fifteen independent central banks who are not willing to cooperate between themselves (see Sachs and Lipton, 1992). Many trade barriers, mostly illegal, still exist between CIS countries, contributing to the economic disintegration of the rouble area. It seems that the lingering mentality of the shortage economy is the main cause of these continued barriers.

Second, the Russian government is also faced with serious inter-ethnic conflicts both inside the Russian Federation and in the other CIS countries, undermining these countries' political and economic stability. The Russian federal system too is a source of many political problems.

Alternative Concepts of Reform

As the authors of the EPICENTR report (Yavlinskii *et al.*, 1992) correctly noted, the Yeltsin–Gaidar cabinet never published any clear formulation of the government programme. President Boris Yeltsin and Vice-Prime Minister Yegor Gaidar had only made general statements in their public presentations. But this is not to say that the new government had no comprehensive concept for economic reform at the onset. Indeed, the concept was drafted by Gaidar's 'team' just before its nomination to government. In October and early November 1991, a special working group, appointed by President Yeltsin and headed by Gaidar, gathered in a government dacha in Arkhangelskoe (near Moscow) to perform this task.

Stabilisation and Reforms, the name of the unofficial working document prepared by this special group (Russian Government, 1991), proposed a gradual stabilization and liberalization package to be implemented over the course of one year. In the first stage, most prices were to be deregulated and foreign economic relations were to be partially liberalized: foreign exchange auctions were to be introduced, and export and import transactions were to be partially liberalized. However, this was to be done without convertibility for the rouble and without a unified exchange rate. After eight to nine months, the next stage of reform was to be implemented, namely, currency reform. A new Russian rouble convertible to Western currencies was to be introduced.

The group's proposal was widely criticized by foreign experts, including this author (Dabrowski, 1991b) on the following counts:

First, the proposal aimed to transform hidden (repressed) hyperinflation into open hyperinflation for a period of at least half a year, risking that inflation would get out of control altogether.

Second, under hyperinflation, the indexation of wages and other incomes creates a very strong inflationary thrust making it difficult to break the hyperinflationary spiral.

Third, a longer transition period means that undesirable compromises must be made, such as maintaining the system of administrative allocation of resources.

Fourth, the continuing macro-economic crisis, combined with plans to introduce the new currency will contribute to the disintegration of the rouble area, which can run counter to the economic and political interests of Russia.

Fifth, currency reform is a very complicated operation technically, and very risky politically. Reducing effective nominal money balances through currency reform, while it is a frequently used means of monetary adjustment in countries with hyperinflation (Dornbusch, 1991, pp. 174–6), seems difficult, given the current Russian circumstances.

Sixth, political and social support for a new government will not be long-lived. Therefore it is better to apply one big shock than a series of shocks over an extended period. Otherwise, the government may lose political support before embarking on the decisive phase of monetary reform. Moreover, gradual implementation of reform can provide the traditional bureaucracy with a better opportunity to consolidate anti-reform forces.

The concept Gaidar and his colleagues sought to follow was the Polish transformation step-by-step. First, partial liberalization and the 'opening' of repressed inflation would take place, as under the Rakowski government from the end of 1988 until August of 1989. Only afterwards would they move on to full liberalization, monetary and fiscal adjustment, and the introduction of current account convertibility, as in Balcerowicz's programme (see Dabrowski, 1991a, pp. 121–2). However, it is important to note that this sequence of events in Poland was a result of the political situation rather than of a conscious plan for transformation. Moreover, Poland had certain political reserves: Mazowiecki's government was available to start the second, decisive stage of liberalization and transformation. Russia seems to be in another situation – the first post-Communist government is already under fire.

Most foreign experts (Dabrowski 1991b) advised implementing one single complex shock operation which would contain:

1. Elimination of the huge monetary overhang through price liberalization and restrictive monetary policy.
2. Deregulation of prices for all goods and services except railway and electricity rates and housing rents. However, prices remaining under administrative control should be increased significantly.
3. Elimination of the budget deficit through a sharp reduction of subsidies (made possible by price liberalization) and comprehensive tax reform.
4. Unification of the exchange rate, introduction of current account convertibility for the rouble, and radical liberalization of foreign trade.
5. Massive demonopolization of industry and trade, including the administrative 'de-concentration' of all cartel-like branch organizations, free entry for all enterprises to each specific product market, and elimination of all existing barriers to entrepreneurship.

Incomes policy was a controversial point in discussions among experts. A number of them, like Stanislaw Gomulka and Richard Layard (see Gomulka,

1991), considering the Polish experience, proposed to retain wage control using tax instruments. Other advisers, such as Jacek Rostowski and this author, were more hesitant about recommending incomes policy in Russian circumstances.

Results of the First Half-Year

Starting at the end of November 1991 the Yeltsin–Gaidar cabinet began to implement measures for liberalization and stabilization. But despite the warnings of foreign experts, the scenario of gradual changes proposed in the *Stabilisation and Reforms* document was chosen. The one important deviation from this proposal was the abandonment of the currency reform idea. Instead, they intended to tackle monetary adjustment through a corrective inflation.

The results of this policy seem to confirm my reservations regarding the two-stage scenario. By mid-June 1992 Russia had accomplished only a partial domestic liberalization, and neither monetary stabilization nor the elimination of the shortage economy had taken place.

Price Liberalization

The main effort in the first half-year was focused on price liberalization a crucial step on the way to a market economy. This is a very difficult operation politically, especially difficult in a country like Russia where for 60 years almost all prices have been controlled by the government. The liberalization of prices at the beginning of January 1992 was extensive, but in June 1992 it is still not complete. Two important targets have yet to be achieved, namely, the elimination of a shortage economy and the introduction of market allocation of goods.

Unpublished statistical data from the Centre for Economic Reform of the Russian Government show that most food products became more readily available in retail trade in February and March of 1992 compared to the last months of 1991. However, the number of cities with shortages of specific goods was still high. A survey of 132 cities taken on 25 February 1992, when the market situation was at its best for the first half of 1992, shows that specific shortages were experienced. Three per cent of cities had a shortage of eggs, 4.5 per cent of milk, and 9 per cent of potatoes. Moreover, in more than 50 per cent of cities, acute shortages existed in the case of wheat flour, macaroni, rice, rye bread, cheese, milk powder, tinned fish, and sweets. According to the same data, from the end of February to the end of May, the situation *per saldo* did not improve. In the case of some goods (meat, milk and some flour products) the number of cities with shortages decreased slightly. However, there are also product markets (especially for fruits and vegetables) where the situation worsened since the end of February.

Turning to the allocation mechanism, we can still observe the administrative system of goods rationing, compulsory regional and inter-enterprise barter, and different forms of inter-regional trade restrictions (Yavlinskii *et al.*, 1992). This situation should be viewed as evidence of the survival of the shortage economy and of the shortage mentality among economic actors.

There are many reasons why the shortage economy lingers on. First, not all prices were deregulated, in particular oil and energy prices, and transport rates. Second, administrative control of many prices (bread, milk, margarine, and some transport rates) was simply decentralized to the local level (ibid., 1992). Third, anti-monopoly price controls are repeatedly applied too widely. Fourth, monopolist producers are not interested in selling at market equilibrium prices. They prefer barter transactions and 'producer diktat'. Fifth, high inflation and powerful inflationary expectations have stimulated speculative behaviour (hoarding goods in expectation of price increases). An accommodating monetary policy reinforces such behaviour.

Far more limited results have been accomplished in the external liberalization. Most import barriers have been removed, and all enterprises have had access to foreign currency through the auction system, direct transactions with exporters, or central allocation. But the Russian economy in the first half of 1992 was still a closed economy. The main reason was the extremely high exchange rate of the US dollar (and other convertible currencies) *vis-à-vis* the rouble.

The over-valuation of the US dollar against the rouble has been caused by several factors. First, expansionary monetary policy has undermined faith in the rouble. Second, the system of multiple exchange rates has caused the main free-market exchange rate to rise further than it otherwise would. Third, many export barriers such as export duties, regulations requiring enterprises to surrender part of their foreign currency, export licences, and quotas have limited possible export revenues and worsened the current account balance of the Russian economy. On the other hand, the real over-valuation of the dollar has been decreasing since December 1991. The free market nominal exchange rate of the rouble was rather stable from the beginning of 1992 to the middle of the year, while domestic prices and wages increased several times during this period.

Fiscal Policy

A second area where relative success has been achieved, at least in the first quarter of 1992, is in fiscal policy. In this period the cash deficit of the consolidated state budget did not exceed 2 per cent of GDP if one uses the official Russian methodology (data of the Ministry of Finance of the Russian Federation). According to international statistical methods the level of the first quarter deficit is higher — about 5–6 per cent of GDP. This is still not high compared to the situation in 1991 (especially in the fourth quarter). Moreover, according to the official reports of the Ministry of Finance, the budget was almost balanced in April 1992 as well. However, some negative signals in this area are evident for the future, namely, a number of wage concessions in the budgetary sphere and tax exemptions (see below). The government did not pay all its obligations in the first months, and thus part of them will have to be paid later.

The second accomplishment in the area of fiscal policy is in comprehensive tax reform. On 1 January 1992 the Russian government introduced an entire package of tax instruments typical to a real market economy: a value-added tax, an excise tax, personal income taxes, and corporate income taxes – an impressive achievement from a legislative point of view! But the organizational difficulties of tax collection remain unsolved. The Russian tax authorities have had great difficulties trying to collect VAT and export duties for the first months of 1992. The problem of tax collectibility can become more dramatic in the future when privatization and demonopolization will have advanced further. Here also there are lessons to be learned from Polish experience.

The tax policy has other weak points. First, there is poor coordination between CIS states, especially in VAT collection. Second, the government often gives in to pressure for tax exemptions. This is an unfortunate ailment of the late Communist economy, and it is now threatening Russian public finances. New tax exemptions were allowed at an increasing pace in the second quarter of 1992, as a direct result of several political concessions of the government towards the industrial and agricultural lobby. Third, the VAT rate is extremely high (28 per cent) in comparison with other countries, where the maximum does not usually exceed 20 per cent. This high rate makes it even more difficult to withstand pressure for exemptions. It would be desirable to decrease this rate to around 20 per cent in the near future.

Monetary Policy

Given the absence of wage control and of a fixed exchange rate, monetary policy should play a key role in the stabilization process. Aside from these two potential nominal anchors, the Russian government has only one feasible option for stabilization – a money-based orthodox programme.

According to the monetary statistics of the Central Bank of Russia, money supply was truly restrictive only in January 1992. From February 1992 both base money (see Table 3.1) and M3 began to grow quickly again. In the balance sheet of the Central Bank of Russia, credits to commercial banks, net credit to the government, and credit to other republics (through their correspondent accounts in the Central Bank of Russia) were the main sources of base money increase. In the consolidated balance sheet of the commercial banks, the rapid increase of short-term credits to enterprises is the cause of monetary expansion (see Table 3.2).

This is a reaction to the rapid increase of inter-enterprise arrears and to a kind of political hysteria connected with these arrears.

The result of fluctuations in monetary policy is the continuing high inflation rate of 10–20 per cent monthly, shortages of goods, the passive market behaviour of most state enterprises, and the over-valuation of the dollar. The latter problem is also compounded by a negative real interest rate. While the nominal interest rate was increased gradually from 6–9 per cent a

Table 3.1   Base money December 1991–April 1992

Date	Amount in bn roubles	1 Jan 1991 = 100	Previous month = 100
1 Dec 91	301	100.0	x
1 Jan 92	382	126.9	126.9
1 Feb 92	327	108.9	85.6
1 Mar 92	451	149.8	137.9
1 Apr 92	617	205.0	136.8
1 May 92	832	276.4	134.8

Source: monetary statistics of Central Bank of Russia

Table 3.2   Short-term credits of commercial banks

Date	Amount in bn roubles	1 Jan 91 = 100	Previous month = 100
1 Dec 91	366	100.0	x
1 Jan 92	394	107.7	107.7
1 Feb 92	474	129.5	120.3
1 Mar 92	635	173.5	133.9
1 Apr 92	767	209.6	120.8
1 May 92	848	231.7	110.6

Source: monetary statistics of Central Bank of Russia

year at the end of 1991 to 20 per cent in January, 50 per cent in April, and 80 per cent in May 1992, it is still considerably lower than the level of inflation. It is not enough to increase the demand for domestic money balances and to limit the demand for credit. The increase in reserve requirements to 20 per cent for demand deposits and to 15 per cent for time deposits also came relatively late — at the beginning of April 1992. All these attempts at discipline, however, are repeatedly being undermined by political pressure for special credit lines to specific sectors and industries, such as the agro-industrial complex and the energy sector. A number of decisions taken in the end of May 1992 on these matters could be a dangerous precedent.

The huge shortage of cash is yet another aspect of the monetary problem. It was brought on by several factors: the huge credit expansion, and some technical and organizational mistakes, including the Supreme Soviet's refusal to print banknotes of higher denominations at the end of 1991. The government must begin to ration cash between CIS states and regions of the Russian Federation as a means of political bargaining and pressure. The cash shortage has been disastrous for the effecting of monetary settlements. The black market exchange rate of the cash rouble against the credit rouble was as high as 1:2 in some regions at the end of May. Some other CIS states such as Ukraine and Belarus have introduced coupons as money surrogates, which has compounded the monetary and trade disintegration of the former USSR territory. The Russian government must also give special compensation to employees who have not received their wages and salaries on time.

Two Scenarios of Further Developments

After half a year of economic transformation the Russian government must again make a fundamental choice — either to quickly make a decisive stabilization effort or to continue a policy of 'controlled' high inflation. The two other options are: to accept open hyperinflation or to return to overall price and wage control (Russian Government, 1992). Neither of these scenarios are desirable and should not be considered. Both economic theory and the empirical experience of other countries tell us that only through quick and consequent stabilization can the Russian economy change into a real market system and have a lasting recovery. Nevertheless, there are some Russian economists and politicians who would rather see a variant of 'controlled' inflation for a longer period, such as a year (Yasin, 1992).

A few good arguments against a scenario of 'controlled' inflation come to mind. The danger of indexation, inflationary inertia, and political impatience were named above. In addition, high inflation is very difficult to stabilize, especially in a post-Communist economy. At any moment it can turn into hyperinflation. It is also naïve to expect that chronic high inflation can protect an economy from deep recession, enable state enterprises to adjust to the new market economy, or stimulate private entrepreneurship. Instead, it would be likely to prolong uncompetitiveness and pathological behaviour. It would make it very difficult to introduce effective current account convertibility for the rouble. All chances of reaching an agreement with the IMF and receiving Western financial support would probably be forfeited.

The road to quick stabilization must start, however, by solving the crucial economic and political problems. The first of these is to quickly reach an agreement with the other CIS states and with the Baltic states to either form a coordinated monetary policy inside the rouble area, or to divorce these states from the rouble (Sachs and Lipton, 1992). The second task is to liberalize oil and energy prices. Third, negotiations with the IMF must be completed quickly to make a stand-by loan and stabilization fund available to the Russian Central Bank and the government of Russia. Fourth, monetary policy, and also to some extent fiscal policy, needs significant tightening, which is closely dependent on the previous point.

Polish and Russian Transformation: Mutual Lessons

Although there are many differences in the economic and political conditions for transition to a market economy in these two countries, the Polish experience can be very useful for Russian reformers. The limited scope of this chapter does not allow a comprehensive analysis, but I shall name a few specific conclusions.

First, it is important to make optimum use of the 'political credit' and time given to the reform government to go as far as possible in reform policy. This amount of political credit is only available to the first really post-Communist government, and it lasts for a limited time only. This necessitates shock therapy rather than a gradualist approach.

Second, the Polish experience shows that most of the painful decisions should be built into the initial decisive stabilization and liberalization package. There are plenty of examples where important reforms were put aside in the end of 1989, and have still not been implemented. These postponements have in turn delayed necessary budgetary policy changes and structural reforms. I have in mind reforms such as the deregulation of the coal, energy, and transport industries, of the housing sector, wage indexation in the 'budgetary sphere', and elimination of several branch privileges.

Third, monetary policy plays an absolutely crucial role in the process of stabilization and liberalization. There is a lesson to be gained here from the Czechoslovakian experience of 1991. The importance of incomes policy (wage control) is rather secondary and controversial from a micro-economic point of view. But, the refinance interest rate of the .central bank is a key instrument of monetary adjustment in a post-Communist economy, at least in the first stage of transition. The high nominal interest rate in the first two months of Balcerowicz's programme, together with the radical fiscal adjustment were the main reasons for the success of the stabilization effort in early 1990. The lack of similar measures in Russia has made the Russian results far more limited.

Fourth, if drastic anti-inflationary measures are relaxed too early, the results of stabilization can be quickly undermined. Take, for example, the Polish experience from the second half of 1990 (Dabrowski, 1992b) when monetary, fiscal and income policies were relaxed too early and brought on the next wave of inflation.

Fifth, it is absolutely necessary to adopt a long-term approach in fiscal and other accompanying policies (especially in the social safety net). The main budgetary troubles will come in the second and third year of the transition process.

Sixth, macro-economic stabilization and domestic liberalization must be combined with at least current account convertibility and with significant external liberalization. Otherwise results will be limited.

Seventh, Central and Eastern European experience so far shows that deep recession is unavoidable after the collapse of a Communist economic system, even without stabilization and external liberalization measures. There are no trade-offs between recession and inflation. Deep institutional changes and quick privatization, while they do not bring immediate results, appear to be the only way out of a transformation depression.

Eighth, Polish, East German and Hungarian experiences also prove the necessity of pragmatic, non-ideological attitudes toward privatization. A multi-faceted approach, with a significant role for decentralized decision-making, seems to bring faster privatization. Russia still has a chance of avoiding some of Poland's mistakes made in the first year of the Balcerowicz programme.

And finally, Russian experience has at least one lesson to offer Poland. Many Polish economists and politicians still argue that Balcerowicz's programme was too restrictive in the sphere of monetary, fiscal and incomes policy, and that this made the recession unnecessarily deep (Kolodko, 1992). These critics of Balcerowicz's policy argue that a softer stabilization package with more gradual liberalization, especially in the external sphere, and with more government interventionism, would have given better results in terms of the level of the GDP, and no worse results in terms of macro-economic equilibrium. The results of the Russian transformation in the first half of 1992 cast great doubt on this approach. In fact, this kind of gradualism can only lead to a closed economy with continued high inflation and the lingering traits of a shortage economy, coupled with deep recession and growing social impatience. The critical task of reform is to radically change market behaviour and the economic mentality, and this task still lies ahead.

Notes

1. From 15 September 1989 until 21 September 1990 I held the position of a Secretary of State in the Ministry of Finance (First Deputy Minister of Finance). Since April 1991 I have held the post of Chairman of the Council of Ownership Changes, advisory body to the Prime Minister of Poland. Since 25 November 1991 I have been a member of the Sejm (the lower house of the Polish Parliament).
2. It was in principle the typical administrative price reform, but with some liberalization components, especially in the sphere of producer goods. In the subsequent months, effective price control weakened due to the political decomposition of the all-union government.
3. I use quotation marks around the word 'real' to show that I mean it in the formal, statistical sense. In reality the increase of 'real' wages does not produce an equal increase in welfare market equivalent due to increasing market shortages.

References

Cottarelli, C. and Blejer , M. I. (1991) 'Forced Savings and Repressed Inflation in the Soviet Union: Some Empirical Results', IMF Working Paper, June, Washington DC.
Dabrowski, M. (1991a) 'The Polish Stabilisation Programme: Accomplishments and the Prospects', Communist Economies and Economic Transformation, 3:1, pp. 121–33.
Dabrowski, M. (1991b) 'Stabilizatsiya i liberalizatsiya rossiiskoi ekonomiki. Skorost' i sekventsiya nuzhnykh shagov', (unpublished memo), Moscow, 15 November.
Dabrowski, M. (1992a) 'Interventionist Pressures on a Policy-Maker During the Transition to Economic Freedom (Personal Experience)', Communist Economies and Economic Transformation, 4:1, pp. 59–73.
Dabrowski, M. (1992b) 'The Polish Stabilisation 1990–1991', Journal of International and Comparative Economics (JOICE), 1, pp. 295–324.
Dornbusch, R. (1991) 'Strategies and Priorities for Reform', in P. Marer and S. Zecchini. (eds), The Transition to a Market Economy, OECD, Paris, vol. I, pp. 169–83.
Gomulka, S. (1991), 'The "Gaidar Plan" and the "Letter of Intent"' (unpublished memo), Moscow, 4 December.
IMF (1992), Economic Review: Russian Federation, Washington, DC, April.
IMF, The World Bank, OECD and EBRD (1990), The Economy of the USSR. Summary and Recommendation (A study undertaken in response to a request by the Houston Summit), Washington, DC, 19 December.
Kolodko, G. W. (1991) 'Transition from Socialism and Stabilization Policies: The Polish Experience', IMF Seminar Paper, Washington DC, 11 June.

Kolodko, G.W. (1992), 'Transition from Socialism and Stabilization Policies: The Polish Experience', in M. Karen and G. Ofer (eds), *The Trials of Transition: Economic Reform in the Former Communist Bloc*. Westview, Boulder, CO.

McKinnon, R.I. (1991) 'Financial Control in the Transition from Classical Socialism to a Market Economy', paper prepared for the IPR-IRIS Conference 'The Transition to a Market Economy — Institutional Aspects'), Prague, 24–27 March.

Russian Government (1991) 'Stabilizatsiya i reformy. Ekonomicheskaya politika Rossii v perekhodnii period (noyabr' 1991–dekabr' 1992 gg)', unpublished working document, Moscow, November.

Russian Government (1992) 'Srednesrochnaya programma (kontseptsiya)', unpublished working document, Moscow, May.

Sachs, J., and Lipton, P. (1992) 'Making the Rouble Area Work', unpublished memo, 11 May.

Yasin, E.G. (1992) 'Liberalizatsiya i stabilizatsiya ekonomiki', unpublished manuscript, Moscow, 11 May.

Yavlinskii, G.A. *et al.* (1992) 'Reformy v Rossii, vesna-92', *Moskovskie novosti*, no. 21, pp. 9–16.

4 Problems in Foreign Trade Regulation in the Russian Economic Reform

Petr Aven

First published in 1994

The historic role of Yegor Gaidar's government (at least as it was seen by its members) was to provide an 'institutional shock' to the economy, i.e., to destroy the traditional stereotypes and mindset of the centrally planned economy (CPE). The deepest beliefs had to be changed; the systemic features of the CPE that had been untouchable earlier, were now to be demolished. These features were the absolute dominance of state ownership, the non-convertibility of the currency, huge military spending, and the regulation of almost all prices. The short-term goal was to prove that 'the unfeasible is feasible' and to create the basis for a market economy. Although macro-economic stabilization was proclaimed as the central objective of the government, by April 1992 it became clear that Gaidar would have to sacrifice this goal for the sake of 'marketization' (including privatization and general liberalization). Reform measures that are normal for an established market economy, such as the complete abolition of import subsidies or tax reform, had to be left for the next stage of the reform and, probably, to the next government.

The main problem was that this institutional shock had to take place during an extremely deep economic crisis. Therefore, the government had to try to avoid collapse and simultaneously attempt a revolutionary reformation of the system.

From the viewpoint of reform, the foreign trade sphere was a very typical example. It was in a very deep crisis and its regulation mechanism was inefficient and obsolete. Two main issues were on the agenda: the introduction of tariffs and currency convertibility. The significance of these issues was huge, just as the other changes implemented by Gaidar's Cabinet, and were previously unknown to the Soviet economy. Their introduction

56

changed the mentality of economic agents and the heart of the system. However, before we examine what has been done, let us look at foreign trade at the end of 1991, when the reform began.

Foreign Trade Performance at the End of 1991

During 1984–91, exports from the territory of the former USSR diminished by more than one-third. Three major reasons for such a decline may be singled out. First and foremost, exports declined due to the sharp decrease in oil extraction and accordingly in exports of oil. Oil export revenues fell from $22 bn in 1986 to about $7 bn in 1991. Second, the collapse of COMECON, which was followed by a radical, though rational, shift to mutual hard currency payments, was an additional reason. Finally, the overall economic crisis also played a role.

A further dramatic slide of exports took place in 1991; during that year exports dropped by 24 per cent. In addition to these factors, the general decentralization of decision-making revealed that a large share of trade was unprofitable either to one, or even to both, partners. When making decisions about where to sell and where to buy, the state often based its choices on non-economic grounds (or on no grounds at all). Such a policy could not be acceptable for independent economic agents, such as trade firms or enterprises that did not care about political relations among specific countries but were interested exclusively in mutual comparative advantages. Therefore, the dramatic decline in Russia's trade with countries such as Cuba or India was not a disaster but had an economic rationale.

In the Soviet economy, imports of know-how and modern equipment were always used as an important lever of change. They were supposed to promote import substitution, making the USSR more independent and competitive. In the end of the 1980s imports formed the core of the accelerated development of machine-building. A vast inflow of oil dollars from the middle of the 1970s made domestic consumption of consumer goods also highly dependent on imports. Therefore, the maintenance of high imports has been considered a primary task.

Since exports were decreasing, only two means were available for the support of imports: heavy external borrowing, or the accumulation and 'proper' use of the hard currency possessions of domestic holders. From 1985 till 1992, the external debt of the country more than doubled, soaring by almost $50 bn. In 1991 alone, it grew by almost $20 bn. Mikhael Gorbachev regarded new credits ('given to him', as he viewed it) as the salvation of the country. However, debt service absorbed more than one-third of total export revenues in 1991.

Nevertheless, external borrowing was not sufficient, and in 1990 Vnesheconom-bank started spending its clients' money, later claiming internal bankruptcy. The amount of clients' money that was spent totalled $10.6 bn. Although the clients who were hit were exclusively Soviet entities and citizens, foreign firms which exported goods to the USSR were in fact among the main victims because they were not paid. Mounting arrears in payments for deliveries to the Soviet Union, which had been unknown before, constituted the first blow against lenders' confidence in the Soviet state.

However, despite external and involuntary domestic borrowing, Gorbachev's government was only able to maintain the level of imports until the middle of 1991. Finally the artificially maintained imports started plummeting; for 1991 they decreased by 44 per cent. In our view, this was the main reason for the decline of production in Russia in 1992.

Regulation Mechanism

The basic principle of organizing foreign trade in a centrally planned economy was through a state monopoly on foreign trade. The USSR not only had a state monopoly, it even had a monopoly by the Ministry of Foreign Trade until 1985. The absolute majority of firms involved in export or import operations were directly subordinated to this Ministry.

A gradual decentralization of decision-making was one of the main developments of the Soviet-type 'bargaining economy'. At first, branch ministries were given the right to participate in foreign trade: during 1986–88 about half of all foreign trade organizations left the Ministry of Foreign Trade to join different ministries, mainly industrial ministries.

Soon afterwards enterprises gained the right to conduct trade themselves. After 1989 any entity could legally get access to trade, but it was necessary to obtain a special certificate as a 'participant in foreign economic activities' in order to begin operations, though it was fairly easy to acquire such a certificate.

All export was also regulated by licensing, but again it was fairly easy to receive a licence for exporting anything except raw materials and military equipment. Export licences were issued by the central USSR government, and the distribution as well as the certification of exporters became a major source of corruption.

When the approaching collapse of the USSR became obvious, republican authorities, along with the all-union bureaucracy, obtained the right to issue licences. As an immediate result, the scope of licences for oil and oil products exports almost exceeded the quantities of extracted and refined oil by the end of 1991.

The sharing of export earnings between an exporter and the state was regulated by hundreds of 'currency coefficients', i.e. individualized exchange rates (specific not only to goods, but also to enterprises). The system of multiple rates was intended to introduce some order and fairness into the relationship between exporters and the budget, while domestic prices remained regulated. In reality, 'currency coefficients' turned into another bargaining point, and the amounts of hard currency that were left at the exporting enterprises' disposal gradually grew larger.

Imports were controlled through the centralized distribution of hard currency. Similar to the distribution of export licences and revenues, currency for imports was allotted on a bargaining basis. Hard currency constraints remained 'soft' for imports of modern technology and consumer goods, and since the official (and unrealistically high) exchange rate (1.6

roubles per dollar at the end of 1991) was applied to all buyers of hard currency, import subsidies grew to 20 per cent of GNP. Tariff regulation for both export and import was basically non-existent.

After the collapse of the USSR at the end of 1991, the situation in Russia was aggravated by the absence of state borders and a desperately obsolete banking system.

Reforms of 1992

Administrative (Non-Tariff) Regulation

The substitution of administrative foreign trade control by a usual system of tariffs was the first task of the reform in foreign trade. Unnecessary restrictions, such as the certification of foreign trade participants, had to be abolished as well. However, the first step of the Gaidar government ran contrary to liberalization: all previously issued licences for the export of oil and oil products (for a total of $1 bn) were annulled. This step was politically controversial, but it showed the decisiveness of the new government and its will to play by the rules. The rest of the measures introduced since 1 January 1992 may be regarded as liberal. Thus, the process of certifying foreign trade participants was abolished and all economic entities acquired equal privileges to export and import.

The list of commodities subject to export quotas and licences was cut considerably. At the beginning of 1992, the list still included oil and oil products, gas and coal, metals, fertilizers and a few other chemical products, timber, fish, and weapons. In the course of the year, this list continued to shrink; ferrous metals, coal and some fertilizers were removed. No civilian machinery required export licences. Despite that, the government succeeded in significantly reducing the number of goods restricted by export quotas, it was heavily criticized for its lack of radicalism. Critics, and the IMF team in Moscow, considered the preservation of any quotas unnecessary.

Rightly, critics noted that these commodities which remained subject to export quotas stood for more than 70 per cent of total Russian exports. Nor is there any doubt that the export tariffs that had been introduced were theoretically sufficient to control the exported volumes of these goods. Nevertheless, it was (and is) necessary to preserve a certain amount of administrative control, for reasons which I shall explain below.

The first of these issues is supplies of key products, such as oil. A sharp decline in the supply of number of strategic resources to the domestic market is unacceptable. There are purely technical reasons for maintaining the minimal supply of oil to the domestic market, currently amounting to 250–270 mn tons per year. If this amount of oil does not reach Russian enterprises today, losses in industry will be excessive both from a political viewpoint and from the viewpoint of efficient adjustment. Remember that the domestic price of oil was only 3 per cent of the world price, and the Russian economy's traditional orientation towards cheap inputs could not be overcome overnight. Even more important, attempts to alter prices overnight might be extremely destructive. To find a road between the inefficient use of resources (from the comparative advantage standpoint) and the collapse of industry was a key task of the government in 1992. I believe that, in principle, the government has chosen the right speed: for example, the domestic oil price is now equal to 30 per cent of the world price. A better result could hardly have been reached in one year, especially in the difficult Russian political environment.

This issue concerns more than oil; according to government assessments, domestic supplies of various commodities were minimal in 1991–92. The implication is that there was no more room for further increases of certain exports. That is why restrictions on exports were a reasonable choice for the Russian economy, and full liberalization was required only for those export goods needing promotion.

The second issue is domestic pricing. Regulation through export tariffs alone is feasible only if prices are relatively stable. In an environment of permanently and hazardously swinging domestic prices, the task of regulating exports by tariffs alone would require weekly alterations and amendments, which is practically impossible. And after prices were liberalized in Russia, no price stability could be expected. Moreover, the prices of certain exportable goods (oil, coal, gas) were not liberalized at all in January 1992. Therefore, attempts to regulate significant exports solely by tariffs would have been senseless.

An additional reason for temporarily controlling exports by administrative means is that as long as state ownership prevails, managers care little about economic rationale from the enterprises' point of view, though they do care about personal benefits, such as bribes and foreign travel. In 1991, for example, non-ferrous metals were being sold at only 20 per cent of the world price in a few cases. Therefore, purely economic regulation was not sufficient for all situations – price control through licensing was necessary.

Due to the reasons mentioned above, the government saw as its task the introduction of a system of tariff regulation, but not the immediate abolition of administrative control over exports. Economic agents had to be used to pay export duties. Only later, when these payments had become common and the system sufficiently advanced, should administrative control be completely eliminated. The government planned to conclude this work during 1993–94, and the introduction of export tariffs in 1992 was regarded as a first step in that direction. At this first stage export tariffs and quotas (and licences) had to co-exist.

Let me remind the reader that other economies in transition also used non-tariff control over exports at the beginning of their economic reforms. In Poland in early 1990, export restrictions were introduced for 24 items. In Czechoslovakia in 1991, about 20 per cent of merchandise exports remained controlled through licensing.

However, the system of allocation of export quotas had to be revised drastically. Since 1 January 1992, the formalities of licensing were radically altered in order to become more expedient and 'automatic'.

The Ministry of the Economy was given the task of determining the total quotas for exports of certain goods from Russia. It was to forward these quotas through various branch ministries to export-producers and regional authorities. It was presupposed that the producers' quotas would be allocated in proportion to the production capacity of their facilities. Regional quotas, which were to be supervised by the respective local administration had to be equal to 10 per cent of all the quotas given to the local producers. Like other goods, quotas could be bought and sold.

Provided that both export quotas and export contracts were available, the Ministry of Foreign Economic Relations was to issue export licences. Thus, the role of an export licence was purely price control. The Ministry of Foreign Economic Relations was also supposed to receive a part of national export quotas (though rather limited in 1992) for sales through auctioning. The idea of auctioning was to execute state obligations, primarily with regard to politics and foreign debt, and to ensure the flexibility of the internal transformation process.

In general, the intentions of updating the administrative supervision was to eliminate discretionary choices and to reduce the leeway of central authorities to determine who would carry out exports. It was a major anti-corruption measure. Imports, however, were not affected by any administrative interventions.

Even in Czechoslovakia, four categories of commodities (crude oil, gas, drugs, arms and munitions) remained subject to import licensing in 1991, and later some agricultural products were added to this list. In Hungary annual quotas were introduced in 1992 on imports of fifteen various steel products from Czechoslovakia and the republics of the former USSR. Thus, from this viewpoint, Russia and Poland were more 'liberal'.

Tariff Regulation

Export tariffs, which were introduced in the beginning of 1992, covered almost the same articles that were subject to administrative controls. Tariffs did not apply to those goods that were export priorities, such as machinery and the majority of other industrial goods. Currently, export tariffs vary from 20 to 30 per cent of the world market price. As domestic prices approached world market prices, the level of export tariffs was to diminish gradually. This process has in fact taken place in 1992–93.

The introduction of export tariffs came as a shock to a large number of exporters who had been extracting excess profits from their trade. It also came as a shock to certain foreign importers and countries, such as Finland, whose prosperity was heavily based on cheap imports from Russia. By setting the level of tariffs as a percentage of the world price, exporters could not escape the tariffs by understating prices.

As a result, the pressure on the government to abolish the new tariff system was strong from exporters. Some exporters stopped exports and tried to show that these new tariffs made all trade unprofitable. The drastic decrease of exports in the beginning of 1992 was at least partially artificial: exporters hoped that the new system would be eliminated. To tell the truth, this decline was also brought about by certain technical mistakes and the lack of coordination between the government and the Central Bank in the installation of the export duties payment system. But the government was able to withstand the pressure, and while making certain changes in the level of tariffs in February, and some exemptions from payments, it preserved the system. In 1993 tariffs became a stable source of income for the budget.

With due consideration to the extraordinary monopolization of the Russian economy and the collapse of domestic supply, at the end of 1991, the government decided to refrain from introducing any import tariffs and to remove all obstacles to accelerated imports. The under-valued rouble itself played the role of an import tariff. During the first six months of 1992 import tariffs did not exist.

However, harder budget constraints and growing rivalry among suppliers made the industrial lobby cry out for protectionist policies. Also, purely fiscal considerations brought forth by the IMF resulted in a unified 5 per cent import tariff, introduced in July 1992 and rising to 15 per cent in September.

The level of tariffs introduced in Russia was similar to those chosen in other economies in transition 'from Marx to the market'. At the start of liberalization, the average level of import tariffs was 16 per cent in Hungary, 12 per cent in Poland, and 5 per cent in Czechoslovakia, where it later was significantly increased.

The ability to introduce more advanced (non-unified) tariffs in Russia in 1992 was very limited. Nobody could tell which industries actually needed protection that would be efficient from the medium-term viewpoint. However, starting in January 1993, import tariff rates were diversified. Currently the tariff is zero for foodstuffs and pharmaceuticals, 5 per cent for raw materials and semi-processed items, and 15 per cent for ready-made goods.

Until 1993 imports were not subject to any additional taxation in the form of excises or value-added tax. But in January 1993 these were introduced. The list of goods subject to excise taxes is similar to the corresponding domestic list, though tax rates may vary. Vodka, production of which fell sharply in 1992 in Russia, is the one example of different levels of excises.

Currency Regulation

Although currency exchanges were already operating in Russia in 1991, before 1992 the purchasing of hard currency for imports was troublesome, if at all possible. Enterprises had long stayed in the dark about how to purchase hard currency, which was fully in keeping with the spirit of a barter economy. Hard currency, just like everything else, was another 'bargaining item', and it was not considered decent to buy it at outrageous prices, but it was acceptable to squeeze it out of the government. When the Minister of Foreign Economic Relations, speaking in Parliament, announced for the first time that in the following year all importers would have to, and would be able to, buy hard currency from banks, the MPs began to laugh. The common argument was: 'There is not enough currency in the country to buy.'

As regards the consumer market, for decades it had been alienated from hard currency, whose circulation was strictly forbidden, with the risk of criminal persecution for the disobedient. In this environment, it is quite understandable that the task of completely reforming the currency regulation system was the most important part of reforming the foreign trade mechanism.

As a first step, the multiple 'currency coefficients' (exchange rates) were abolished. Exporters were obliged to surrender 40 per cent of their hard currency earnings at the fixed rate of 55 roubles per dollar to the Central Bank. At the time 55 roubles was equal to 50 per cent of the auction rate. (For private citizens, a different black-market rate did exist, which was slightly higher than the auction rate.) An additional 10 per cent of revenues had to be surrendered to banks at the auction (market) exchange rate.

The rate of 55 roubles per dollar arose as a compromise between the government and the central bank, which had insisted (with the silent backing of some officials from the Ministry of Finance) on preserving either multiple surrender coefficients or on introducing a fixed artificial rate, proposed at the unrealistic level of 3 roubles per dollar. Later the proposed figure grew to 5.4 roubles which was regarded to be high enough, taking into consideration the official rate used then for importers: 1.6 roubles per dollar.

The level of the exchange rate was not the main thing, though the level proposed by the government was tied to the level of export tariffs. What did matter was to break the old way of thinking which viewed hard currency not as 'money', but simply as an ordinary commodity, taken (not bought) by the government from those who possess it, and allocated by the government, again for free.

Two tasks had to be solved in order to destroy this old pattern of behaviour. First, exporters had to be paid for the currency they surrendered to the state, and the price had to be real. It did not matter whether the price was 40 or 60 roubles per dollar, but the non-price of 3–5 roubles had to go. Moreover, this price had to be unified, and the bargaining connected with currency coefficients had to be avoided.

Second, importers also had to be forced to pay the real price for hard currency. And this price naturally had to be equal to the price paid for the currency by the state. In other words, the Central Bank's surrender rate had to be equal to the rate applied for importers who received hard currency from the government. The rate set at currency auctions was to be used in all transactions except those that were state-related.

Of course, using an artificial exchange rate instead of the auction rate had no economic rationale. However, in January the government was not powerful enough to push beyond this compromise. After the extremely low rates (both for surrender and purchasing) were abolished, it was much easier to implement a unified market exchange rate later in July.

From July 1992, the exchange rates for hard currency surrender, currency auctions and 'purchase-for-import' were actually unified. The auction (market) rate applied to all transactions, with a few exceptions, such as 'centralized imports'. From that time 20 per cent of hard currency earnings were to be sold compulsorily through the currency market, and another 30 per cent to the Central Bank. However, the market (auction) exchange rate was employed in both cases, and it was based on the rate set at Moscow

Interbank Exchange Auctions which took place once a week in 1991, increasing to twice a week in 1992.

In discussing the reform, I would like to mention that it was especially difficult to overcome the habit of importers of technological equipment to receive hard currency for free. Their main argument was: 'Nobody has enough roubles, you will stop the country.' A similar argument ('There are not enough roubles') was used by certain Ministry of Finance officials when the problem of currency surrender was discussed. Obvious answers, such as: 'The state will receive roubles from the export duties and from those who buy the currency', or: 'If you would like to subsidize, do it directly, but not through the exchange rate' did not always help. In fact, during the whole year the government used special 'subsidy coefficients' applied to imports of certain goods if it took place by a government decision within centralized imports. These were in fact individualized exchange rates. However, in the second half of the year centralized imports began to evaporate, so the role of these coefficients decreased drastically. At the end of 1992, only a small number of foodstuffs (mainly grain and sugar) were actually subsidized through the exchange rate.

The unification of the exchange rate and the reduction of import subsidies were backed up by a new procedure for distributing hard currency credits received under government guarantees. Instead of their nearly free allotment (at the official rate of 1.6 roubles per dollar) with vague requirements for repayment, a compulsory 15 per cent pre-payment of the utilized credit was introduced in July. Payment had to be made in roubles based on the market exchange rate. Also, the enterprises had to pay for the received credits in full compliance with their terms. As a result, there was a serious decline in the number of enterprises' requests for hard currency credits.

One controversial question that remained on the agenda was obligatory surrender. From my point of view it was justified to push the economic system, even artificially and administratively, towards the creation of an adequate currency market. Regretfully, the overthrow of the finance and banking system brought about a notable time gap between when hard currency was surrendered by an exporter and when the rouble equivalent of sold hard currency was surrendered by an exporter and when the rouble equivalent of sold hard currency ended up in the exporter's account. This gap sometimes exceeded two months. Given the heavy inflation, this meant an additional export tax of at least 20 per cent. Apart from that, some exporters had a special relationship with their banks, which made it possible to avoid obligatory surrender. However, artificial support to the hard currency market, as in the beginning of 1992, helped to spread know-how of currency operations and promoted a gradual growth in the amount of hard currency offered for sale and purchase.

In fact, the new mechanism of hard currency regulation allowed residents to enjoy current account convertibility. Moreover, import contracts were sometimes faked, which means that hard currency in reality was bought and sold without any real commitment. The private currency market has now been completely legalized. I strongly believe that rouble convertibility was one of the major achievements of the Gaidar government.

Special Exporters

As mentioned earlier, state ownership affects the behaviour of enterprise managers, who are frequently more interested in their personal income than in maximizing export revenues for 'their' companies. Under-invoicing became an acute problem in 1991–92. The lack of experience and amateur rivalry between many newly emerged exporters led to falling prices on several major export items. Anti-dumping procedures aimed at Russian exporters became common in Europe, US and Japan; ferrous metals and fertilizers were frequently under investigation.

The government realized that it was impossible to control prices exclusively through licensing. There were also political considerations which forced the Cabinet to show that it would not 'sell out' Russia. It was decided to decrease the number of exporters in those spheres where under-pricing was most common. The idea was to make it possible to monitor exporters of 'strategic' commodities. From autumn 1992 permission to export 'strategic' goods, such as oil and oil products, gas, ferrous and non-ferrous metals, and timber, was granted only to 'skilled exporters'.

In practice, the list of 'strategic' goods was almost the same as the list of goods subject to export quotas. (The former was even a bit larger.) Through this step all items were clearly divided into two groups. The first group embraced commodities covered by all forms of export control: quotas, licences, tariffs and certification of exporters. The second group included goods that could be freely exported. Obviously, raw materials constituted the core of the first group, and goods with a relatively high level of processing belonged to the second. Only a few items were in between. Thus, ferrous metals were not subject to export quotas, but had to be traded through 'special exporters' and with export tariffs.

I have to admit that the introduction of 'special exporters' was a mistake (or an unnecessary concession). In principle, it could have made sense if the number of exporters could truly have been limited, as when this system was initially introduced in September 1992. At that time the list of 'special exporters' embraced all major producers of relevant commodities, and also those trade organizations which had proved to be competent. In general, the number of exporters was reduced several times. However, under strong pressure from enterprises, the list of 'special exporters' started to grow again, and it grew several times. Similar to the 'participants of foreign trade' in 1991, now almost everyone can acquire the necessary permission, and thus it is yet another source of bribes and corruption.

One important lesson can be drawn from this experience, namely, that any obstacle to economic activity, especially one which assumes the existence of a discretionary choice, will be circumvented in Russia, and therefore, this country has to be more liberal than any other.

Certain steps have been taken in 1992 in the area of trade policy and export promotion, but they were not of a very reformist nature.

Results of 1992

In my view, the foreign trade performance in 1992 was generally satisfactory. For the first time since 1989, the monthly volume of exports stopped falling and even started to grow. The physical volume of exports in 1992 was even with 1991. Due to the slump in world market prices, export revenues fell by 12 per cent, to $45 bn. If we do not count the 'gratuitous' part of 1991 exports (to countries such as Cuba or Mongolia), the drop could be assessed at a mere 7 per cent.

Imports in 1992 decreased by 6 per cent, to $42 bn. Imports fell less than exports, due to the lower share in Russia of all-union imports (63 per cent) as compared to exports (80 per cent). Contrary to the previous year, the trade balance was positive at $3.1 bn. The current account balance was negative at $3.0 bn.

The creation of an adequate hard currency market was another success of the reform. In January 1992 the monthly currency exchange turnover totalled only $18 mn. It came close to the billion mark by the end of 1992, equalling one-third of exports. At least the same amount was sold by banks outside the auctions. The rouble proved to be *de facto* convertible for current transactions.

When the new government took office in November 1991, state hard currency reserves were less than $100 mn. By the time Yegor Gaidar resigned, they were more than $1.5 bn. During the first five months of 1993 this figure increased at least threefold.

The dynamics of the exchange rate were also positive. Within the first six months of 1992, the dollar became 15 times cheaper in real terms in Russia. From November 1992 until March 1993, the dollar again depreciated twofold against the rouble. While the nominal rouble exchange rate fell by about 15 per cent a month, the average monthly inflation rate was 20–25 per cent. The appreciation of the rouble (not only in real terms, but later even in nominal terms) continued into 1993. However, foreign trade performance, and in particular exports, responded slowly to the ups and downs of the exchange rate. According to our estimates, only ferrous and non-ferrous metals exports correlated modestly with the exchange rate fluctuations.

Due to the introduction of the tariff system, export and import revenues became a stable source of income for the budget. Now they account for about 20 per cent of all budgetary revenues. This figure could be much larger if numerous regions and enterprises had not been granted tariff privileges.

Unfortunately, the number of exemptions from export or import duties is not decreasing. In 1992 about 100 decrees of the government or of the President gave tariff privileges for a total sum of more than $2.8 bn ($2.5 bn for exports, $0.3 bn for imports). During the first three months of 1993 new privileges were given for $3.6 bn.

In principle, the first quarter of 1993 exceeded most of the trends achieved in 1992. However, the introduction of a value-added tax and excises for imports resulted in a notable decrease of imports (by nearly 50 per cent), while exports stayed even. As a result, Russia had a positive balance of trade in the first three months of 1993 totalling $5 bn. After four months, the trade surplus reached $7.6 bn.

Although certain attempts to partially centralize trade took place in the beginning of 1993, they did not change the basic features of the system introduced in 1992. Moreover, the majority of decisions made continued at the pace initiated a year before. Thus, certain goods were excluded from the list of goods subject to export quotas (for example, timber).

As before, exporters have to surrender 50 per cent of their hard currency earnings, but only to commercial banks and not to the Central Bank. Therefore, state intervention has become less important and the supply of hard currency on the market more guaranteed.

The subsidization of imports has been decreasing gradually. As early as 1992, import subsidies fell from over 20 per cent to 5–6 per cent of GNP, and I hardly believe that the government could have done better at the time. However, centralized imports were further decreased in 1993, and now it appears that only grain will be subject to further import subsidization.

Thus, in concluding, it seems that the reform of the foreign trade sphere has become irreversible.

5 Main Issues of Privatization in Russia

Anatoly Chubais and Maria Vishnevskaya

First published in 1993

Status of the Privatization Process

The start of orderly privatization in Russia can be dated to July 1991, when the Law on Privatization of State and Municipal Enterprises in the RSFSR was adopted. Yet by the end of 1991 privatization had been implemented on an extremely limited scale. This was for a number of reasons, ranging from the lack of a clear strategy for enforcing the new legislation to the absence of a clear division of state property rights. The legal framework for privatization was clearly insufficient, and the institutional infrastructure was under-developed.

In the whole of 1991 the value of state property transferred to private and/or collective ownership equalled 2 billion roubles, while budget revenues resulting from privatizations amounted to less than 200 million roubles. By January 1992 only 70 enterprises had come under private ownership and 922 under collective ownership.

In practice, the privatization process was launched only after adoption of the 'Basic provisions for the privatization of state and municipal enterprises in the Russian Federation in 1992'. The legal basis for starting the organizational work came from the decree of the Supreme Soviet 'On the division of state property into federal property, state property of the federation's constituent republics, krais, oblasts ...', approved in January 1992 along with a set of normative documents governing the privatization procedure.

State property management committees have been set up in almost all the 20 republics of the Russian Federation and in all its 86 okrugs, krais and oblasts. Such committees now function in all regional centres, as well as in many other cities. The establishment of property management committees at district (i.e., raion) level is soon to be completed. A massive sell-out of

68

municipal property – primarily of shops and establishments providing consumer services – was launched in early 1992. By summer 1992 Russia was approaching the end of the first stage of the privatization process, the purpose of which was:

1. to elaborate the legal framework for privatization;
2. to create the organizational structure of privatization at all-Russian and local levels, including provision of office facilities;
3. to move on to the substance of the process, i.e. to have local privatization programmes adopted and implemented leading to a sharp increase in the number of concluded privatizations, and of revenues obtained from them.

In this context, mention should be made of the negative experience of small-scale privatization in Moscow. It shows that the free transfer or preferential direct sale of shops and enterprises to labour collectives is a method of privatization to be avoided. Clearly, no improvement was made to management in these businesses, and this threatens to discredit the very idea of privatization among the population.

Fortunately, all segments of society now seem to approve of the notion of privatization by vouchers. Growing support for this method represents a particularly welcome development, since it is the method preferred by the government in privatizing large state enterprises and in bringing them under the control of responsible owners.

Yet, several critical issues remain to be tackled. One is the problem of sabotage of privatization by local authorities and government employees. Another is the problem of 'nomenklatura' privatization. Of immediate concern has been the insufficient preparation for mass and large-scale privatization, as in summer 1992 the commercialization of large-scale industry was only beginning and distribution of vouchers was yet to start. Also, the legal system is in a state of flux, and various management bodies are engaged in conflicts over their respective powers in the process of privatization.

Principles of State Privatization Programme

The first main stage of privatization in Russia is to implement the 'State privatization programme for the state and municipal enterprises in 1992', drawn up in March of that year. The guiding principles of the programme can be summed up in these points:

1. to create effective owners;
2. to quickly obtain and demonstrate the results of privatization by transforming the major part of property immediately, and transferring it – for a charge or free – to Russian and foreign shareholders;
3. to boost revenues from privatization, as progress in privatization closely depends on the extent of success in economic stabilization;
4. to ensure priority of privatization from above by means of mandatory

targets laid down in the State privatization programme, by means of strict control by the State Committee for State Property Management (Goskomimushchestvo – GKI) of the procedure of privatization, and by means of assistance in the staging of pilot privatizations on request from below;

5. to secure fairness, thus attracting broad popular and political support;
6. to coordinate the interests of those who will participate in privatization: workers, managers, public service employees, local authorities and federal government;
7. to make provision for the use of privatization procedures that are simple and have low organizational costs, thereby avoiding complicated methods of asset valuation.

Russia must meet the challenge now confronting her. Our policy is to speed up the process of establishing a private sector and of swiftly finding effective management for the state enterprises. Unless we succeed in this, state enterprises will remain an easy prey to spontaneous privatization by their old directors seizing the opportunity created by the present vacuum in enterprise management.

Entering the second stage of privatization we intend:

1. to implement 'small-scale' privatization;
2. to create conditions for 'large-scale' privatization in 1993–94; to convert all large enterprises into public joint stock companies;
3. to distribute among the citizens of Russia a special means of payment in the form of vouchers;
4. to set up a system of financial institutions (investment funds, holdings, stock exchanges, etc.), to facilitate capital movement, including vouchers;
5. to provide for the wide participation of foreign investors in privatization;
6. to organize effective management in the enterprises still under state ownership.

Small-Scale Enterprises Up For Sale

Eligible for small-scale privatization are enterprises with assets valued at up to 1 million roubles and with up to 200 employees operating in wholesale and retail trade, construction, agriculture, food industry and cargo transport.

The basic method of 'small-scale' privatization is through auctions, organized by local state property management committees (local GKI departments). The plan is to privatize 50–60 per cent of those enterprises by the end of 1992 and most of the rest in 1993. The revenues from privatization will be distributed between local and central government with local authorities taking the major part (65 per cent).

Buyers of small-scale enterprises will help establish the foundation of a market economy. In many cases a local entrepreneur will be the buyer. In other cases, employees will get together to buy out their own enterprises. It will also be possible for enterprises to be bought by managers and employees together. As in auctions and tenders, the assets will go to the highest bidder. Thus, auctions will become an important means for local authorities to collect revenues. Moreover, auction sales of small-scale enterprises are likely to improve the quality of consumer services and to give privatization a good image.

Mass Privatization of Large-Scale Industry

In restructuring the economy, privatization of large and medium-sized enterprises plays a key role. The Russian Programme sets the start of 'large-scale' privatization for autumn 1992, and plans to accelerate its implementation thereafter.

Obviously, this task would be impossible if privatization were conducted by stages on the model of privatization developed in Great Britain and in many developing countries of Asia and Latin America. Instead of this 'classical' approach, mass privatization will be used in Russia, with the exception of some enterprises and sectors that should be privatized in the 'classical' way.

Mass privatization refers to the distribution of shares of state enterprises among the population free of charge, or at minimum charge, as a rule through the medium of vouchers and privatization accounts. The Russian programme lays down the various steps of mass privatization and provides for the use of a wide spectrum of incentive schemes.

The first necessary step in the process of privatization of large and medium-sized enterprises is to commercialize them, i.e. to transform them into public joint stock companies, allowing the free sale of shares. This part should be completed by autumn 1992.

Some positive effects will make themselves felt in enterprises immediately upon commercialization. First, they will have to introduce modern management structures, such as a board of directors. Second, using their preferential right to buy shares in the enterprise, managers will have an incentive to increase enterprise profits.

The privatization programme provides for substantial advantages to managers and the workforce of an enterprise. In designing a privatization plan enterprise managers, together with the workers, will have the option to choose one of three 'privilege schemes':

1. *Scheme 1*. Employees are given a one-time gift of non-voting shares in the enterprise, equal to 25 per cent of the charter capital and up to a maximum of no more than twenty times the minimum monthly wage of each employee. They are also entitled to buy up to 10 per cent of the voting shares of the enterprise at a 30 per cent discount off the nominal value and with the right of deferred payment for up to 3 years (up to a maximum of no more than six times the monthly wage per employee). Enterprise officials and managers are, subject to contracts signed with them, given an option to acquire shares up to 5 per cent of the charter capital at its nominal value. Moreover, 10 per cent of revenues gained from the sale of

shares is deposited into the personal privatization accounts of the employees of the privatized enterprise.

2. *Scheme 2.* Enterprise employees are given the right to buy (by closed subscription) voting shares equal to 51 per cent of the charter capital. Note should be taken of the requirement that enterprise assets be evaluated according to GKI methods. In this case there is no free-of-charge transfer of shares, nor any sale of non-voting shares.

3. *Scheme 3.* By contract with the competent property management committee, a group of employees of an enterprise may assume responsibility for the improvement of the financial situation of the enterprise to be privatized, while also undertaking to maintain the competitiveness of enterprise products and keeping the number of jobs as defined by the privatization plan. If the contract is signed with the consent of the workforce, and for a period of not less than two years, and if the terms of the contract are fulfilled on expiry of the contract, the members of such a group are entitled to acquire 20 per cent of the charter capital in the form of voting shares in the enterprise at its nominal value and with the right of deferred payment for 3 years. If the group fails to fulfil the clauses of the contract, this right (option) is not valid. The group enters a contract with the local GKI department, which stipulates the liabilities of its members, including material liabilities for the property in their private ownership (contributed on mortgage).

In scheme 3 all the enterprise employees (including group members) are subsequently given the right to acquire further shares up to the amount of 20 per cent of the charter capital, but for a sum of no more than 7000 roubles per employee at a 30 per cent discount off nominal value, and with deferred payment of 3 years. (As we have said, the amount of the initial contribution must not be more than 20 per cent of the nominal value of the shares.)

Thus, in the first stage of mass privatization the government is seeking support primarily from workers and management, giving them unprecedented privileges and prompting them to corporatize enterprises and participate in privatization. It should be noted that the basic position of the GKI is to not give the workforce voting shares free of charge, despite strong pressure to do so from enterprise management, workers' councils and trade unions. The point of privatization is not to simply change owners, but to transfer property into the hands of the most effective owners. This will reinforce a new type of owner, who is able to act in a responsible and concerned way in order to increase his capital. It seems doubtful that this type of desired behaviour could be brought about through the free distribution of property. Moreover, the typical attitude of the workforce would not be to make investments in production, but to exploit existing capacities to squeeze out maximum profits with the help of price rises, especially when the enterprise has a monopoly position on the market. This would later lead to totally run-down machinery and equipment and to the shut-down of the enterprise.

Of course the subsequent sales and purchases of free-of-charge shares would eventually bring a change of owners. However, this process would take a long time, since far-sighted national or foreign investors tend not to invest in worker-managed enterprises.

Vouchers

The second phase of the mass privatization, beginning from autumn 1992, involves introducing registered privatization accounts (vouchers). In this way we can involve the majority of society, including groups working outside the sphere of material production — doctors, teachers, military personnel, etc. — in the purchase of property.

The voucher project has a number of objectives:

- all Russian citizens should gain from privatization, so that the process will be fair;
- society's support for the privatization process should be gained;
- extra pressure should be placed on the administrative framework to make it speed up privatization;
- the demand for property must be stimulated since, if the mass privatization programme were not available, the savings of the population would be enough to buy only a small portion of state property (even at book value).

The voucher project contains five main provisions:

1. Every citizen of Russia gets a voucher (B) with a certain nominal value, if he pays a small fee to cover practical costs. The initial portion of B is offered in the fourth quarter of 1992 and extra portions will be available in 1993 and 1994. (The GKI estimate is that about 40–50 per cent of the property in Russia can be privatized by means of vouchers.)
2. The voucher-holder may use his voucher together with money to buy shares of companies to be privatized. He may also exchange it for shares in investment funds or sell it for cash.
3. The federal government will get its proceeds from privatization in the form of vouchers. All vouchers accruing to 'property funds' (committees) from sales of shares will be transferred to the federal 'property fund' and will be written off there.
4. The voucher project will cover all regional and federal companies (except those that are already leased). Every enterprise of this category converted into an open joint stock company will earmark a part of its shares for sale by vouchers.
5. The voucher will be valid during a limited period of time (the initial series of vouchers will be valid until the end of 1993, and the second one until the end of 1994).

The procedure for selling shares for vouchers will be described in the privatization programme.

Problems with Vouchers

The principal problem of the voucher project is the need to take the leading position in offering shares of companies to be privatized and in the conversion of many state-controlled enterprises into open joint stock companies, in order to prevent the invitation surge.

Moreover, additional problems can arise in the circulation of the vouchers due to: the simultaneous use of money and vouchers in the course of privatization; possible attempts to issue special regional vouchers; possible sabotage of privatization at the managerial level of enterprises; and the risk that the population would all want to sell their vouchers at the same time.

Investment funds will be badly needed to facilitate the voucher project. They will serve as intermediaries between households offering vouchers and money and companies offering shares. Moreover, investment funds help to protect the wealth of small-scale investors (i.e. the population) by spreading their assets over many enterprises. They should be established 'from the bottom' and will be rather varying in size, and in industrial and regional affiliation. For a certain part of the population the investment funds will be the sole chance to make efficient use of their vouchers. Some investment funds can be established by privatization authorities, i.e. property funds and committees for property management.

A wide system of holding companies will appear. By buying a large quantity of shares, holding companies and investment funds can considerably reduce the problem of ownership being spread among too many small shareholders during the issue of the vouchers. Vouchers can be used to modify the pension system. Pension funds will be advisable for this purpose.

The law stipulates several methods of privatization for the medium- and large-scale companies. Almost all of them are competition-based schemes. First, a company can be sold to the highest bidder by auction or by competitive tender (where company management will be subject to certain conditions in the future). Sale to the highest bidder will probably be used for selling medium-sized companies both as a whole, and for selling major blocks of shares in them. Second, very large companies can be sold through 'investment biddings' (direct sales), where bids will be evaluated by a number of criteria. Here commitments on future investment and employment, ecological requirements, etc. will be considered along with price. If there is only one client at the auction, tender or investment bidding, direct sales will take place.

There are a number of advantages in using the competitive approach as the cornerstone of the Russian privatization programme. This approach will facilitate the emergence of large-scale owners who possess enough shares to take actual control of the company and manage it in a proper way. Competition means that companies will go to the highest bidder, and as a rule this is a client who can maximize the company's profits and efficiency. The highest-bidder basis will give substantial government revenue. This approach will rule out corruption and bribery, and thus privatization will be associated with open information and democratic methods.

In cases when less than 100 per cent of shares are offered at the auction, tender, or investment bidding and nobody gets a large block of shares, then the other shares will be offered at an auction or tender of small blocks of shares. These can be acquired for cash or vouchers. Such auctions are a key part of the programme, because all shares left under the control of the government will be transferred to the population or investment funds, thus completing the privatization process. The privatization profits will go to budgets on various levels and to state committees on privatization, and will mainly be spent on social benefits for the population.

The basic reason for local authorities to participate in the privatization process is their urgent need to improve their budgets and thus limit the inflation, which would otherwise imperil the reform effort, including privatization.

Thus the programme of mass privatization in Russia will provide all potential 'owners' (employees, managers, local authorities, private business-men, households, etc.) with an economic incentive to support the privatization policy. A major intention of the programme is to ensure a 'balance of interests' for the different levels of society, and to let this be a guide in the process of economic reform.

Preparing for Large-Scale Privatization

During the second phase of the preparation for Russian privatization (summer–autumn 1992) attention is focused on preparing and elaborating 'large-scale privatization', that is, the conversion *en masse* of state-controlled enterprises into public companies and the distribution of vouchers among the population, preparing pilot programmes for privatization in all large companies, and on improving methods for attracting foreign investments. This is also the time when we begin to privatize insolvent companies controlled by the state.

It is planned to sell state property for a total value of 70–80 billion roubles and to give away (as gratis shares distributed among the employees) property valued at another 150–200 billion roubles. A certain part of property (the accurate figure is difficult to forecast) will be acquired by the population by means of transfer from the registered accounts (vouchers). The total amount of privatized property can reach 15–20 per cent of the value of fixed assets by the end of 1992.

In 1992 privatization will cover the small-scale companies subject to compulsory selling to private owners. Most probably they will be sold by means of competitive and non-competitive tenders, and in some regions, for lack of demand, they will be sold directly to the only customer interested, namely the enterprise workforce.

Resentment over the 'fat cats' who bought up property at auctions should begin to decline when the real mass sell-out of shops starts, leading to substantial price decreases for trade and service properties, and after the distribution of vouchers among the population.

Survey data give reason to suppose that the majority of employees (from one-half to two-thirds) will use their vouchers for acquiring shares in their companies. At the same time a considerable part of the society will have no desire to become owners and they will sell their free shares. Marketing surveys show that one-third of employees will not take part in the privatization. In 1992 the most likely buyers of the privatized property will be its workers and representatives of new commercial groupings.

The third phase of the privatization (roughly 1993—94) will be devoted to selling shares of large industries and other spheres of the economy. This will be the main concern of the government, including regulation of the share sale, creation of conditions for free transfer of the capital including vouchers, issue of new portions of the vouchers and distribution of them among the population, regulation of the investment fund activities and holding companies' work, etc. Special attention will be paid to stimulating faster privatization (including the distribution of Western aid as investment subsidies to privatized companies).

The final phase will involve special procedures for privatizing companies that have not yet been privatized, in particular, loss-making enterprises, and those whose functioning is harmful to the environment.

Foreign Investment and Privatization

Particular attention should be paid to foreign investment, since this can be a decisive factor for the success of privatization as a whole. Today the basic obstacle to foreign investment is the poor legal framework. Foreign investors very often cannot get an answer to very simple questions such as: Who are the partners? Who do we negotiate with? Who is the decision-maker? And so on.

The government is supplementing the legal structure, know-how, and practical mechanisms for receiving foreign investments. The basic principle here is that local and foreign investors should be subject to similar conditions. In particular, the competitive approach and a lack of general restrictions should prevail (100 per cent of shares can be sold to a foreign investor). Nevertheless, there are a few distinct industries and services where restrictions and bans have to be imposed on foreign investment.

Privatization in Russia is now entering a decisive phase. In the second half of 1992 it will become the main focus of the economic reform programme. Based on the organizational, legal, and institutional work already done, the government intends to widely extend small-scale privatization, and to start to implement mass privatization. The success of privatization will be decisive for the Russian reform programme.

Part III
Macro-economic Stabilization

6 Remaining Steps to a Market-Based Monetary System in Russia[1]

Jeffrey Sachs and David Lipton

First published in 1993

Introduction

The monetary problems facing Russia are perhaps the most complex in world history. At the beginning of 1992, the fifteen newly independent states of the former Soviet Union each had central banks issuing rouble credits without coordination. Recently, Estonia and Latvia have successfully introduced new currencies and others are sure to follow. Russia faces the challenge of coordinating monetary policies throughout the rouble area. At present, it remains difficult to make payments and settlements in a banking system that was designed for central planning. The enormous and mounting inter-enterprise arrears require urgent attention. And Russia must also develop payments mechanisms for its trade with countries leaving the rouble area.

Russia began its economic reforms lacking the basic monetary arrangements necessary for a market economy. It is essential to undertake fundamental monetary changes in several areas. The areas of greatest importance are:

1. establishing clear and unified control over monetary policy in the rouble area;
2. establishing mechanisms for market-based trade with states that leave the rouble area;
3. unifying the rouble exchange rate;
4. improving the payments mechanism of the banking system, to eliminate delays which now threaten the economy;
5. overcoming the cash crisis, and unifying the cash rouble (*nalichnyi*) and non-cash rouble (*beznalichnyi*) markets;
6. establishing central bank independence; and
7. managing the huge build-up of inter-enterprise arrears.

79

This chapter outlines the basic issues in each of the areas. Most of what is presented is straightforward and well known. Perhaps the less-well-known areas include: the mechanisms for trade with countries that leave the rouble area; improvement of the payments mechanism of the banking system; and unification of the cash and non-cash rouble markets. In any event, the goal of the chapter is to pull together suggestions for the key remaining actions in one document.[2]

The Rouble Area: Rules and Sharing Procedures

For monetary policy to be effective and for the stabilization effort to succeed, there must be a single monetary authority with adequate control over the instruments of monetary policy. To make this possible, the states that use the rouble must adopt a common set of rules and procedures for the management of the rouble monetary area. Most importantly, *the Russian central bank should become the sole bank of issue of the rouble.* There are several important principles that should be followed in establishing the rules and procedures of the rouble area, and these are outlined below.

In the event that another central bank refuses to agree to Russian control over the rouble issue, the country should politely be invited out of the rouble area. In effect, Russia must nationalize the rouble, but in a fair and transparent way, that is equitable among the states that remain in the rouble area.

Earlier this year, the IMF proposed that each of the central banks in the rouble area retain the right to issue roubles, and that credit policies be coordinated by negotiation among the members of the rouble area. In our view, there is no realistic possibility of controlling credit in a system in which several independent central banks each have the independent authority to issue credit. The reason is simple. There is an overwhelming pressure in each of the states to 'free ride' by issuing rouble credits at the expense of the rest of the system. Even IMF conditionality will not be strong enough to make friendly agreements stick.[3]

Monetary economists take it as a nearly self-evident proposition that a single currency area should have a single bank of issue:

> The key feature of a unified currency area is that it has at most one central bank with the power to create money – 'at most' because no central bank is needed with a pure commodity currency. The U.S. Federal Reserve System has twelve regional banks, but there is only one central authority (the Open Market Investment Committee) that can create money. Scotland and Wales do not have central banks.[4]

Our recommendations for rules and sharing procedures within the rouble area are as follows:

1. *One authority over monetary policy.* There should be one institution, which could be called the Rouble Monetary Authority, with the sole jurisdiction over monetary policy. This Authority should include representation from all states using the rouble, but voting should be based on membership

quotas calculated to reflect the economic size of the participating states. In other words, Russia should have 55 per cent or more of the votes and should unilaterally control the decisions of the Authority, subject to the safeguards spelled out below.

2. *One bank of issue.* The Charter of the Rouble Area should establish that the Central Bank of Russia will be the sole bank of issue for roubles. What this must mean is that only the Central Bank of Russia will extend credits either in the form of currency emission or in the form of bank reserves. Centralizing control over credit creation is necessary, because it is the best way to prevent an abusive creation of credit by other states, a process that would be fatal to the effort to establish price stability.

3. *Fair treatment of member states.* To make these terms for membership in the Monetary Authority (and the continued use of the rouble as legal tender) acceptable to other states, the Articles of Agreement of the Authority should set out clear procedures that establish fair treatment of member states. The fair treatment procedures should be changeable only by a super-majority (e.g. 66.6 or 80 per cent).

First, the gains from the creation of rouble cash money (seigniorage) must be distributed fairly among member states. In other words, the cash issue should be distributed routinely to the governments of member states according to an equitable distribution formula.

Second, credit creation by the Central Bank of Russia must be apportioned fairly among the member states. There must be an agreement on a sharing formula for the allowable amount of credit to member state governments to finance budget deficits. If there are to be refinancing credits to commercial banks, there must be a sharing formula for the allowable amount of refinancing credits so that banks in each of the member states have access to their fair share. Under a credit-sharing arrangement, the central banks of member states would serve as the conduits for refinancing credits from the Central Bank of Russia to commercial banks, but would issue no net credit themselves.

Third, the Monetary Authority must also take responsibility to coordinate foreign exchange market intervention throughout all member states, so as to guarantee equal access to foreign exchange and a unified exchange rate in all member states.

With these procedures, potential member states should be attracted to joining the Monetary Authority for two main reasons. First, each member is protected from the abusive behaviour of other members by the fact that Russia has strong control over the Authority and that there are rules to prevent member states from abusive credit creation. And second, the system will be administered in a way that is fair to all members. Monitoring by the International Monetary Fund will help to assure all members that other states are not abusing the procedures of the system to their own advantage.

4. *Freedom to join or leave.* All of the states using roubles at present should be given the choice to join the Rouble Monetary Authority, or to leave the rouble area by introducing their own currencies. There should be no active dissuasion of any state that wishes to have its own currency. When a state

leaves the rouble area, it would do so under rules of behaviour that will protect the remaining members of the rouble area (as described below). In particular, Russia would insist that any state introducing its own currency should do so via a currency exchange that withdraws the cash roubles circulating in the state, and that converts the bank balances into the new national currency. Roubles withdrawn from circulation should be returned to the Rouble Monetary Authority. Russia should request that the International Monetary Fund help enforce the rouble withdrawal requirement as part of its conditionality.

5. *Rouble Monetary Authority.* Once established, the Rouble Monetary Authority should take responsibility for the conduct of monetary policy. The Authority would set interest rates on credits of the Central Bank of Russia (mainly refinance credits to the commercial banks). The Authority would also establish reserve requirements (and the interest rates for remuneration on reserves) that would obtain for commercial banks in all member states. The Board would also manage exchange rate policy, either pegging the exchange rate (and devoting foreign exchange reserves to the defence of the pegged rate) or declaring a floating or managed exchange rate system.

6. *Member states' central banks.* As a consequence of membership in the Rouble Monetary Authority, the central banks of member states would cease to be independent monetary authorities. These central banks would not create credit, would not issue currency, and would not make monetary policy. They would serve a coordinating role in the monetary system, and would operate in cooperation with the Rouble Monetary Authority. They would retain an important role in the supervision of commercial banks in their state and would be involved in inter-republican settlements.

7. *National currencies.* It will be possible to accommodate other states in a symbolic way by allowing a distinct national cash money to circulate on a rigid one-for-one basis with the rouble (akin to Scottish pounds or banknotes of the Federal Reserve Bank of Boston). In effect, the money in circulation would be redenominated, and replaced with new currency notes (e.g. the Belarus rouble), but the republican central bank would have no monetary authority except to change Belarus currency into Russian roubles, and vice versa, on a one-to-one basis. In effect, the republican central bank would become a strict currency board, attached to the Russian Central Bank.

8. *Reorganizing balance sheets.* There are important issues of transition to a centralized Rouble Monetary Area. The balance sheets of the member central banks must be reorganized in line with the principal goal of establishing a single bank of credit issue.

Trade and Payments with the Non-Rouble Area

Estonia introduced its own currency, the kroon, in June 1992, becoming the first state of the former Soviet Union to introduce a new currency.[5] Latvia followed in July 1992, introducing the lat. In the coming months, Ukraine will probably introduce its own currency as well. In each case, the new currencies will be the sole legal tender for transactions within these states. There are a number of technical issues that must be resolved for those states that elect to leave the rouble area, and we shall discuss these issues using Estonia as an example (the same principles should apply to Ukraine and other countries introducing new currencies). These issues include the return of roubles circulating in Estonia, the nature of the exchange regime between the rouble and the kroon, and the features of the settlements mechanism between the Russian and Estonian banking systems.

Return of the Cash Roubles

Estonia agreed to return to Russia the rouble cash in circulation. This measure has prevented Estonia from incurring a trade deficit with Russia by purchasing goods in Russia with the outstanding rouble cash, and thereby adding to the money supply in Russia (this issue obviously is much more important in the case of Ukraine). To accomplish this, the Russian and Estonian central banks agreed that there would be an exchange of kroon for rouble cash in circulation over a short and limited period of time.

The Estonian central bank and commercial banks have also swapped roubles for kroon in bank balances (and in the denomination of contracts). There are some technical issues to be resolved in converting rouble bank balances to kroon. It would have been irregular for Estonia to insist that deposits of non-residents (e.g. Russian enterprises holding accounts in Tallinn banks) should be converted involuntarily. The possibility of allowing Russian enterprises to maintain rouble balances in Estonian banks could be taken up in connection with discussions about the payments mechanism to be adopted for trade between Russian and Estonian enterprises.

The Rouble–Kroon Exchange Rate

In order to absorb the rouble cash in circulation, Estonia converted ten roubles into one kroon. Once the exchange was complete, both Estonia and Russia agreed to allow the exchange rate to float. Estonia was uninterested in maintaining a peg to the rouble, as it is trying to escape from the tight link to Russian monetary policy. For Russia, a commitment to support the kroon at a stable rate in the foreign exchange market would be tantamount to supplying an open credit line of roubles to Estonia. Of course, it was precisely this obligation that Russia wanted to avoid.

Estonia decided to peg to the deutschmark. Note that if Russia, in time, decides to peg to a convertible currency, the cross-rate of the kroon and rouble will also in effect be pegged. But in this case, Russia will have no obligation to support the kroon, and Estonia will have no obligation to support the rouble. Foreign exchange interventions in each country will be against convertible currencies, not against each other.

Settlement of Trade Transactions

Once the former republics have their own currencies, it will be important to have a settlements mechanism that allows trade to operate without long payments delays or cumbersome procedures. One possibility, to conduct trade in hard currency settlements, would require a large holding of foreign exchange reserves, and is therefore too expensive. More realistically, trade should continue to be settled in roubles, *but strictly on a market basis*. For rouble trade to continue, however, a new settlements mechanism must be put in place.

This could be done through a series of correspondent banking accounts, held by republican banks in Russian banks. To see how this would work, consider how Russia now trades with Germany (or any other hard-currency country). Enterprises are not supposed to own German bank balances directly (although, of course, some do). Instead, they own bank accounts in Russian banks, while the Russian banks hold bank accounts of the same amount in German banks. Thus, when an enterprise owns a deutschmark (DM) bank balance in Moscow, it is really holding an account in a Moscow bank that is backed by the bank's ownership of the same amount of DM in a German bank. The bank accounts of Russian banks held in German banks are correspondent bank accounts.

When an enterprise without DMs wants to make an import from Germany, it purchases a DM-account on the inter-bank auction market. In effect, it becomes the (indirect) owner of the bank account in Germany, by owning a DM claim on a Russian bank which is backed by the Russian bank's ownership of the DM claim on the German bank. When a Russian enterprise makes an export to Germany, the German buyer deposits its DMs with the German correspondent bank of the Russian exporter's bank. The Russian bank increases its correspondent account with the German bank (or at least is supposed to do so!).

In principle, Estonia will now trade with Russia in exactly the same manner as Russia trades with Germany. Trade will (mostly) be denominated in roubles (though some trade will naturally be denominated in hard currency as the rouble is not yet stabilized), with Estonian banks holding correspondent accounts in Russian banks. When an Estonian exporter to Russia earns roubles, the correspondent account will rise. When an Estonian importer wants to make an import from Russia, the correspondent account will fall. Also, the rouble accounts will trade freely against kroon in an auction market in Tallinn or Leningrad.

In the past, the Central Bank of Russia has opposed a system of direct correspondent accounts between commercial banks on the grounds that '(it) would no longer have the necessary information on flows between the two countries'. This view was a relic of the old 'control mania', when money flows were used to track the planning process rather than to facilitate market-based trade. However, there are no crucial facts that can be learned under this system that could not be gathered by customs houses and direct reporting by banks and enterprises on cross-border shipments. (In any event, the Central Bank has been completely overwhelmed administratively, and has not even been able to process in a timely way the inter-republican transfers through its correspondent accounts).

Therefore, a system of correspondent accounts should be established between Russia and each republic's commercial banks.[6] This will require a change of Russian Central Bank procedures to allow republic banks to hold rouble accounts directly with commercial banks in Moscow.

Moreover, to make the new trading system function well, banks will have to acquire and maintain adequate rouble balances in their mutual correspondent accounts. There is a simple way to accomplish this. The major commercial banks in each country and Moscow should arrange to swap correspondent accounts. For example, Russian banks would receive a rouble account in Tallinn, which could be used by their customers to make import purchases from Estonia, while Estonian banks would receive rouble accounts of the same amount, in order to facilitate imports from Russia. The central banks in each country should take care to make sure that these correspondent accounts are set up before the central bank correspondent accounts are discontinued.

To the extent that the major banks are illiquid, there may be a role for a one-time central bank loan in each country to their respective banks for the purpose of establishing the correspondent accounts. These central bank loans would take place at the refinance interest rate.

Unification of the Exchange Rate

In preparation for the stabilization of the rouble, the foreign exchange market should be simplified and the multiplicity of exchange rates should be unified so there is a single exchange rate for all current account transactions. At present there are several exchange rates, because of regulations that segment the exchange market and reserve special rates for certain current account transactions.[7]

Our recommendations for the unification of the exchange rate are as follows:

1. The commercial exchange rate, currently set at half of the central bank's quasi-market exchange rate, should be eliminated. This rate is used solely for exchange surrender of 40 per cent of the proceeds of energy and raw materials exports that take place at the commercial rate. When the commercial rate is eliminated, an explicit export tax on these products could raise an amount of revenues for the budget equivalent to the penalty involved in surrender at a sub-market rate.
2. The special budget rate used for centralized imports and external debt service should also be eliminated. Purchasers of centralized imports should pay the full market exchange rate, and receive explicit budget subsidies if necessary for distribution of the goods to the final customer (e.g. in the case of medicine). Budget accounting should use true, market exchange rates so that the economic cost of transactions undertaken by the government is reflected accurately in the budget. The use of accounting

exchange rates distorts budget accounting and provides a misleading impression of budget outcomes.

3. The official exchange rate set by the central bank should be set routinely and frequently to reflect the outcome of transactions in the auction market for foreign exchange. The present system of setting a quasi-market rate with only a loose connection to market outcomes should be replaced by an automatic process (based on averages of the most recent auctions from around the country). The period of adjustment should be shortened, and the exchange rate should be adjusted every few days to reflect the result of the auctions. To make it possible to have a market-based official exchange rate, the auction market for foreign exchange must be broadened to permit greater access for buyers and sellers.

4. This will be made easier if the value of the rouble is strengthened. There are two instruments of policy that can make this occur. First, the central bank will have to limit the creation of credit and raise interest rates to positive real levels. Eliminating the abundance of deposit money held by enterprises will heighten the demand for roubles and strengthen the exchange rate. Second, the central bank should sell foreign exchange in the auction market in much larger quantities as soon as it is feasible to do so.

5. There should be 100 per cent repatriation of foreign exchange earnings, but no surrender requirement. This means that the dollar earnings would have to be returned to Russia in the form of a bank balance held in a Russian bank. However, the Russian bank account could remain in dollars, rather than being converted to roubles. The Russian commercial bank would then be required to hold an equivalent amount of foreign exchange in its correspondent accounts with foreign banks. In effect, there would be a 100 per cent reserve requirement on the foreign currency deposits.

6. To the extent that the Russian government requires dollars, it should either take them from revenues (e.g. export taxes paid in hard currency), or purchase them for roubles, on the auction market.

Banking System Reform: Managing Bank Liquidity in a Market System

The Stalinist payments system in Russia has not yet adjusted to the new market system. The old division between cash money and non-cash money remains the law, and even the practice, for most state enterprises. Cash is used for retail purchases and wages, while non-cash money must be used between enterprises. The banking system does not serve the most basic function that it does in a market economy: allowing the depositor to withdraw deposits in the form of cash.[8] Nor does cash serve its most basic function, as legal tender for all transactions in the economy.

The commercial banking system is completely unreliable, so the present arrangements have very high costs. When an enterprise makes a cash deposit, there is no sure (or even legal) way to get the deposit out in cash again, except in the form of wage payments (and even for wages, the access to cash has become unreliable). Therefore, private enterprises find it difficult, or impossible, to rely on the banking system, and they tend to rely on cash instead, despite the high transactions costs of using cash. Moreover, since the legal circulation of cash is completely regulated, there is little innovation by commercial banks and enterprises in the efficiency of cash utilization. At the same time, as cash is drawn into the private trading system, the central bank has become unable to guarantee that cash circulates within the official channels to be available to state enterprises for wage payments.[9]

It also appears that the division of cash and non-cash markets causes serious problems for macro-economic control. Consider what happens if bank credit is expanded while the supply of cash in circulation is left unchanged. The credit expansion leads to a rise in producer prices, and these higher producer prices are passed along to retail prices. Since the supply of cash remains unchanged, however, nominal demand in the retail sector remains unchanged. With higher prices, and constant nominal demand, real demand by households actually falls. The result is that the expansion of enterprise credit leads to inflation and a fall of consumer purchases. Presumably, arrears increase as well, as retailers are unable to repay their suppliers from sales.

The huge arrears build-up in the first half of 1992 probably resulted, in part, from the discrepancy of cash and non-cash money (there were other causes as well, which are discussed below). Most observers agree that: enterprise credit conditions were more expansionary than cash conditions during 1991; that, upon price liberalization, enterprise prices thereby increased by more than could be absorbed in the retail market; that retailers therefore were unable to sell their goods; and that this has contributed to the rise of arrears. Interestingly, a 1977 description of the classical Soviet payments mechanism similarly pointed to shortfalls in retail sales as the main reason for arrears build-ups:

> Delays in settling for goods occur mainly when consumer goods reaching retail outlets are selling slowly or not at all. this is the point in the deposit transfer circuit where the greatest 'unplanned' use is made of short-term bank credit. It takes the form of an automatic (but not unlimited) extension of loans, either to the seller to bridge the settlement gap, or to the purchaser to enable him to make payment on the date due.[10]

Note that an expansion of credit to primary producers in the current environment could actually *worsen* the arrears problem rather than improve it. Production would continue, and producer prices would remain high, but the goods would still not be sold at the retail level.

In view of the end of the planning system, and the introduction of a market-based economy, it is necessary to recreate the payments system on a normal basis, in which bank depositers can convert their sight deposits into cash upon demand. In order to do this, there are four major changes that must be made:

1. The supply of cash money relative to the supply of non-cash money must be increased, by printing more cash and restricting the issuance of non-cash credits.

2. The attractiveness of non-cash money should be enhanced by raising interest rates on bank deposits, especially on Sberbank deposits (Sberbank is the household savings bank).
3. The legal distinctions governing the use of cash and non-cash money should be eliminated. Both cash and bank deposits should be legal tender for all debts, public and private. All enterprises should be free to use cash or non-cash money in any transactions, and to hold cash or non-cash money balances.
4. The Russian Central Bank should stand behind the reserves in the banking system, in the sense of providing cash *upon demand* to commercial banks that seek to draw down their reserves held at the Central Bank.

To back up these changes:

1. Credit expansion should be low.
2. Foreign exchange should be sold into the non-cash market auctions, in order to absorb liquidity (this should also be done to strengthen the exchange rate).
3. Cash money should be printed in large amounts, including very high denomination notes.
4. Households should be encouraged to shift out of cash money and into savings deposits, by raising interest rates on Sberbank deposits.

Sberbank Interest Rates and the Cash Crisis

One key way to ease the cash crisis is by encouraging households and enterprises to economize on cash. Many enterprises, for example, already pay wages directly into Sberbank accounts of their workers, rather than in cash payments at the workplace. This practice is typically resisted, however, since workers prefer the convenience of receiving cash, especially during a period of high inflation. Sberbank deposits can, and should, be made more attractive to workers, to encourage the practice of economizing on cash payments.

This can be done in several ways. First, and perhaps most important, the Central Bank should ensure that Sberbank itself remains liquid, so that deposits are readily available in cash. It will be much easier to guarantee the liquidity of Sberbank than of tens of thousands of workplaces at which wages are now paid. Second, special attention should now be given to creating a Sberbank checking account system. Third, interest rates on Sberbank deposits should be raised significantly, in order to protect the real value of deposits. The government has already declared that it will pay 80 per cent nominal interest rates on delays in wage payments owing to cash insufficiency. The government should encourage a similar interest rate on savings deposit accounts.

The balance sheet of the Sberbank is essentially as follows. There are liabilities, in the form of household savings accounts. These liabilities are matched by Sberbank claims on the Treasury, in the form of Treasury bonds (there are also some claims on the non-budgetary sphere, including loans to enterprises). The Finance Ministry has insisted that its interest payments on Treasury bonds held by Sberbank should remain very low, in order to avoid strains on the budget. As a result, the Sberbank has also insisted on maintaining low interest rates on household deposits, in order to maintain its own solvency.[11]

The government has so far resisted a rise in interest rates on Sberbank deposits, on the grounds that this would substantially increase the budget deficit. This is a mistaken position, as the increased deficit arising from higher interest rates could readily be financed in a non-inflationary way, if the government were to issue Treasury bonds to Sberbank in order to pay the interest due to the bank. Moreover, the real (inflation-adjusted) value of those bonds would not increase rapidly as long as the real interest rate on deposits remains low. In fact, since interest rates (even after a substantial increase) may well remain below inflation rates, the real value of the government's debt could actually decline.

Consider an illustration. Suppose that the Sberbank begins with exactly 200 billion roubles of household deposits, matched by 200 billion roubles of claims on the Treasury. The nominal interest rate on the Treasury debt and on the deposits are set at 20 per cent per annum, at a time when the annual inflation rate is 100 per cent. At the end of one year, the nominal value of household savings accounts will have risen to 240 billion roubles (200 × 1.2), while the real value will have fallen to 120 billion roubles measured at beginning-of-year prices. Similarly, the public debt to Sberbank will have risen to 240 billion roubles (presuming that interest payments are redeposited in new Treasury bills, an assumption we return to momentarily), but the real value will have fallen to 120 billion roubles.

According to standard definitions, the interest payments to Sberbank would contribute to budget expenditures of 40 billion, which would increase the deficit if these are not financed by tax revenues. In real terms, by contrast, the budget would record a budget surplus of 80 billion roubles, reflecting the fall in the real value of the public debt from 240 roubles to 120 roubles. In essence, the Treasury is paying a negative real interest rate so that the real budgetary burden of the debt to Sberbank is negative not positive.

Now let us consider what would happen if interest rates were raised to 100 per cent per year, to match the inflation rate. Clearly, household deposits would rise to 400 billion by the end of the year, as would the public debt. Measured in real prices, there would be no change in the value of deposits or Treasury debts to Sberbank. The budget burden of the debt would show 200 billion of interest payments, which would be matched by an equivalent budget deficit (assuming no other sources of revenue). In economic terms, however, the budget deficit would be zero, since the real value of the public sector's indebtedness would remain unchanged. There is no risk to the public finances in raising the interest rates to Sberbank, since the real value of the debt (and its burden on the budget) would not increase.

One important problem could arise, of course. If the Treasury had to pay the interest in cash, rather than new bonds, the interest payments would still generate inflation (even though the real value of the debt to Sberbank would be falling). Thus, it is important that Sberbank should accept payment from the Treasury in the form of new Treasury bonds, rather than in cash. It will be in a position to do this under two conditions: (1) that households are not attempting to liquidate their accounts at Sberbank, but rather are prepared to maintain their value in real terms; and (2) that the Treasury bonds are tradeable (if only to the Central Bank), in the emergency event that Sberbank faces a sudden and large withdrawal. To provide further protection to the budget and the Central Bank, the highest interest rates should apply only to time deposits, with a significant penalty in the form of early withdrawals.

To summarize, the government should encourage a rise of interest rates on Sberbank deposits. To do this, it should be prepared to raise the interest rates that it is prepared to pay to Sberbank on the bank's Treasury bonds. Interest payments should be in the form of new bonds issued to Sberbank. The bank should be required to accept these bonds, perhaps with the understanding that they will be repurchased in part by the Central Bank in the event of a run on Sberbank deposits. In this way, the higher 'deficit' of the Treasury would be financed by bonds, rather than by money printing (except in the event that the Central Bank had to repurchase the bonds).

It is thus important that the measure of the budget deficit should be adjusted to reflect the real value of the interest payments on the debt, instead of the nominal value of interest payments.

Bank Reform: Payments Mechanisms

There is an urgent need to simplify the system for payments transfers between banks. When an enterprise with a deposit in one bank wants to pay an enterprise with a deposit in another bank, the process of transferring accounts can take *several days* if the two banks are within Moscow; *two weeks* if one of the banks is outside Moscow; and up to *two months* if one of the banks is in another republic. By simplifying the payments mechanism, most of these delays could be eliminated, and the majority of settlements could be done in a day or two.

The payments delays are wreaking havoc with the economy. They are one of the major factors causing the inter-enterprise arrears: enterprise B cannot pay enterprise C because it has not yet received payment from enterprise A.

These delays will occur as long as the Central Bank tries to monitor every transaction that takes place in the economy, and to maintain a paper document for every transaction. This is a relic of the old planning system, in which the settlements process was used as a control mechanism to make sure that plans were being implemented. The result, of course, is that the whole system is breaking down, and the Central Bank actually controls nothing: it has no time (or reason) to analyze the millions of paper documents being generated in the payments system.

Consider just one example of the perversity of this system. If an enterprise with a deposit in one branch of a Moscow bank wants to make a payment to an enterprise with a deposit at another branch of the same bank, each branch bank must maintain a separate correspondent account at the Central Bank. A payment order must be sent from one branch of the bank to the Central Bank, which then sends the payment order to the other branch of the bank. The central bank then credits the account of one of the banks and debits the account of the other bank.

In a normal market economy, such a transaction has nothing to do with the central bank! The bank, including all its branches, maintains just one account at the central bank. This account is used only when there are settlements between the bank and a completely different bank. For settlements between two branches of the same bank, however, transfers are left to the internal accounting of the bank, which has nothing to do with the bank's account at the central bank. It is crucial that each bank consolidate its accounts at the central bank into one correspondent account so that intra-bank settlements (i.e. transfers between branches of the same bank), would not involve the central bank at all.

Banks should also open correspondent accounts directly with other banks so that transfers between banks linked by correspondent accounts will not require Central Bank settlements. Consider the following example. Suppose a depositor at Moscow Business Bank wants to make a payment to a depositor at Menatep Bank. Instead of sending the payments order from the Moscow Business Bank to the Central Bank and then to Menatep Bank, Moscow Business Bank would hold its own account directly at Menatep Bank. To make the transfer, Business Bank would debit the account of its depositor; Menatep bank would debit the account of Business Bank; and Menatep Bank would credit the account of its depositor (the enterprise receiving the payment). In this way, there would be no change in the correspondent account balances of either bank held at the Central Bank, and the Central Bank would not have to be involved in the transaction.

A group of banks should also be allowed on a voluntary basis to organize a clearing-house for payments orders, outside of the Central Bank. Suppose that there are three banks (A, B, and C). Each is ordered (by depositors) to make transfers to other banks. A is to transfer 50 roubles to B; B is to transfer 75 roubles to C; and C is to transfer 40 roubles to A. In the current system, all three transactions must be processed separately by the Central Bank. In a clearing system, the banks would get together (once a day in Moscow, and without the involvement of the Central Bank) and they would establish net positions. A's net position for the day is − 10 (40 receipt less 50 payment); B's net position is − 25; and C's net position is +35. Obviously, the net positions add to zero.

After the banks agree on the net clearing, they would report just three numbers to the Central Bank (in a document signed by all of the banks): A, − 10; B, − 25; C, +35. The Central Bank would then debit or credit the central bank correspondent accounts of each bank by the requisite amount (e.g. A's reserves at the Central Bank would be reduced by 10 roubles). There would be no paper flows to and from the Central Bank, except the one sheet recording the changes in the net positions.

Central Bank Independence

History clearly shows that the legal arrangements surrounding a cental bank play a critical role in determining central bank policies. The independence of the German Bundesbank from direct political interference, for example, has been a central reason why the deutschmark has consistently been a stable currency. Independence should have the following features:

- Chairman (Governor) of bank appointed for several years, fixed term;
- Board of Directors appointed for several years, fixed term;
- no requirement for government approval of monetary policy;
- no requirement for Parliamentary approval of monetary policy;
- statutory requirement that the Central Bank should pursue the aim of monetary stability;
- legal protection of Central Bank in conflicts with government and Parliament;
- no automatic financing of budget deficit;
- deficit financing at market rate of interest;
- ceiling on total government borrowing from Central Bank;
- discount rate set by Central Bank, not Parliament or government.

Even with central bank independence, both the government and the Parliament would retain some prerogatives. The Parliament would continue to monitor monetary policy, in committee hearings and debate, but not through explicit directives to the Bank. The government (or President) would make appointments of the Chairman, and the Board of Directors, that must be confirmed by the Parliament. Neither the government, the President, nor the Parliament, would have the power to remove the Chairman of the Bank, nor the Board of Directors, except for malfeasance in office. Terms of the Chairman and the Board would be confirmed for several years, independent of the government and the Parliament.

It may seem naïve to expect that the assignment of political responsibilities could be worked out now, in view of the feuding between the Parliament and the government. But perhaps there is a way to make progress on central bank independence, by having both the government and the Parliament simultaneously renounce operational control over the Central Bank of Russia, in favour of a properly independent central bank.

We recommend that the government and the Parliament reach an agreement on the overall organization of the Russian Central Bank. A Board of Directors of the Bank would govern general policy, and the day-to-day management would be under the direction of the Governor of the Bank. Members would be nominated by the President of the Russian Federation, and approved by the Parliament. There would be a fixed term, say of three years, for the first board. Similarly, the Governor of the Central Bank would be nominated by the President and approved by the Parliament.

The Central Bank should also have an establishing charter. The goals of the Central Bank would be clearly stated, in order of priority:

1. To guarantee a stable value of the rouble, on domestic markets and in international exchanges.
2. To organize an efficient payments system in conformity with the needs of a market economy.
3. To guarantee the international convertibility of the currency.
4. To maintain credit conditions conducive to overall macro-economic stability, as a basis for long-term economic development.

The Charter would clearly state that the Central Bank is to undertake monetary policies conducive to these goals, and is proscribed from financial operations that would be detrimental to these goals.

The Central Bank should be obligated to make timely reports on monetary conditions and monetary policy to the Parliament, and to hear recommendations of the Parliament and government on the conduct of policy. Parliament and the government, however, would be explicitly barred from interfering in the operation of monetary policy.

The Central Bank would be proscribed by its Charter from making subsidized loans in the economy, except as provided explicitly by the budget.

Managing Inter-Enterprise Arrears

It is now well understood that there is no single explanation for inter-enterprise arrears. There are, in fact, many important contributing factors. Final demand has fallen more than production. The cash shortage has contributed to a squeeze of final goods purchases, while producers have continued to produce at old levels. As mentioned earlier, there has been a breakdown of bank payments mechanisms. Because of the archaic methods used to clear payments between banks, there are large delays in receiving payments. Enterprises therefore lack the money to pay their suppliers because they have not yet received payments from their own customers. This is exacerbated by the breakdown of payments between republics. There has been a particularly sharp breakdown in the clearing of settlements between Russian and non-Russian enterprises. Settlements can sometimes take up to two months.

At the same time, military–industrial enterprises continue to produce. Despite the cutback in budgetary spending, the military sector has maintained production even where there is no demand from the government budget. These enterprises are not paid, and therefore they cannot pay their own suppliers.

The micro-economic incentives governing shipments and payments are also deficient. There is an absence of incentives to clear arrears. Enterprises in arrears are still able to pay wages, and even to raise wages. In addition, interest charges on arrears are negligible, so that there is a strong incentive to delay payments. Moreover, there is a lack of clear sales-verification mechanisms. There is not yet a system of bills of exchange, letters of credit, bank checks, and so forth, to allow shippers to guarantee that they will be paid by suppliers. Finally, there is a lack of bankruptcy provisions. Since there are no legal bankruptcy mechanisms in place, there are very limited means for enforcing debt contracts.

These problems have several clear implications. Increased credit is dangerous. Credit might allow some production to continue, but it will not raise final demand of consumers. For that reason, it is crucial to overcome the cash shortage, which can only be done by raising the amount of cash relative to the amount of bank credit. Therefore, more credit will simply lead to inflation, higher inventories, and even higher arrears because of unsold goods. An improvement in the payments mechanism is crucial. There will be no way to prevent a further growth in arrears unless there are reliable ways to make payments between customers and between banks. And, incentives are needed to encourage firms to pay their bills. Incentives should include higher interest rate charges on arrears; legal mechanisms for creditors to seize assets of debtors; restrictions on wage increases to enterprises in arrears; and finally, a bankruptcy law.

A strategy for solving the arrears problems should aim at three things:

1. *Postponing the repayment of arrears*. These should be postponed for a period of several months, perhaps one year. The goal of this step is to prevent the old arrears from destroying future production. Many firms lack the liquidity needed both to pay off their arrears and to buy inputs for future production. By postponing the repayment of arrears, firms are given the opportunity to continue current production.
2. *Stopping the accumulation of new arrears*. Steps should be taken in several ways. We urge the immediate improvement of the payments system between enterprises, and between banks, according to specific suggestions. Penalties should be levied on enterprises in arrears (including wage limitations and high interest rates on the arrears). Bankruptcy proceedings should be imposed on enterprises that cannot pay of the old arrears and that continue to generate new arrears.
3. *Providing a way to settle past arrears*. A clearing system should be established for the old arrears, by netting them out, and then providing a new schedule for repayments. To give incentives for the eventual repayment of these arrears, we recommend that enterprises with arrears be subjected to strict wage limitations until the arrears are cleared.

Managing the Old Arrears

A date should be chosen to separate old arrears from new arrears. All arrears between Russian enterprises that are bona fide (e.g. registered in *Kartoteka dva*) would be registered with a payments agent. These debts would be converted into [one-year] loans, with [one-third] of the debts due in each [four-month] period. The loans would carry an interest rate [equal to] the Central Bank discount rate. (Obviously, a different maturity and interest rate of the debt could be selected. We are merely aiming to provide a specific illustration here.)

At this point, after the conversion of the arrears into securities, there are two possible variants.

1. *Variant 1*. The debts remain in the form of inter-enterprise claims, between specific enterprises. These claims would be marketable, so that the creditor enterprise could sell its claims to other enterprises, or even to the debtor firm, at a discount. At the end of the period, when the claims come due, failure to honour the debt could lead to the initiation of bankruptcy proceedings (under new procedures being established by the State Property Committee).
2. *Variant 2*. The debts would be converted from bilateral obligations between particular enterprises, into obligations to and from a central Clearing House (CH). The purpose of establishing the CH would be to permit the multilateral netting of claims and debts. For example, if Enterprise A owes 50 million roubles to Enterprise B, and 70 billion to Enterprise C, while at the same time it is owed 60 million from Enterprise B, and 20 million from Enterprise C, the CH would establish a net claim on Enterprise A of 40 billion roubles (50 + 70 − 60 − 20). Since the CH would lead to a significant netting out of claims, thereby reducing the stock of gross arrears into a much smaller stock of net debt either owed to, or owed by the CH.

In both variants, additional sanctions would be imposed on enterprises in arrears, as the terms for winning a debt workout, and as a disincentive to any further increases of arrears. For example, such enterprises would be subjected to strict wage limitations. Also, if the enterprise does not pay off the debt on the new [one-year] schedule, the enterprise would be subjected to bankruptcy proceedings. In particular, the management and workers in the enterprise would stand to lose their equity claims in the enterprise.

Clearing House Mechanics

If variant 2 is selected, the precise CH mechanisms might work as follows. All arrears owed by an enterprise to other enterprises would be converted into debts owed by the enterprise to the CH. All claims by an enterprise on other enterprises would be converted into claims by the enterprise on the CH. The CH would then cancel out offsetting arrears and claims of each firm, and calculate a net debtor or creditor position for each firm with the CH. Thereafter, enterprises would pay their debts into the CH (managed by the Central Bank), and enterprises would receive their payments from the CH. This system obviously applies only to the old arrears, before June 1. Consider the following illustration in Table 6.1.

Note that Enterprise 1 has total arrears of 120, and total payments due of 80 from the other firms. Therefore, Enterprise 1 has a net position of 40 in arrears (i.e. a net debt of 40). Enterprise 2 has total arrears of 100, and total payments due of 95 (net arrears 5). Enterprise 3 has total arrears of 65, and total payments due of 110 (net arrears are −45, i.e. a net credit position).

Table 6.1 Example of arrears

Arrears Owed by	Enterprise 1	Owed to Enterprise 2	Enterprise 3
Enterprise 1	–	50	70
Enterprise 2	60	–	40
Enterprise 3	20	45	–

Total arrears are 285 (= 120 + 100 + 65). These arrears are converted into net claims to or from the Clearing House, as follows:

	Debt to CH
Enterprise 1	40
Enterprise 2	5
Enterprise 3 (i.e., net credit)	−45
Total	0

Now, if we add up the net debt of the debtor enterprises, the outstanding balances have been reduced to 45 (= 40 + 5). By construction, the CH has a net worth identically equal to zero.

Payments made to the CH by debtor firms would simply be passed along to the creditor firms, on a *pro rata* basis. Thus, if Enterprise 1 and 2 each pay half of their respective debts (20 from Enterprise 1, and 2.5 from enterprise 2), that amount would be passed along to enterprise 3. The Clearing House would, by construction, never run a surplus or a deficit on a cash-flow basis. It would simply pay out what it takes in from debtor firms. If the debtor firms default (in part or in whole) on their payments, the creditor firms would receive only a fraction of what is owed to them.

In general, the CH would have the responsibility of trying to enforce the debt claims. Firms that owe money to the CH will be under a wage freeze, and with the threat of closure and bankruptcy if the debts are not paid on time to the CH. The CH could also try to sell its claims on specific enterprises into the capital market (at a discount on face value), and let the new creditors that purchase the debt try to collect.

Since the arrears are being turned into one-year debt, the CH would have several months to start up operations. For example, the arrears recorded at the commercial banks (in the *Kartoteka dva*) could be registered in 60 days, and netting could take place in the next 30 days. Firms would then be notified of the payments falling due, and would have another 30 days to come up with the first payment. Therefore, many of the administrative problems could be resolved *after* the CH is set up.

Two further comments are in order. First, the debts would probably be eroded by inflation, as long as the real interest rate is negative. Second, there would no doubt be political pressures on the CH to make payments to the creditor enterprises even when they fail to receive payments from the debtor enterprises. It would be essential to resist these pressures.

Each variant has its advantages and disadvantages. Variant 1 has the following advantages. First, it is administratively straightforward, since no new CH must be set up. Second, it preserves the legal status of creditors and debtors, and thus does not set a precedent that debts might be cancelled or taken over by some other entity. Third, it allows a decentralized approach for working off the debt, since creditors and debtors can bargain amongst themselves for debt reduction, debt buybacks, etc.

Variant 2 solves one problem, which may be enormous and worth solving: the complex web of claims in which enterprises are both creditors and debtors. The CH allows for a rapid netting out process, which can simplify matters immensely *if the gross arrearages are much larger than the net debts*. For example, if most enterprises are both creditors and debtors on inter-enterprise arrears, than netting could be hugely advantageous. If most enterprises are either creditors or debtors, but not both, then the clearing house would not be advisable, and smaller amounts of netting could take place on a decentralized basis. Remember that the CH alternative has the serious disadvantage of making it much harder to reach decentralized, bilateral settlements, and that disadvantage must be weighed against the possible benefits of netting.

Once the government has investigated the extent of the gains from a netting operation; it will be better able to decide between variant 1 and variant 2. All claims arising from arrearages before the chosen date would be transformed into one-year claims. An international investment firm could assist the Central Bank of Russia in analysing the extent to which a clearing house would reduce the overall amount of debt. If the total arrears (on the order of 3.0 trillion roubles at end-June 1992) would be reduced to, say, 1 trillion in net claims, by the CH operation, then establishment of a CH probably makes sense. If the net claims were to remain above 1.5 trillion roubles, on the other hand, then leaving the debts in bilateral hands probably makes sense.

Preventing Future Arrears

It would be extremely important to prevent a new build-up of arrears after the conversion of the old arrears into one-year debt. Enterprises should be warned to make shipments only to enterprises with the money available to make the purchase. Banks should issue letters of credit or other conditional payment instruments to guarantee the suppliers of the capacity to pay before shipments are made. Work on improving the settlements system should proceed more rapidly. There are many easy things to do, such as allowing banks to consolidate all of their branches into one account at the Central Bank; allowing the major banks to do their own clearing among themselves; and allowing banks to set up correspondent accounts with other banks. Interest rates on new arrears should be at a punitive rate of interest, even higher than the refinance rate.

Firms in arrears (whether old or new) should be subject to a wage freeze, and ultimately to bankruptcy procedures.

Conclusion

The steps we have outlined towards achieving a market-based monetary system in Russia are aimed at creating monetary institutions that will restore the usefulness of the rouble as a money, support price and exchange rate stability, and depoliticize monetary policy. Russia must abandon the structures and practices held over from the Stalinist economic system and perpetuated by the mentality of central control over monetary matters. In its place, Russia must build a monetary system that places the key instruments of money and credit policy firmly in the hands of a single, independent monetary authority. Not only must the Central Bank of Russia be made independent, but the independent states must quickly decide whether to remain in the rouble area (and join a monetary authority) or introduce new currencies (and take full responsibility for domestic stability).

With the instruments of monetary control firmly in independent hands, the rouble must be made a real, usable currency. The distinction between cash and non-cash money, which exists nowhere else in the world, must be eliminated. The multiplicity of exchange rates must be eliminated, so that international trade and finance can develop naturally. And, the commercial banks should be freed to conduct their domestic and international banking business without undue interference from the monetary authority.

The actions we have outlined are the most urgent. Further banking sector reforms will be needed over the years to come. These should include: enhanced banking sector supervision, including capital adequacy and portfolio diversification requirements on the vast proliferation of banks that have opened in the past two years; securities trading and disclosure laws; and efficient bankruptcy procedures, including mechanisms for converting debt into equity of existing state of enterprises.

Notes

1. The authors would like to thank Stanley Fischer for many discussions, and for collaboration on an earlier version of the discussion of inter-enterprise arrears.
2. These actions are the most urgent. The next round of banking sector reforms should include: enhanced banking sector supervision, including capital adequacy and portfolio diversification requirements on the vast proliferation of banks that have opened in the past two years; securities trading and disclosure laws; efficient bankruptcy procedures, including mechanisms for converting debt into equity of existing state enterprises.
3. The problems has been acutely underscored by Ukraine's announcement on 12 June 1992, of its intention to proceed – unilaterally and without consultation – on an enormous credit expansion (between 300 and 600 billion roubles), in order to settle inter-enterprise arrears. This massive amount of credit issue threatens to re-ignite explosive inflation in Russia unless the currencies of

Ukraine and Russia are quickly separated. Ironically, there are far superior ways to address the inter-enterprise arrears in any case, as we document later in the paper.

4. Milton Friedman (1992, p. 242).

5. The introduction of the kroon took place over the weekend of 20-21 June 1992. This chapter was prepared in the weeks leading up to this event. The following discussion of the mechanisms being adopted reflects our understanding of how the new system will function.

6. It would be possible, in theory, to maintain the existing system. Up until the introduction of the kroon, Estonian commercial banks have held correspondent accounts only with the Estonian Central Bank, which holds a correspondent account with the Russian Central Bank, which in turn holds correspondent accounts with Russian commercial banks. Under the new system, it is conceivable that every time that an Estonian enterprise wants to make a purchase in Russia, it would debit its account at its bank; its bank would debit its account at the Estonian Central Bank; the Estonian Central Bank would debit its account at the Russian Central Bank; and the Russian Central Bank would credit the correspondent account of the exporter's bank. But this cumbersome procedure, through long delays in settlements, has already contributed to a collapse of inter-republican trade.

7. Some of the changes recommended here were adopted by the Central Bank of Russia on 1 July 1992. The exchange rate system was unified and the CBR began to set the official exchange rate at the level prevailing in the interbank foreign exchange auction.

8. The convertibility of bank money into currency and vice versa is considered such a central role of a banking system that it is rarely even questioned. Deposit banks in operating the payments mechanism play the role of converting notes and coin into bank money and bank money into notes and coin.

9. In the classic central planning system, households spend cash in retail markets. Retail shops deposit the cash in the Central Bank. The Central Bank then allocates the cash among the 'commercial' banks (where state enterprises maintain deposits) to allow enterprises to withdraw their wage payments in cash. Under present circumstances, a smaller proportion of cash is being redeposited in the central bank, so that the central bank is unable to maintain the banks in cash that the enterprises need to make wage payments.

10. Garvy (1977).

11. It has been able to do this, in part, because the new commercial banks have not attempted to lure away household deposits by offering higher interest rates on household deposits. The new commercial banks argue, by and large, that they lack the facilities, branch offices, and technical capacity to service small household depositors.

References

Friedman, M. (1992) *Money Mischief: Episodes in Monetary History*, Harcourt, Brace and Jovanovich, New York.

Garvy, G. (1977) *Money, Financial Flows, and Credit in the Soviet Union*, National Bureau of Economic Research, Cambridge, MA.

Hansson, A. and Sachs, J., (1992) 'Crowning the Estonian Kroon', World Bank *Transition*, vol. 3, no. 9, October, pp: 103, Washington, DC.

International Monetary Fund (1992a) *Economic Review: Russian Federation*, Washington, DC, April.

International Monetary Fund (1992b) *Economic Review: The Economy of the Former U.S.S.R. in 1991*, Washington, DC, April.

International Monetary Fund *et al.* (1991) *A Study of the Soviet Economy Vol. 1*, Washington, DC February.

Moody, S. (1992) 'Eastern Approaches: Rubles, Western Aid and Ruble Stabilization', *Perspectives on Change*, vol. 1, no. 2, March.

Sundarajan V. (1992), 'Central Banking Reforms in Formerly Planned Economies', *Finance and Development*, vol. 29, no. 1, pp. 10–13, March.

7 Farewell, Rouble Zone

Brigitte Granville*

First published in 1995

Falling inflation was a cardinal feature of the Russian economy in the first quarter of 1994. The average monthly inflation rate of 12 per cent was about half that of the equivalent period of 1993 (23 per cent). One of the reasons for this comparative improvement is the end of the rouble zone in the autumn of 1993.

Inflation in Russia is strongly linked to the growth of the money supply, which had resulted from extra-budgetary central bank subsidies to enterprises, credits to finance the budget deficit, and credits to other former Soviet republics (FSRs).

The rouble zone was especially costly in the first year of transition. Credits to other FSRs amounted in 1992 to 8.5 per cent of Russian GDP[1] if delivery of cash is excluded, and 11.6 per cent otherwise, in terms of central bank credits alone (see Table 7.1).

This chapter is organized as follows: section 1 presents the argument against the rouble zone based on inflationary and trade effects. Section 2 relates the history of the zone up to the latest Belarus agreement signed on 12 April 1994. Any attempt to restore the rouble zone with one currency, even with a single centre of emission, is viewed as highly unstable.

Arguments Against the Rouble Zone

The 'rouble zone' indicates here the fifteen former Soviet republics (FSRs) which inherited a common, unconvertible currency, the Soviet rouble, upon the break-up of the USSR in December 1991, and those FSRs which continued to use the same currency as Russia in the succeeding months.[2] For more than a year after the collapse of the Soviet Union, the EC, IMF and other international financial institutions urged the FSRs to preserve a single currency. This poor advice was based largely on the notion that these states should seek to minimize the dislocation of central planning's organic enterprise links. As early as 1991, however, some economists pointed out the advantages of the rouble zone's replacement with national currencies.[3] These

Table 7.1   Financing of resource flows from Russia to other states of the former Soviet Union

	1992 bn roubles	1992 per cent of GDP	1993 Jan–Sept bn roubles	1993 Jan–Sept per cent of GDP
Central bank correspondent account and technical credits[1]	1545	8.6	1032	1.1
Government loans	2	–	119[2]	0.1
Commercial bank correspondent accounts	−30	−0.2	−675	−0.8
Enterprises Trade credit arrears	163	0.9		
Total identified financing (in bn USD)	1680 (8.5)	9.3	476 (0.6)	0.5
Memorandum Currency Issue	565	3.1	1928	2.1
Implicit trade subsidy at 1992 average exchange rate	2385	13.2		
Russian GDP	18 064.50		89 953	

Source: IMF (1994), Table 1, p. 25 and Goskomstat.
Notes: 1. Preliminary data subject to revision. Data may differ from balance of payments figures partly because they include financing provided to Georgia and Tajikistan, and partly because of data inadequacies, including those for financing among states other than Russia. 2. Government loans for 1993 are through 8 October 1993.

advantages included: creating incentives for sound macro-economic policy, especially in terms of controlling budget deficits and inflation; increasing trade benefits; and formulating optimal medium-term restructuring policies. However, it is important to recall the peculiarities of the monetary system in a command economy before evaluating these arguments.

The Twin Monetary System

The rouble zone owed its peculiarity to the monetary system inherited from the former regime. Until 1988, when a two-tier banking system was introduced, the functions of both central and commercial banks were performed by the State Bank (Gosbank). There were four exceptions: the Bank for Foreign Trade (Vneshtorgbank) which was in charge of international reserves, the Savings Bank (which became Sberbank), the construction bank (Promstroibank), and the bank for agriculture (Selkhozbank).

Gosbank was charged with allocating financial flows to government, enterprises and households according to a credit and cash plan. Firms received credits according to their production and investment plan financed from budgetary transfers. Enterprise profits were transferred to the government to support the budget, while the State Bank provided the additional credits necessary to these enterprises facing shortfall of revenues against expenses. For households, wage payments were received in cash. The only alternative financial assets were deposits in the state savings bank (Sberbank) which were re-deposited in Gosbank and hence made available for the government to use. In effect, two roubles existed: the cash rouble used by households and the bank deposit (non-cash) rouble used by enterprises.[4]

Under the Soviet regime, each republic had its own branch of Gosbank. When the republics declared their independence/sovereignty in 1990–91, they took over the local Gosbank branches and transformed them into national central banks.[5] However, the only service these banks could provide was issuing credits ('non-cash' roubles). The emission of cash roubles remained the monopoly of the Central Bank of Russia (CBR), as Russia was able physically to take control of all cash rouble emission. All 'Gosznak' bank-note printing plants were located inside the former RSFSR.

The dichotomy of the monetary system between cash and non-cash roubles led to an extremely unstable situation. On the one hand, there was a single currency, the cash rouble, whose emission was controlled by the CBR. On the other hand, there were as many non-cash roubles as independent central banks, all aiming to extract as many resources as possible from Russia. For the other FSRs, this system meant an unchecked supply of credit, but a hard constraint on the delivery of cash. For Russia, it meant high inflation, i.e., a 15 per cent monthly inflation rate over several months.

Inflation

The choice of a single or separate currency is determined by the criterion of fiscal discipline. If a country has its own currency, it is forced to confront the consequences of its own profligacy. Tough decisions on which loss-making enterprises should be allowed to go bankrupt can be made directly by national authorities, which are best equipped to weight costs and benefits in light of local conditions and prospects. Preserving the rouble as a single currency without any means of controlling budget deficits encouraged the countries to compete in running up the highest deficit. These deficits, in the absence of non-monetary financial assets, were necessarily financed out of money created by Russia.

The other FSRs had a permanent deficit with Russia (see Table 7.2), with the exception of Azerbaijan and Uzbekistan. This situation had to be corrected, or Russia would be forced to transfer resources to cover these deficits. The solution was that the FSRs introduce their own national convertible currencies and let their currencies float.[6] Their exchange rates could then move to a level which could eliminate this deficit, by reducing the demand for Russian roubles. Foreign exchange markets such as the MICEX in Russia were organized very quickly in almost all FSRs.[7]

Table 7.2   Trade between Russia and the FSRs, 1993 (bn roubles)

	Supplies from Russia	Supplies to Russia	Balance
Total	13 870	8621	5249
of which			
Armenia	69	17	52
Azerbaijan	167	181	−14
Belarus	2205	1966	239
Georgia	42	26	16
Kazakhstan	2386	1414	972
Kyrgyzstan	208	112	96
Moldova	402	112	290
Tajikistan	97	34	63
Turkmenistan	194	86	108
Ukraine	7365	3647	3718
Uzbekistan	735	1026	−291

Source: Goskomstat

Trade

The case against the introduction of national currencies was based on the need to protect trade links among the FSRs. It was argued that since these states would have no use for each other's new national currencies, payments would be made in hard currency, draining already meagre reserves. In fact, the supposed connection between the degree of intra-regional dependency in trade among FSRs and the introduction of national currencies is misleading. In intra-regional trade, the important aspect is not a common currency but rather free trade at free prices[8] and current account convertibility.[9] The best way to improve resource allocation is to value trade at world prices.[10] Otherwise: 'Mispricing of raw materials and intermediate goods leads to their hoarding or diversion to world markets with the result that final goods production grinds to a standstill.'[11]

This is exactly what happened to intra-regional trade before price liberalization. Much trade was effected through barter. Trade protocols were signed with each state, defining all commercial relations within the former Soviet Union (FSU). They were, however, poorly conceived and never implemented. As soon as prices were freed, barter diminished.[12] Further, Michalopoulos and Tarr (1992) demonstrated that ensuing breakdowns in trade relations were due to 'export licences introduced as a result of the different degrees of price liberalisation in the different FSR'.[13]

Convertibility is equally vital. If the FSRs' national currencies are convertible for trade transactions, payments can be made in roubles.[14] Trade between FSRs requires the purchase of roubles from the central bank of the FSR. If an FSR is a net importer from Russia, the central bank of that FSR would find its reserves of roubles dwindling. Thus, the volume of reserves serves as a limit to the imbalance in trade. Where there was only one currency (the rouble), trade imbalances did not manifest themselves as a change in the reserves of the central bank. Instead, FSRs' enterprises continued borrowing from the FSR government or from Russian enterprises (causing inter-enterprise arrears) without a natural check to the process.

Convertibility also has the advantage of introducing international competition, stimulating domestic production and trade. Most of all, it helps to do away with the old type of trade, based on products for which there is no demand. Many Russian enterprises were interested in keeping the rouble as the sole currency because they were unable to sell their output in a competitive market and wanted to continue to receive state subsidies. Such enterprises behaved as if they were still operating in a single country and under a soft budget constraint. Other republics were supplied with goods, regardless of their capacity to pay, while settlement was provided for by credits from the CBR.

Estonia's case illustrates the usefulness of introducing a national currency. In 1990, Estonia was dependent on intra-regional trade within the USSR for 91.6 per cent of its GNP, as one of the most dependent FSRs on Soviet trade.[15] Nevertheless, it introduced its own currency on 20 June 1992 at the rate of DM 1 for 8 new Estonian crowns. After one year the DM exchange rate of the crown had remained stable. The share of intra-regional trade had fallen to 47 per cent in 1992 and for 1993 it is estimated at 32 per cent.[16]

The example of Estonia shows that even if 'trade among the members of the CIS[17] certainly has an important geographic motivation', quite varied trading zones are developing.[18] With convertible currencies, free trade and free prices, trade links will be based on true comparative advantage rather than on patterns imposed by the central planning authorities.[19] For instance, the Central Asian States and the Transcaucasus are turning towards Turkey, Iran, the Gulf States and Pakistan and India. The Slavic and Baltic States are developing ties with Europe. The largest countries, Russia and Kazakhstan, are the least dependent economically on intra-regional trade. Ukraine, however, remains very dependent on Russia for energy supplies.

There are two main counter-arguments to the proposition that FSRs cannot afford raw material and energy imports from Russia at world prices. First, Russia is a country in too severe an economic plight to pay huge sums for the development of other FSRs. Second, it is not to the long-term advantage of the FSRs that Russia would suffer from subsidizing other FSRs.

Russia had much to lose from the rouble zone's existence, given the extent of subsidies, open or hidden, which it provided to the other FSRs mainly in the form of underpriced oil and raw materials (see Table 7.1). In some cases, these cheap natural resources were re-exported by the receiving FSR at world prices, generating windfall profits.

In the long term, the economic benefit of other republics was eroded by overdependence on Russia, because it dissuaded them from stabilizing and restructuring their economies to develop their own comparative advantages. Furthermore, it can be argued that if Russia has no reason to sell its oil at subsidized prices, the FSRs have no reason to buy Russian products if they can afford Western products of higher quality. In short: 'It is a quite awful idea to maintain a currency area between sovereign nations based on an unstable centre currency.'[20]

The Four Phases of the Rouble Zone

The Introduction of Correspondent Accounts (January–June 1992)

Although the rouble zone was a direct inheritance from the Soviet Union, comprising all FSRs, the CBR remained responsible for cash emission in the entire area. The CBR also handled non-cash emission, but only inside Russia. As of 1 January 1992, commercial banks were instructed to direct all transactions with FSRs through correspondent accounts at the CBR. The correspondent accounts of the central banks of the FSRs centralized the payment clearing system for inter-FSR transactions.[21] Payments were supposed to occur only if funds were available. In fact, since the FSRs traditionally had a trade deficit with Russia, they were able to finance their deficits by money creation in Russia.

Ickes and Ryterman (1992) explain well how the Russian surplus *vis-à-vis* the other FSRs was financed:

> First the surplus is financed by domestic expansion of non-cash rubles. The technical delay in clearing non-cash transactions in the ruble zone contributes to the high level of inter-enterprise debt in Russia. Second the surplus is financed directly by Russian enterprises, which deliver inputs without receiving payment. In this case the ultimate lender may be the Russian government, which provides the Russian enterprise with an implicit supply of credit.[22]

This undermined Russian efforts to cut inflation by means of tight monetary policy. In 1992 the automatic extension of Russian trade credits alone (excluding delivery of cash) to the FSRs amounted to 1,545 bn roubles (see Tables 7.1 and 7.3). Approximately 56 per cent of these credits were provided to Ukraine, 15 per cent to Kazakhstan, 7.6 per cent to Uzbekistan, and about 7 per cent to Turkmenistan. Cash supplies to the FSRs in 1992 amounted to 565 bn roubles or 3.1 per cent of GDP (Table 7.1) as compared to 1,928 bn roubles (2.1 per cent of GDP) during the first nine months of 1993.

In the period January to June 1992, the main events were the introduction of parallel currencies and the tightening of control over the FSR central banks' correspondent accounts in the CBR.

Russia embarked on its price liberalization programme in January 1992 without waiting for the other FSRs to follow its example. Consequently, the rouble zone became a dual price system, with predominantly free prices in Russia and predominantly controlled in the other FSRs.[23] Preserving the rouble as the common currency was difficult in such a situation. Parallel (coupon) currencies were introduced for two reasons:

Table 7.3 Financing of other states by the Central Bank of Russia, 1992

	End-1992 CBR Correspondent Account Position		End-1992 CBR position, Adjusted to exclude currency	
	bn roubles	per cent of GDP	bn roubles	per cent of GDP
Russian Federation	−2109	−11.7	−1545	−8.5
Armenia	34	49	9	12.8
Azerbaijan	51	25.8	34	17.4
Belarus	102	10.7	69	7.2
Estonia	4	4.0	4	4.0
Georgia	69	51.4	38	28.4
Kazakhstan	407	25.5	235	14.8
Kyrgyzstan	42	22.9	20	10.9
Latvia	2	1.0	2	1.0
Lithuania	9	3.2	9	3.2
Moldova	27	11.3	18	7.5
Tajikistan	36	90.7	17	42.5
Turkmenistan	172	53.3	111	34.4
Ukraine	862	21.7	862	21.7
Uzbekistan	292	69.9	117	28.1

Source: IMF (1994), Table 2, p. 26.
Note: Preliminary data subject to revision.
1. Currency deliveries amounted to 3.2 per cent of Russian GDP and 6.5 per cent of non-Russian GDP. Currency deliveries to Uzbekistan are estimates. No data are available on how much currency was used for financing Russian exports in 1992.
2. Includes Rbs 408 bn in offset arrears but excludes swaps of Rbs 80 bn.
3. The table includes a country breakdown for financing through correspondent account overdrafts, technical credits, and currency deliveries, but no country breakdown is available for financing in the form of arrears and commercial bank lending. These amounted to 0.8 per cent of Russian GDP and 1.6 per cent of non-Russian GDP in 1992. See Table 7.1 for a summary of aggregate data.

1. Rationing. Instead of freeing prices, most of the FSRs (e.g., Ukraine) resorted to administrative price hikes.[24] It then became cheaper for Russians to shop in the other FSRs. Some FSRs introduced coupons to confine the supply of foodstuffs and price-controlled goods to their own domestic markets.[25]
2. Coupons as additional money. We noted above that Russia strictly controlled the printing of cash, but excessively so. Repressed inflation turned into open inflation after price liberalization, and was further fuelled by the lack of control over the non-cash money supply. Instead, the cash money supply was overcontrolled in the mistaken belief that it would ward off inflation. This action produced a liquidity squeeze in Russia and the other FSRs.[26] In the absence of a well-developed monetary and banking system, cash was the predominant means of payment. The other FSRs

responded to the lack of roubles by issuing coupons as additional currency to pay for wages and consumer goods.

Although the original understanding was that correspondent accounts were to be used on the condition of strict availability of funds, inter-state payments continued to be processed automatically and unchecked. This practice was the result of payment delays and the CBR sub branches continued to independently process payments.[27]

Measures employed in Ukraine illustrated the instability of the payment system. Russia was left with no choice but to control further the correspondent accounts, in its efforts to limit the growth of the non-cash money supply. On 12 June 1992, Ukraine announced a massive increase in credit, approximately doubling its money supply to clear inter-enterprise arrears.[28] The Russian government was not consulted.

To limit the inflationary effect of this measure, and to ensure that no other FSRs would follow the Ukrainian example, the Russian government responded on 21 June with a decree effective from 1 July aimed at making the restrictions posed by the correspondent accounts effective. Two measures were intended to halt automatic credit to other FSRs. The national banks of the FSRs could only withdraw credits from correspondent accounts held at the CBR, if deposits existed to cover the transaction. All national banks were notified of this measure on 29 June 1992. Also, a new line of credit, called 'technical credits' and subject to negotiation, was opened for trade. The rate of interest charged was the CBR's normal refinance rate at that time (80 per cent yearly).

At the same time, the CBR encouraged FSR commercial banks to clear payments by establishing correspondent accounts with each other and without recourse to the CBR. Such a policy was formally reflected in Russia's agreement with Estonia, which specified that banks in Russia, which were allowed to open correspondent accounts under the general foreign exchange licence, might also open correspondent accounts in the FSR.[29]

The CBR's imposition of limits on the growth of correspondent accounts rendered the non-cash roubles of FSRs separate and non-convertible currencies.[30] With credit limits on each correspondent account of the FSRs, the price of the non-cash rouble began to vary from country to country. The exchange rate depended on differentials between FSR deposit demand, which depended in turn on the possibility to convert this deposit into either purchasing power in Russia or cash. The ultimate determinant, therefore, was the availability of credit and cash in the correspondent account of the country concerned. Moreover, if a rouble zone country wished to increase its money supply, it required a balance of payments surplus with Russia or to negotiate technical credits with the CBR.

Unfortunately, these rules were not adhered to. The central banks of the other FSRs continued to issue credits without providing any assets in exchange. Bills were simply sent to Moscow, forcing the CBR to finance them. This was possible for two reasons: first, the lobby of Russian firms trading with the other FSRs was strong and they wanted to be paid. Second, the CBR got a new chairman, Viktor Gerashchenko.

The End of the 'Old' Rouble Zone (July 1992–September 1993)

Viktor Gerashchenko's appointment as head of the CBR on 17 July 1992 was an event of major importance to the rouble zone. His policy was obvious: granting the requests for new credits from not only Ukraine but also from Kazakhstan, Kyrgyzstan and Belarus, with the professed aim of protecting commercial ties with these states. Consequently, the direction of policy towards the other FSRs was reversed.

Gerashchenko's policy caused credits to FSRs to skyrocket. This stock of credits reached 1,545 bn roubles at the end of 1992 (see Table 7.1), while at the end of June 1992 it had amounted to 325 bn roubles (i.e., an increase of 1,220 bn). Previously the limit had been fixed, in agreement with the IMF, at 215 bn roubles for the second half of 1992.

Moreover, the cash supply now became less regulated than the supply of non-cash roubles, and the cash squeeze was relaxed.[31] The CBR provided cash roubles more or less on demand, with the restriction that only bank notes issued between 1961 and 1992 (with a denomination of less than 10,000 roubles) could be delivered to FSRs. Their claims for cash supplies increased sharply in the second half of 1992 and still more in 1993, when cash supplies were the main source of total financial transfers to FSRs, and no regulations existed on delivery of cash to the FSRs (see Table 7.1).

The other defining event of this period was the appointment of Boris Fedorov as Deputy Prime Minister and Minister of Finance in December 1993. From then on, the fight against inflation and against the lax policy of the CBR became a major priority, and credits to FSRs a major target. In the spring of 1993, the negotiations with the IMF on a new credit line facility especially designed for Russia, the Systemic Transformation Facility (STF), provided a strong incentive to limit the cost of the rouble zone for Russia. By this time, the IMF had recognized the necessity for each of the FSRs to introduce their own national currencies. Most technical credits had exceeded their ceilings and needed renegotiation. Therefore, it was easy to renew them.

In agreement with the IMF, the government and Supreme Soviet of Russia decided to abolish technical credits in April 1993. All previous credits to FSRs accumulated during 1992–93 were transformed into state debts, denominated in USD and with interest expressed in LIBOR (London Inter-Bank Offering Rate). The advantage of such a measure was that state debts were regulated and channelled through the budget. The Ministry of Finance (Fedorov) was then in a position to control directly the volume of financial transfers to the FSRs.

At the same time, credit lines were opened to FSRs for the remainder of 1993. They were limited to 895 bn roubles, but in fact never exceeded 595 bn (Ministry of Finance data). Unlike technical credits, however, these were tied credits for purchasing specific Russian goods. Also, they could not be allocated without the approval of the Ministry of Finance, which further limited Gerashchenko's generosity to the other FSRs.

Following the unification of a Russian exchange rate in July 1992, new bank notes with Russian emblems had been issued in 5,000 rouble denomination. The new bank notes circulated parallel to the old Soviet ones (depicting Lenin), but only Soviet notes were delivered to the other FSRs. With the tightening of the credit policy to FSRs, their demand for cash increased dramatically.[32] As noted, this demand became the main source of Russian transfer to the other FSRs.

While the supply of non-cash roubles were more or less under control, the supply of cash roubles became the main danger for Russian monetary policy. Most countries of the rouble area had already introduced coupons as a complement to cash roubles, freeing some of their rouble liquidity to be spent in Russia.[33] At the same time, the supply of cash had increased tremendously. If Russia was serious about lowering the inflation rate, the Lenin bank note had to go.

On 24 July 1993, the CRB carried out a monetary reform aimed at isolating Russia's cash circulation from the other FSRs. Pre-1993 Soviet roubles were withdrawn and those countries of the rouble area still using these notes found that their money was no longer legal tender in Russia.[34] Without detailing the disorderly and chaotic mechanism devised to implement this reform, the reform's principal advantage is evident: the FSRs were forced to choose between introducing their own currencies or opening negotiations with Russia for a 'new style ruble zone'.[35]

The New Style Rouble Zone (NSRZ), (September 1993–April 1994)

A multilateral agreement on the NSRZ was signed on 7 September 1993 by representatives of Russia, Kazakhstan, Uzbekistan, Tajikistan, Belarus and Armenia.[36] Subsequently, all the signatories signed standardized bilateral agreements with Russia on the harmonization of economic policy and legislation during September. The Russian motivation for the agreements was partly political, based on concern for the fate of Russian populations in the FSRs. The FSRs' motivation was to avoid any abrupt interruption in obtaining easy credit, even at the price of some loss of control to Moscow.

The multilateral agreement on the NSRZ mainly focused on the rules for the 'transition period' to a monetary union based on the Russian rouble. These rules included coordination of monetary, fiscal, banking and foreign exchange regulations and commitment to maintain stability of national currencies against the Russian rouble. The main indicators to be agreed with Russia were the money supply, deficits of consolidated budgets, refinance rates of the central banks, and reserve requirements. At the end of the transition period, the rouble was supposed to become the only legal tender in the states of the NSRZ. These states also committed themselves to establishing a unified exchange rate of the rouble against hard currencies, and a joint currency reserve to support the rouble.

From the start, it was clear that the fixed deadlines for the convergence of legislation and regulatory mechanisms were unrealistic. For example, it had been agreed that the transition period would end in 1994. During this time, the future members of the NSRZ were supposed to unify their economic legislation with Russia, and demonstrate that their monetary and budgetary policies were in line with Russia's. If, and only if, this was successful, Russia would replace cash money with the 'new' roubles and transfer bank non-cash accounts from national currencies into roubles. Various points in the agreements remained obscure, such as how the NSRZ members would finance their future trade deficits with Russia and service the debts already accumulated. In addition, the principles of cash and credit emission by different members of the NSRZ were extremely vague.

After the dissolution of the Russian parliament on 21 September 1991, Fedorov succeeded in rallying considerable support from all areas of the government including the President's office, isolating Gerashchenko in his desire to revive the rouble zone. The insight spread that macro-economic stabilization could not take place in Russia with disorderly monetary arrangements with the other FSRs. The position of the Russian government became increasingly firm. During visits to Alma-Ata and Tashkent on 22–24 October, Russian negotiators declared that mere unification of economic legislation was not enough and that real economic convergence was necessary. To achieve this, the FSRs should introduce their own national currencies and demonstrate over time that monetary convergence was possible – the European monetary union in reverse.

The controversy between the members of the NSRZ culminated on 26–28 October 1993 when, under pressure from the Uzbek and Kazakh governments to deliver cash in new rouble bank notes, the Russians issued the following conditions:[37]

1. Cash would be provided on credit for half a year for 210 per cent annual interest payments (the CBR refinance rate).
2. One half of the cash delivery should be backed by gold and hard currency as collateral. When the Kazakhs declared that they had no gold reserves, the Russians suggested they mortgage the Baikonur space station and other large assets.
3. Countries receiving Russian cash should refrain from introducing their own currency for a period of 5 years.
4. If after 6 months Russian conditions of monetary integration were not met, the entire credit should be paid back in hard currency or precious metals. If integration proved possible, state debt should be designated as non-interest state credit.

In the face of such tough conditions, Kazakhstan and Uzbekistan decided to introduce their own currencies on 15 November 1993. Table 7.4 shows the FSRs' various monetary arrangements at the end of November 1993. Note that Tajikistan decided form the start to remain in the NSRZ, whatever the conditions, effectively confirming its status as Russian protectorate.

The Belarusian position was not as clear as the Tajik one. Surprisingly, negotiations led to an agreement signed on 5 January 1994 by the chairmen of the Central Bank of Russia and of the National Bank of Belarus. The Russian Ministry of Finance had not been consulted. Evidently, two types of agreement had circulated during the NSRZ negotiations: one backed by the CBR, based on giving credits first and setting conditions later; and the Ministry of Finance model, which set conditions first with the credits to follow.

Table 7.4 Monetary systems in FSRs

Monetary system	Country – currency
Currency board with peg to DM Current account convertibility	Estonia – kroon introduced 20 June 1992
Floating exchange rate Full convertibility	Latvia – lats introduced 28 June 1993
Floating exchange rate Full convertibility	Kyrgyzstan – som introduced 10 May 1993
Floating exchange rate Current account convertibility	Russia – Russian rouble introduced 22 July 1993
Floating exchange rate Current account convertibility	Lithuania – litas introduced 25 June 1993
Foreign exchange auctions suspended November 1993. Transactions has since taken place at different rates; other various arrangements.	Ukraine – karbovanets introduced in November 1992
New Currencies Floating exchange rate	Azerbaijan – manat Moldova – leu introduced 29 November 1993
Temporary legal tender from 2 August 1992. The Lari is under discussion.	Georgia – coupons
Peg to the Russian rouble	Uzbekistan – som introduced 15 November 1993
Rate determined at weekly official foreign exchange auctions	Turkmenistan – manat introduced 1 November 1993
Rate determined at weekly official foreign exchange auctions	Kazakhstan – tenge introduced 15 November Armenia – dram introduced 22 November 1993
New Style Rouble Zone Negotiations with Russia Temporary legal tender	Tajikistan Pre-1993 rouble introduced 8 January 1994
Monetary union conditional on parliamentary ratification	Belarus Belarus only used the zaichik (coupon) since 1 June 1994, waiting for monetary union

Source: Dabrowski (1993), press reports, *Interfax*, IMF (1994), Annex 3, pp. 48–9.

The relative failure of the reformers in the December 1993 elections gave Geraschenko the necessary window to impose at last his support of the rouble zone. To understand the extent to which this agreement was unacceptable, one has simply to imagine the governors of the Bank of France and the Bank of England meeting, without consulting their respective governments or people, and deciding that from that point on the pound sterling would replace the French franc as legal tender! The agreement claimed with Belarus was immediately disowned by the Russian Ministry of Finance, and for a time it was believed that the rouble zone was dead.

The Threat from Minsk (April 1994)

Then, quite suddenly, a monetary union treaty was signed on 12 April 1994 by Russian Prime Minister Viktor Chernomyrdin and Belarusian Prime Minister Vyacheslav Kebich. The main points of the agreement, to be carried out in stages, follow.

First, a customs union was duly implemented on 1 May 1994. Customs barriers have been abolished and tariffs unified. Removal of Russian export duties on oil/gas will be worth $1.4 bn to Belarus in 1994. Russia will not pay Belarus rent on its military bases in Belarus (a cost of 6.2 trillion roubles in 1994) or transit fees for oil and gas pipelines, and other raw material transit from Russia ($200 mn in 1994). Also, at the end of 1994, Russia should provide Belarus with energy at domestic Russian prices. The hope for Belarus is that this will mean cheap energy. In fact, by this time, prices of Russian energy are likely to be about the same as world prices.

Second, Belarus will effectively give up its central bank. This measure will require changes to Belarus' constitution. Kebich has said that he will take the issue to referendum if Parliament refuses. Kebich's domestic rivals, including the Head of State Grib, have argued in favour of a 'compromise' on the central bank issue, avoiding the need for any constitutional amendment. With the Belarusian leadership divided, this question and the issue of ratification were shelved pending the presidential election on 23 June 1994. The Russians, for their part, insisted on a referendum to ratify what amounts to a loss of sovereignty for Belarus, to create the political conditions necessary to enable the Russian Central Bank to take charge.

Third, bank notes would be exchanged at a rate of 1:1, up to a ceiling (200,000 cash zaichiks (coupons) for each Belarusian citizen and 1 million non-cash zaichiks held by companies). In any case, the exchange of bank notes would be a gift from Russia to Belarus of at least 2 trillion roubles, or about 10 per cent of the April 1994 Russian monetary stock.

As Kebich lost to Alexander Lukashenko in the presidential elections in July 1994, the whole issue of a monetary union seems to have fallen through. A monetary union would have entailed substantial costs for both Belarus and Russia. The exchange of the zaichik for roubles at the rate of 1:1, while limited, will mean at the very least an inflation blip. The different in inflation rates of the two states is also notable: the monthly inflation rates in Belarus during the first quarter of 1994 were 43 per cent in January, 24 per cent in

February and 11 per cent in March;[38] in Russia, the monthly inflation rates were 17.4 per cent, 10.7 per cent and 7.4 per cent respectively.

In addition, it should be remembered that a common currency supposes goods and factor mobility between both countries. In case of real shock, if the nominal exchange rate cannot be used to correct relative prices, this mobility makes the adjustment possible. Obviously, Russia and Belarus are both in transition to market economies, but as quite different stages and subject to different shocks. For instance, at a time when Russian unemployment should rise due to restructuring of state enterprises and the end of the lax CBR credit policy, one may wonder about the readiness of the Russians to welcome the Belarusian workers laid off after relatively tough policies were implemented in the monetary union process.

Consider also that, even with a single central bank, both Belarus and Russia will view this arrangement as a means of exploiting the other, and both will try to manipulate the central bank policy. Russia will aim to lower the global inflation rate, while transferring the costs onto the Belarus economy. Belarus will increase government spending and therefore pressures on the global inflation rate, even though the budget spending should be subject to limits set by both countries.

In the end, both would lose. If Russia succeeded (and the inflation rate was lowered), Belarus would blame Russia for the adjustment costs (unemployment). If Belarus succeeded (and government expenditures were increased), Russia would blame Belarus for the failure of the stabilization policy. The result would be a reinforcement of nationalism, a possible backlash and most likely the end of the monetary union.

Conclusion

In this chapter it has been argued that national convertible currencies and free trade at free prices are necessary conditions for a successful stabilization programme in these countries. If Russian aid to other FSRs cannot be stopped altogether, assistance should be financed from non-inflationary measures backed by some collateral, preferably not by Russia. All FSRs have become members of the IMF. Their IMF membership can facilitate external financing of comprehensive reform programmes, and therefore is a crucial element in a successful transition to a market economy. Other international organizations could contribute as well.

Notes

*   Many thanks to Anders Åslund, Marek Dabrowski, Jacques Delpla, Michael Ellam, Peter Oppenheimer and Simon Johnson for their comments and discussions.

1.   Sachs (1993a) and others give the figure of 10 per cent of GDP. The reason for the difference is that Goskomstat kept changing its GDP figure for 1992. The very first estimate of GDP for 1992 given by Goskomstat was Rbs 15.6 trillion (first

published in January 1993). This figure was later revised by Goskomstat to Rbs 20 trillion then to Rbs 18.064 trillion at the end of 1993 (which is the one used here).

2. With the introduction of a unified market exchange rate in Russia in July 1992, the CBR began to refer to the 'Rouble of the Russian Federation'.

3. Williamson (1992), discussed by Granville (1992).

4. Williamson (1993), p. 309.

5. See IMF, IBRD, OECD and EBRD (1991), p. 11. According to the 1977 Soviet constitution, the fifteen union republics had the right to secede and to enter into relations with foreign states. By December 1990, all fifteen republics had declared their independence or the sovereignty of their laws over those of the Union.

6. Sachs (1993a).

7. IMF (1994), p. 39: The IMF lists the various exchange markets as for instance in Kyrgyzstan, Latvia, Lithuania, Ukraine. Adding that 'the development of exchange markets for national currencies was limited in most countries in part because country authorities began to operate multiple exchange rate systems'.

8. Dornbusch (1992a), p. 7: 'Price reform is the only absolute prerequisite to maintain trade. ... Without price reform goods will not move, at least not in official hands'.

9. A national currency is convertible if the issuing authority refrains from imposing restrictions (not control) on payments and transfers for current international transactions.

10. Michalopoulos and Tarr (1992), p. 5.

11. Dornbusch (1992a), p. 8.

12. Michalopoulos and Tarr (1992), p. 10: 'With the price liberalisation that occurred in early 1992, the pressure for barter within each state was significantly reduced. Some preliminary estimates indicate that the percentage of sales among enterprises within Russia that are based on barter declined to 20 per cent in March 1992, from 80 per cent in January 1992 and an even higher percentage in late 1991.'

13. Michalopoulos and Tarr (1992), p. 6.

14. Granville (1992), Michalopoulos and Tarr (1992), Sachs and Lipton (1992).

15. Michalopoulos and Tarr (1992), Table 1.

16. Hansson (1994), p. 2: 'The 1993 figure will be around 32 per cent, of which one-quarter is with the other Baltic States. Finland with about one-third of Estonia's trade, replaced Russia (with about 19 per cent) as the major trading partner. Germany and Sweden each account for about 9–11 per cent of Estonia's foreign trade.'

17. Commonwealth of Independent States.

18. Dornbusch (1992a), p. 2.

19. Granville (1992).

20. Dornbusch (1992), p. 419.

21. IMF (1994), p. 33: 'In the U.S.S.R. payment system, each branch of Gosbank had correspondent accounts with virtually every other branch, so that it was always possible to know whether a given branch was in deficit or in surplus with the rest of Gosbank. However the system was not set up to track 'regional' balance of payments as opposed to 'branch' balance of payments. the CBR's correspondent accounts, in contrast, allowed central banks to begin monitoring payment imbalances in inter-state trade on a regular basis.'

22. Ickes and Ryterman (1992), p. 16.

23. This was already the case but before price liberalization the price duality obtained as between the official market and the black market or farm market.

24. Ukraine, following the liberalization of prices in January 1992, introduced coupons, which were initially designed to protect its domestic market (they were only used as payment for staple goods). But then, there began to be cash rouble shortages, and the coupons became a real substitute currency.
25. In Ukraine, coupons were introduced on 10 January 1992.
26. The cash shortage had already started in late 1991: by the time of the dissolution of the Union, bank deposits could not be converted into cash and firms started to sell those deposits for cash at a discount.
27. IMF (1994), p. 34: 'The accounts of the sub-branches were consolidated by the CBR only once a month, with a lag of two to three weeks; from the point of view of the branches, the new correspondent account system simply meant that accounting had changed, but not the processing of payments.'
28. Ukraine left the rouble zone on 12 November 1992.
29. Article No. 2 of the Agreement between the Government of the Russian Federation and the Government of Estonia concerning the Procedure Governing Settlements for Mutual Deliveries of Goods and the Rendering of Non-Commercial Payments.
30. IMF (1994), p. 35: 'The new financing limits led to non-uniform discounts on the non-cash (deposit) rubles of various states in the region, depending on the extent of their excess demand for rubles. This effectively made their deposits mutually inconvertible.'
31. IMF (1994), p. 43: 'The cash shortage in the ruble area during the first half of 1992 was eliminated in the third quarter by the printing of bank notes with larger denominations'.
32. IMF (1994), pp. 44: 'In the period April–21 July, currency issue to the other members of the ruble area increased by Rbs 674 bn, compared with Rbs 97 bn during the first three months, and yet there reportedly was still an excess demand for currency in many of these states.'
33. For instance in Azerbaijan, Belarus, Georgia and Moldova (Table 7.4).
34. The 1993 bank notes were only distributed in Russia therefore to withdraw the circulation of the pre-1993 notes meant to introduce a Russian national currency.
35. IMF (1994), p. 6: 'By mid-1993, only the Baltic countries, Ukraine and the Kyrgyz Republic had left the ruble area.'
36. Granville and Lushin (1993).
37. Lushin (1993).
38. Data from the *Interfax*/CIS statistical Committee Report, 13 May 1994, no. 18–19.

References

Åslund, A. (1993a) 'The Gradual Nature of Economic Change in Russia', in A. Åslund and R. Layard, (eds) (1993) *Changing the Economic System in Russia*, Pinter, London.
Åslund, A. (1993b) 'Key Dilemmas in the Russian Economic Reform', mimeo, September.
Bornefalk, A. (1994) 'The Ruble Zone: A Case of Irrationality', Stockholm Institute of East European Economics Working Paper No. 90, August.
Dabrowski, M. (1993) 'From Soviet Ruble to National Rubles and Independent Currencies: Evolution of the Ruble Area in 1991–1993', paper presented at the Third Trento Workshop, third revised version, May.
Dornbusch, R. (1992a) 'A Payments Mechanism for the Commonwealth and Eastern Europe', mimeo, MIT, Cambridge.

Dornbusch, R. (1992b) 'Monetary Problems of Post-Communism: Lessons from the End of the Austro-Hungarian Empire', *Weltwirtschaftliches Archiv*, cahier no. 3, vol. 128, pp. 391–424.

Granville, B. (1992) 'Price and Currency Reform in the CIS', Special Discussion Paper, RIIA, Post Soviet Business Forum, London.

Granville, B. (1993) 'Russian Monetary Policy in 1992: The Threat to Stabilisation', *Business Strategy Review*, London Business School, London.

Granville, B. and Lushin A. (1993) 'The New Style Ruble Zone or the Old Soviet Union "Revisited"', mimeo, 15 October, Macroeconmic and Financial Unit (MFU), Ministry of Finance of the Russian Federation, Moscow.

Hansson, A. (1991) 'Monetary Reform in a Newly Independent State: The Case of Estonia', WIDER, mimeo, 15 October.

Hansson, A. (1993) 'The Trouble with the Ruble: Monetary Reform in the Former Soviet Union', in A. Åslund and R. Layard, (eds) (1993) *Changing the Economic System in Russia*. Pinter, London.

Hansson, A. (1994) 'International Trade and Economic Transformation in Estonia', paper prepared for the European Forum for Democracy and Solidarity Conference on 'The role of International Trade in the Transition Process', January 1994.

Hansson, A. and Sachs, J. (1992) 'The Case of National Currencies in the Former Soviet Union, Crowning the Estonian Kroon', *Transition*, vol. 3, no. 9, October, The World Bank, Washington, DC.

Havrylyshyn, O. and Williamson, J. (1991) 'From Soviet Disunion in Eastern Economic Community?', Institute for International Economics, October, no. 35, *Policy Analysis in International Economics*, Washington, DC.

Ickes, B.W. and Ryterman, R. (1992) 'Inter-Enterprise Arrears and Financial Underdevelopment in Russia', IMF, Research Department, September, Washington, DC.

Illarionov, A. (1993) 'The Cost of Friendship between Russia and the FSU', *Izvestiya*, 16 September 1993, Moscow.

Interfax (1991), (1992), (1993) various issues, Moscow.

IMF, IBRD, OECD and EBRD (1991), *A Study of the Soviet Economy*, Washington, DC.

International Monetary Fund (1992a) *Economic Review: Russian Federation*. April, Washington, DC.

International Monetary Fund (1992b) 'Money and Banking Statistics in Former Soviet Union (FSU) Economies', prepared by R. Calogero, W. Nahar, and T.R. Stillson, WP/02/103, December.

International Monetary fund (1993) *Economic Review: Russian Federation*, no. 8, June, Washington, DC.

International Monetary Fund (1994) *Economic Review: Financial Relations among Countries of the Former Soviet Union*, no. 1, Washington, DC.

Izvestia (1991), (1992) various issues, Moscow.

Lushin, A. (1993) 'Recent Developments in the Ruble Zone: The Death of the Unborn Child', mimeo, November, Macroeconomic and Financial Unit, (MFU), Ministry of Finance of the Russian Federation, Moscow.

Michalopoulos, C. and Tarr, D. (1992) 'Transitional Trade and Payments Arrangements For States of the Former USSR', mimeo, The World Bank, June, Washington, DC.

Sachs, J. (1993a) 'Achieving Monetary Stabilization in Russia in 1993', mimeo, Harvard University, Cambridge, 7 March.

Sachs, J. (1993b) 'Urgent Issues in the Ruble Zone Debate', memo, Macroeconomic and Finance Unit, 17 October, IMF.

Sachs, J. and Lipton, D. (1992) 'Remaining Steps to a Market-Based Monetary System in Russia', in A. Åslund, and R. Layard, (eds) (1993) *Changing the Economic System in Russia*, Pinter, London, pp. 127–62.

Smith A. (1993) *Russia and the World Economy: Problems of Integration*, Routledge, London and New York.

Williamson, J. (1991) 'The Case for a Payments Union', *International Economic Insights*, September–October.

Williamson, J. (1993) 'Comment', in J. Williamson (ed.), *Economic Consequences of Soviet Disintegration*, Institute For International Economics, Washington, DC, pp. 307–11.

8 Macro-economic Policy and Stabilization in Russia

Boris G. Fedorov

First published in 1995

What is Russia's Macro-economic Policy?

The salient feature of today's Russia is the lack of a macro-economic policy in the usual sense of the word. While in 1992 and 1993 there were feeble attempts to formulate some kind of policy, in 1994 all pretence is nearly gone. Nevertheless, the government and CBR (Central Bank of Russia) have learned certain basic lessons such as 'CBR credits spell inflation' and have generally employed the simple instrument of not giving money away. Needless to say, this can be rather efficient.

The usual reaction to the term 'macro-economic policy' is rather derisive. This is not what 'real people' worry about; only some technocrats in the Ministry of Finance really care for the subject. Among the top officials (excluding Mr Anatoly Chubais) only Prime Minster Viktor Chernomyrdin attempted to fathom what all the fuss was about, though never beyond a simplistic level necessitated by the political situation.

Macro-economic policy is considered mostly to be tantamount to anti-inflation policy, always at odds with the much more prevalent approach, which boils down to the slogan 'production volume at any cost', disregarding monetary considerations. Many believe that the more money injected into the economy (whatever the source), the better.

An important factor in the education process was and is cooperation with the IMF and G7, which brought many new issues to the day-to-day attention of state leaders. Never before had foreign dignitaries discussed with Moscow leaders inflation, central banking, or monetary growth. Never before had the Russian Prime Minister telephoned the managing director of IMF while on holiday. Never before had an article by the Russian Prime Minster appeared in The *Financial Times*, not to speak of the bizarre fact that it was originally drafted in the IMF building in Washington.

Still, the basic composition of macro-economic policy is the same as elsewhere: fiscal policy, monetary policy, external factors. The difference is that linkages between different policy instruments are not always obvious, policy-makers do not see eye to eye, and a comprehensive overview of policy issues barely exists.

Stabilization

For Russians, stabilization usually means a solid level of production, full employment, no bankruptcies, a modest but stable standard of living – all the nice touches we allegedly had in the socialist past. No-one likes price hikes, but practically no-one understands the nature of inflation. A post-Communist approach, which disregards the market economy reality of constantly striving for efficiency via competition, dominates. A Russian dream of equality and prosperity for everyone without much effort is all too widespread.

Financial stabilization is snarled at as rather unimportant and secondary to 'vital' things. The foremost proponent of this approach is our CBR governor. Mr Viktor Gerashchenko is under duress to behave like a normal central banker, but never loses an opportunity to stress that the fight against inflation is much less important than a boost to production whatever the cost.

The Russian industrialist approach is that the only way to stop inflation is by stimulating production, even if monetary emission is necessary. At the same time, one should concede that in 1993 and 1994 many more changed their views, which helped to better control the situation.

Fiscal policy

A coherent fiscal policy was never formulated in the last decades of the Soviet period. Deficits were considered bad and thus were practically non-existent. Nor did a tax system exist in the common sense of the term (save for income tax). The whole country was one big factory belonging to the state, which planned everything – from production to consumption – and could take from the enterprise any proportion of profit it deemed necessary.

The generations of the 1970s and 1980s were not properly indoctrinated even in Stalin-style economics. The policy of avoiding big deficits at the expense of population and enterprises gave way to populist policies where deficits were supposed to 'give' something to people, making government more popular.

The advent of 'democracy' Russian-style led to budgets being taken from very conservative financiers and given to mostly ignorant Members of Parliament and to a new wave of government officials, who had been second- or third-tier bureaucrats under the Soviet regime. Contrary to popular misconception, young economists-turned-officials who came in the wake of Mr Yegor Gaidar never had real control over the situation, and in any case were novices in the statesman's world.

Thus budget deficits became inevitable. Mr Gaidar's early dream of a zero deficit budget collapsed within months: 1992 ended with a budget deficit of 18 per cent of GDP. In 1993 attempts were made to curb expenditure and boost revenues. Several breakthroughs were achieved: uncontrolled loans to CIS (Commonwealth of Independent States) countries virtually stopped, import subsidies were abolished, various off-budget items were consolidated into the budget, etc. The year ended with a budget deficit around 10 per cent of GDP, and the deficit remained more or less at this level in 1994.

This size of the budget deficit is obviously excessive, but not catastrophic; the question is how it is financed. More than 95 per cent of the deficit is financed directly from the CBR. Given the fact that this financing is extended at 10 per cent per annum one can understand how undervalued deficit figures are.

The 1994 consolidated state budget was finally approved in June by the State Duma (lower chamber) and was eventually approved by the Federation Council (higher chamber). It has a 70 trillion rouble deficit which is supposed to correspond to about 35 per cent of all expenditures. It does not require special skill to calculate how big the deficit would be if the Ministry of Finance had to budget the interest rate expense at the rate of 185 per cent per annum, which properly compounded in Western equivalent terms, is around 500 per cent.

A breakthrough in formulating a fiscal policy consistent with financial stabilization goals will have to consist of three basic elements: expenditure cuts, revenues measures with a new tax policy, and a change in deficit financing methods.

It must be understood that even a 70 trn rouble deficit figure does not take into account 45 trn roubles of measures promised to the IMF but not implemented, and up to 80 trn roubles of expenses based on various laws which nobody in the government wants to implement. Thus, expenditure cutting seems an enormous task. One will need political will made of steel to go through, with a fine-tooth comb, every single decision included (or not included) in the budget to render the state's financial position at least realistic and controllable. This is very unlikely to happen.

On the revenue side, the government's main instrument is obviously a better collection of taxes and other revenues. Certain efforts have been undertaken, but without real success because:

1. No-one wants to go against offenders on federal issues – it is too politically sensitive.
2. The tax enforcement agencies are ill-managed and prefer to go for easy targets, since they primarily want to collect more fines for their own pocket; non-payment of taxes by huge dinosaurs of industry is looked upon rather benignly.
3. Politically motivated tax exemptions are the rule, and the government is unwilling to take them away.

A tax reform linked to expenditure and revenues measures should be a priority. It should feature overall tax cuts, abolition of certain (numerous) freak aspects of the tax system, and replacement of certain taxes with a capital gains tax. Unfortunately the government at the moment effectively proposes a higher tax burden instead of a comprehensive package to boost the economy.

The importance of issuing securities to finance the budget deficit is now widely understood and efforts are being made to increase the amount outstanding. The main problem in this sphere is the poor credibility of government paper.

Monetary Policy

The concept of monetary policy in Russia was developed during a fierce dispute in 1993 when the CBR was slowly coerced into proper behaviour. After fuelling inflation by injecting large sums of money into the economy in a desperate attempt to boost production, the CBR became a true central bank. Its refinance rate slowly rose from 80 per cent a year to 210 per cent a year to reach positive levels, monetary growth was curbed, and foreign exchange market operations became much more meaningful.

The CBR's main policy tool is its official refinance rate, which is not supposed to sink more than 5 percentage points below the benchmark inter-bank market rate. At this interest rate, officially directed loans are extended via commercial banks into concrete segments of the economy. These loans are intended to respect limits set by the government credit policy commission. The lowering of the official rate in April–June 1994 from 210 to 185 per cent reflected falling monthly inflation rates.

Clearly, directed credits are not anything like real central bank refinancing. The recent innovation is credit auctions, which in the first five months of the year accounted for nearly 30 per cent of CBR credits. Interestingly enough, supply at the auctions so far exceeds the demand. Commercial banks are also now allowed to borrow from the CBR for 7 days at 1.2 times the official interest rate. This refinancing scheme is used to regulate short-term bank liquidity level.

It is planned that in the near future a discounting facility for commercial bills will be opened, but so far no commercial or treasury bills, or any government securities, are traded by the CBR for monetary policy purposes. Quite soon, a lombard loan scheme will be initiated with mostly government securities as collateral.

The other main instrument of monetary policy at the moment is the reserve requirements system. The ratio for the last two years has been 15 to 20 per cent, but it is unclear how effective this system is in combating inflation. For example, centralized loans are excluded from the calculations, which in effect means that the system does not cover 30 to 50 per cent of all credit in Russia and even stimulates loan applications to the CBR.

In 1994, despite clear promises from the Prime Minister 'to correct' the direction of the reform, the monetary policy appears to have become even more restrictive than before. The reason is obvious: political upheavals called for some type of success, and however strange it may seem, getting the second tranche of the IMF STF (Systemic Transformation Facility) was easier than making any real progress in the domestic arena. Hence a successful operation to ensnare the IMF was executed, using all imaginable ploys and pressures.

In the area of monetary policy, real progress is possible only with a much faster switch to real refinancing techniques instead of directed credits, with outright prohibition of central bank loans to the budget. For the moment this is not feasible and the main burden of financial stabilization is obviously on the budget side. At the same time it is clear that the CBR will have to be more flexible as to its official interest rate — carefully lowering it now to avoid outrageously high real interest rates, but then quickly raising it once inflation starts creeping up. In 1992–93 the CBR was always too slow.

External Factors

Russian domestic prices are moving incredibly fast towards the international price level. Russia enjoys record dollar (hard currency) inflation since the exchange rate falls much slower than domestic prices rise. In 1993 prices jumped about 9 times, but the exchange rate dropped only by a factor of 3. The dollar in Russia, then, lost two-thirds of its purchasing power in 1993. Domestic prices now stand at 30 to 40 per cent of the international level.

We did not embrace the idea of a fixed exchange rate as a nominal anchor, but in effect our floating rate grew stronger and in real terms produced the same result. It became a tool for assessing Russian industry competitiveness. It is no longer possible to ship abroad even some standard goods like metal or fertilizers or raw materials without reducing costs and increasing productivity and quality. With the slow dismantling of export duties and the quota system, the exchange rate plays a more important role.

It is a popular misunderstanding that the exchange rate is overvalued and artificial. Only on one occasion in January 1994 did the CBR support the exchange rate for political reasons. The overall strengthening of the rouble was mainly caused by tighter monetary and fiscal policies, changes in the obligatory currency surrender system, and a virtual suspension of credits to the CIS countries. Even more interesting is the fact that for a substantial part of 1993 the CBR tried to cushion the rouble's strengthening rate.

Export and import duties so far have performed a mainly protectionist task: to stop goods in shortage from leaving the country and to handicap foreign competitors. Fiscal reasons obviously were of paramount importance. Then, it became clear that curbing exports was unwise and duties fell considerably, but belligerence towards imports skyrocketed, often beyond reason. This is one of the dangers of opening up the economy and increasing efficiency.

One argument for contending that the rouble rate is not overvalued is that the trade balance and balance of payments in general are in the black, and that the officially declared hard currency reserves of enterprises and banks are higher than ever. The problem is that the real scope of capital flows is largely based on guesstimates.

For example, it is more or less a universally acknowledged fact that there are about 10 to 15 bn dollars in bank notes in Russia, that unorganized imports of consumer goods (in tourists' luggage) in 1993 probably reached 15 bn dollars, that billions of dollars are hoarded illegally in foreign bank accounts and various forms. One thing is clear: Russia is not as poor as some people think.

With this in view, it is important to assess the role of external assistance in Russian reforms. However paradoxical it may seem, the experience of the last five years in the USSR and now Russia tends to reveal that the greater the assistance, the less the desire to reform. Alternatively, the harder the situation, the closer one's back is to the wall – the stronger the reformist drive.

In 1993 and 1994, the situation surrounding the STF tranche disbursement showed that as soon as the decision to release money is made, a certain wandering from the stabilization path occurs. On 20 April 1994, the IMF approved the STF. On 26 April, the Russian Parliament approved amendments to the budgets increasing the deficit by 8 trillion roubles.

If the G7 and IMF are to be criticized, it is not for excessive conditionality, but for a lack of it. Sometimes it seems as if no-one in the West cares where their taxpayers' money goes. Even the commercial bankers often behave like pleaders and borrowers, not creditors. The IMF was created as a financial and monetary watchdog to pursue sound policies; one request I have is that Russia not be treated differently.

Growth Versus Inflation

In Russia, the hottest debate on economic policy always concentrates on the issues of inflation and economic growth. The biggest problem, however, is that neither side is precise in its arguments. Usually there is very little quantification of the policy issues and forecasts are notoriously inaccurate. Nevertheless, there has been a substantial improvement.

The pro-inflation policy proponents, as a rule, are reluctant to prove their points and rely on their 'practical' experience in the Soviet economy. It is very difficult to switch from thinking in terms of tonnes and kilometres to thinking in terms of roubles. The volume of production is an overriding target for many officials and they are not receptive to learning anything new.

Likewise, on the reformist side the problem has been the little attention paid to the basic relationships among such economic parameters as savings, investment, growth, and employment. Reformers failed to explain the significance of savings for investment and talked mostly about tough fiscal/monetary policy. That is where a compromise between 'monetarists' and 'industrialists' could have been reached.

When at last we reached the stage of positive interest rates, savings began to grow very quickly, building a foundation for an economic upturn. If this could be coupled with a careful interest rate policy to avoid punitive lending rates, milder tax policies, and stimulation of equity markets and foreign investment, then a new macro-economic breakthrough could be imminent. The main task for the government nowadays is to continue pursuing its financial stabilization target (more ardently than before) while keeping the upturn in mind.

One major prerequisite of effective reform is still missing: a real constraint on the enterprises to make them behave as market agents, shedding excessive workforce and assets, seeking out investors, new lines of production, and new markets and niches. So far most medium- and larger-sized industrial enterprises, and practically all in the agricultural sector, have failed to become more efficient regardless of their ownership status.

Thus, before we see real stabilization and adjustment, production will fall again, the number of bankruptcies will have to rise to several thousands, and the unemployment rate will increase two or fourfold at least. It is especially important to see this happen in the machinery industry (including military–industrial) and agriculture. For the moment this development can be expected only in 1995.

Politics

In my opinion, it is unlikely that great success in macro-economic policy and financial stabilization and structural adjustment of the economy will be possible without a breakthrough in politics. The situation can be summarized as follows:

1. The priorities of the president and government are unclear.
2. The government has no apparent base in Parliament or in the country, and is in fact rather disunited.
3. The very fragmented Parliament is unlikely to become a driving force for reforms.
4. Grass-roots economic development visibly outpaces politics, the anti-quated government machine, and the legal system (the adjustment could be dramatic).
5. Reformers have been used by politicians and only now have begun to understand that without real power they shall never succeed (a clash between reformers and anti-reformers never occurred).
6. The democratic movement is divided.
7. Future parliamentary and presidential elections could be disasters.

It is not serious to expect that stabilization and real reform progress will be achieved without a political victory affecting the entire government. That is why Mr Gaidar is creating a party and most reformers landed in the Parliament. But democrats and reformers cannot agree among themselves; there is no agreed presidential candidate for 1996 and disagreements will evidently continue.

While a full return to the Communist system is nearly unthinkable, the situation is still very fragile and can easily turn into a neo-Communist muddling-through scenario so characteristic of most countries in the former Soviet Union. The majority of leaders are the same as years ago but with different (updated) titles. Much time can be lost with millions of people losing faith in reform. Only a much faster reform movement can save the situation from deterioration, which could be politically dangerous. Certain recent changes in Russian domestic policy (concerning security, mass media, freedom of movement, etc.) at all levels of executive power may not be very noticeable to the outside world. They do not seem very democratic or reform-orientated and worry us a lot.

At times I think that our most important task at present is to observe our own laws, render the government machinery compatible with the economic environment, and stamp out corruption and crime through democratic means.

Prospects for 1994

It is already clear that macro-economic parameters will improve in 1994 over 1993, but without a real breakthrough; it will rather be an attempt to preserve the achievements of 1993 and early 1994. This will not constitute a stabilization in any sense of the word.

The budget deficit will probably be greater than in 1993 as a share of GDP, but with a slightly higher proportion covered by securities. Monetary policy will be somewhat tighter than in 1993, but the real interest rate could again fall to negative levels. The exchange rate will depreciate slower than the pace of inflation although the discrepancy will be much smaller. Price rises will be smaller than in 1993, but will accelerate in the second half of the year. Production will continue to fall, but not disastrously.

Bankruptcies and unemployment will not be the major problem of the year. The big problem will be whether policies will be tight enough to accelerate adjustment of the economy, to make enterprises act as economic agents. The overall economic and political situation will be that of instability but not a reversal or total collapse. The Russian economic miracle is not yet in the making.

9 Why Russia Has Failed to Stabilize

Jeffrey D. Sachs

First published in 1995

Russian stabilization has been a continuing story of missed chances, by the Russians and the West. As the saying goes, Russia and the West have never missed an opportunity to miss an opportunity. The good news is that Russia has so far avoided hyperinflation. The bad news is that the climate of Russian public opinion *vis-à-vis* market reforms has continued to deteriorate; most reformers have left the government; political extremism and criminality seem to be on the rise; relations are cooling with the West; there are signs of increasing militarization of Russian politics; and inflation remains high and unstable. In short, Russia remains adrift, and still vulnerable to political upheaval.

The sad part about Russian stabilization is that the underlying precepts of a good stabilization programme were discernible at the start of reforms in 1992. Unfortunately, the West failed miserably to speed the needed reforms. The G7 never got deeply involved in the reform process, and certainly never provided vital financial backing at the key moments. Technical IMF advice was highly flawed. The World Bank moved at a glacial pace, probably to avoid getting caught in the Russian thicket. At the same time, the Russians were chronically divided as to what to do. Long-standing patterns of Russian politics – intrigue, chronic lying to the public, improvisation rather than serious administration – all gravely undermined the stabilization effort. Despite all the uproar in recent years about 'shock therapy' in Russia, knowledgeable observers understand that it simply never occurred, an obvious point when one compares Russia's disorganized and partial stabilization efforts with the decisive actions in the Czech Republic, Estonia, or Poland.

What Would Shock Therapy Have Entailed in 1992?

The Russian stabilization programme that was launched early in 1992 should have included:

127

1. a *quick* introduction of national currencies for the successor states of the Soviet Union;
2. a budget deficit of between 5 and 10 per cent of GDP, financed by non-monetary means;
3. Western financial support for the Russian budget, of the order of 5 per cent of GDP;
4. a pegged exchange rate of the new Russian currency as a nominal anchor for Russian monetary stability early in the reform period, backed by a restrictive credit policy and a Western-financed stabilization programme;
5. the early introduction of non-monetary instruments of deficit financing, such as Treasury bills and bonds;
6. a comprehensive rescheduling of Russia's debts.

See Sachs (1993, 1994a, 1994b), Sachs and Lipton (1993), and Fischer (1994) for earlier discussions of the basic components of a stabilization package.

These six points have finally become the foundations of negotiations between the IMF and the Russian government at the end of 1994, but fully *three years* after they should have been put on the table. These basic points were not promoted by the West, nor accepted by the Russian government, in the early stages of reform. The delay in arriving at this basic stabilization strategy has been as unnecessary as it has been costly.

Consider the evolution of thinking on these points. The IMF opposed the early introduction of national currencies during 1992, and instead promoted the 'coordination' of monetary policies under IMF auspices. Among other things, the IMF asserted that the non-Russian republics were not ready to manage their own currencies. In saying this, the IMF failed to recognize that the continued use of the Soviet rouble as a common currency virtually guaranteed highly inflationary policies in the non-Russian republics, and therefore the failure of stabilization during 1992. As a direct result of the use of a common currency among the CIS states, Russia ended up extending credits to the other republics of around 10 per cent of GDP during 1992 (see Sachs, 1994a).[1]

It is certainly true that Russian attitudes towards a separate national currency were divided. In general, there was support for a separate national currency among the reformers, even if they lacked a clear technical understanding of how to proceed. On the other side, the hard-line opposition generally opposed a separate national currency, as they still dreamed of a reunification of the Soviet Union. None the less, an early move on a national currency, backed by the West (and the IMF in particular) could have caught the anti-reform opposition off guard. In any event, a separate national currency proved to be the only feasible course of action in any event, as many of us had predicted in the face of IMF resistance early in 1992.

As for the budget deficit, the IMF position at the start was that Russia should aim for a balanced deficit. This was typical 'wholesome' but naïve IMF advice. The Russian fiscal crisis was deep, and there should have been little expectation that Russia could reduce the budget deficit as a percentage of GDP below levels achieved in almost all of the OECD!

Western financing for the Russian budget – that is, loans and grants to help cover the budget deficit in a non-inflationary way – was simply not part of the West's real policy discussion with Russia until 1994, and the possibility of large-scale budgetary financing was not discussed with Russia until late in 1994. The two aid packages announced for Russia, $24 bn announced in April 1992 and $28 bn announced in July 1993, were never properly elaborated or delivered. These packages were failures even at the conceptual level, since the G-7 and IMF failed to understand that Western support for Russia's budgetary financing was necessary for Russia to achieve financial stabilization.

The notion of relying on the nominal exchange rate as an anchor to stabilization was also strongly rejected by the IMF until late in 1994, when the institution abruptly reversed position. The IMF's advocacy of a floating exchange rate during 1991–93 flew in the face of stabilization experience, including the successful stabilizations in Eastern Europe in the Czech Republic (1991), Estonia (1992), and Poland (1990), and the major recent stabilization successes in other parts of the world, including Argentina (1991), Bolivia (1986), Israel (1985), and Mexico (1987).

Since almost all the official Western advice regarding Russia's budget deficit focused on deficit cutting, rather than non-inflationary deficit financing, there was little attempt among the Western institutions to help spur the issuance of Russian treasury bills as an alternative to central bank financing. Moreover, the chances for successful stabilization would be enhanced by the use of *indexed* or *dollar-linked* treasury bills, but once again, there has been little effort or advice in this direction.

Finally, a comprehensive debt settlement, both conditional and delivered in tranches (as in Poland's two-stage debt cancellation) is a necessary feature of Russian stabilization, given the heavy burden of debt servicing on the budget. But, as is well known, the negotiations over the debt have dragged on for years without being adequately integrated into Russia's stabilization efforts. This was especially true during the first two years of reform, when the debt burden loomed large in the Russian thinking, and with actual negotiations tied up in knots over Western insistence on the 'joint and several responsibility' for the Soviet debt among the successor states. The legal fiction of 'several responsibility' (making each individual state, such as Moldova, legally responsible for the entire debt of the Soviet Union) was hastily forced upon the republics in late 1991 by the G7. This clause then delayed a satisfactory negotiation over the Russian foreign debt burden until late 1993.

A comprehensive and rapid effort towards stabilization along the six dimensions just indicated – in short, 'shock therapy' stabilization – could have succeeded in 1992. Such an effort was politically and financially feasible if the Russian reformers and the Western governments had been alert to the opportunities at hand. Of course, it was a difficult course of action, since it called for a set of sophisticated and consistent policy measures at a time of extreme confusion and upheaval. Active Western involvement and financial backing were needed to provide vital impetus for the overall package. Both Russia and the West would have had to choose, rapidly and unswervingly, to follow the policy prescription.

The basic need for speed should have been clear. The small team of reformers, led by Yegor Gaidar and Anatoly Chubais, needed to lock in certain basic rules of behaviour early in the reforms – such as the introduction of a national currency, deep subsidy cuts, a clear rule limiting credit expansion by the central bank, and private ownership of industry – in order to cut through the political turmoil, corruption, and often ineptitude that afflicted the ruling elites of the Russian bureaucracy, the Russian Central Bank, and the Supreme Soviet. Necessary breakthroughs were, indeed, achieved in a few areas of reform, most notably privatization and the liberalization of international trade (in sectors other than raw materials), but no breakthrough was achieved in the area of the public finances. At the same time, Russia's underlying financial conditions were deteriorating rapidly during 1992 and 1993, as a result of enormous inherited instabilities and political tensions (foreign debt, declining tax revenues, the increasing confrontation between the President and the Parliament, and so on).

There are in fact many reasons to believe that stabilization could have been achieved in 1992. President Yeltsin was at the peak of his popularity, a true national hero with unquestioned moral authority throughout Russia. Moreover, the Russian Parliament had bestowed Yeltsin with emergency powers for one year to enable the new government to stabilize the economy. Public opinion was highly supportive of market reforms and democratization. And despite fears of massive social turmoil, there were almost no strikes or demonstrations against the reforms. Of course, as in Poland a few years earlier, this kind of unity and support for reforms could not be expected to last. But as in Poland, it could have been used to achieve implementation of the basic measures needed for stabilization.

By acting indecisively with regard to the public finances, the Russian reformers and their supporters in Western governments and the international institutions gave time for the anti-reform backlash to take hold. Corruption in the bureaucracy quickly multiplied, and at a very high cost to the budget (this has been especially the case in the areas of agricultural subsidies and energy export quotas). The reformers inexplicably failed to block the return of Mr Viktor Gerashchenko to the leadership of the Russian Central Bank in July 1992, from which position he engineered a highly inflationary policy to support his political patrons in key state sectors. The Russian Central Bank was almost surely home to enormous corruption under Gerashcenko's leadership.

Other fissiparous trends took hold within Russian politics and society at large as it became clear in mid-1992 that the reformers had failed to slay the inflationary beast. Several regions successfully campaigned to withhold or to reduce their tax payments owed to the federal government. Tax evasion and lobbying for tax exemptions by individual enterprises and sectors (e.g. energy) soared. Capital flight increased markedly in step with the Gerashchenko-led flood of a new credits to Russian industry, and in response to the failure of the Russian government to introduce a national currency (leaving Russia exposed to imported inflation from the rest of the CIS).

The eventual political failure of the Gaidar government came for a straightforward reason: the government had promised a quick stabilization, à la Poland, but did not deliver. In his recent autobiography, *The Struggle for Russia*, Yeltsin (1994) depicts the unravelling of support for radical reforms as a result of the government's failures to deliver on its promises. Yeltsin notes ruefully that in the spring of 1992, 'Yegor Gaidar kept giving assurances that stabilization was just around the corner. I was forced to mimic his confidence' (p. 165). Discussing events in the ensuing months, Yeltsin notes: 'By the end of the summer [of 1992], the economy was obviously cracking along two fault lines. It was impossible to attempt any economic measures or plan an economy when the prices on everything were constantly jumping (p. 174).[2] Then, in advance of the Seventh People's Congress in December 1992, in which Gaidar was dismissed, Yeltsin worried that: 'The opposition's gloating over the Gaidar government's unfulfilled promises threatened to escalate at the Congress into the usual harassment campaign, which would destabilize the country and undermine the authority of our policy and our ideas' (p. 176).

What Should the Russian Government and the West Do Now?

Russian governments, since the start of reforms, have failed to deliver on their promises of stabilization. Rather than sticking to clear and transparent rules of actions, backed by the West, these governments have relied on an unending series of improvisations and often deceptions of the public, with little real Western support and a heavy dose of bad IMF advice. Though 1994 was another year of official pronouncements regarding the urgency of monetary stabilization, little progress was actually recorded. The inflation at the end of 1994 was *higher* than at the end of 1993, as December 1994 inflation soared to 16 per cent for the month, compared with 13 per cent in December 1993.[3] The amount of central bank credits to the budget (as a percentage of GDP) during 1994 was probably higher than in 1993, though central bank credits to the commercial banking sector were successfully restrained in 1994, a very important and positive point for a future stabilization attempt. In the meantime, the public's confidence was further sapped by the October rouble crisis (in which the currency lost 27 per cent of its value in one day), and then by the outbreak of war in Chechnya in December 1994.

Delay in stabilization till now has had several adverse financial effects, which make future stabilization attempts more difficult and probably more costly (see Sachs, 1994b, for further analytical and quantitative details on these points). First, the Russian public now places extremely low credibility in the Russian rouble, and thus has engaged in a massive flight of capital, and an unwillingness to buy Russian treasury bills except at enormously high interest rates. As a result of the decline in the ration M2/GDP, the inflationary consequences have increased for any given level of central bank financing of the Russian budget deficit. Second, tax evasion and tax exemptions have grown enormously, so that tax collections have consistently declined as a percentage of GDP, contributing to the chronic budget deficit. Third, the regional governments have successfully claimed an ever-growing share of total revenues, beyond the shift in expenditure functions to the local level. On the positive side, though, we should note the following: Russia now has its own currency; credits to the other republics have stopped; and most credits to the banking system have also been brought under control. Finally, there is certainly increased understanding, both in the Russian government and in the West, as to what is needed to succeed in stabilization.

As of the start of 1995, the greatest single challenge for the Russian government is to win back the confidence and support of the Russian people, a challenge that may prove to be impossible before new elections in 1995 or 1996, or even after. A successful stabilization effort in 1995 will require renewed confidence among several key groups:

- *domestic money holders*, who must trust the rouble enough to stop the flight of capital, who must buy large quantities of T-bills at interest rates that are manageable for the budget;
- *foreign creditors*, who must grant another round of debt-service relief;
- *foreign lenders*, mainly foreign governments, the IMF and the World Bank, who should agree to large-scale foreign loans, on the order of 3–5 per cent of Russian GDP (around $12 billion), to support rapid stabilization;
- *the Duma*, which has a keen political interest in overseeing the government, and passing a budget that is actually implemented.

For these reasons, stabilization will require an open, transparent rule-based economic programme, in order to reassure domestic creditors, to appeal to the Duma's stake in its own laws and oversight function, to protect the stabilization programme from presidential and governmental improvisation, and to help to convince foreign creditors and lenders (a process made vastly harder if not impossible by the events in Chechnya). The core of the stabilization programme should therefore be a prominent set of laws and principles, agreed among the government, the Parliament and President. The laws should include concepts of the following sort (the list is obviously meant to be illustrative, and not exhaustive):

1. The government cannot spend any funds not appropriated by the Duma in the Budgetary Act.
2. The government and the President cannot approve any tax exemptions not voted by the Duma (ending the practice of granting tax exemptions by decree).
3. All existing tax exemptions established by presidential or governmental decree rather than Parliamentary law will be ended, unless reauthorized by law.
4. The Duma will set the limit on overall Treasury bills and bonds that may be borrowed on the market.
5. All treasury bills will be marketable securities. There will be no further issues of forced 'promissory notes' or arrears on government payments, which have been a disguised method of financing (with the promissory notes even constituting a kind of money printed by the Treasury).

6. The Central Bank cannot extend any new net credits directly to the government during 1995. The Central Bank cannot increase its net claims on the government above a restrictive authorized limit, established by law. (The most appropriate limit would be zero net credit in 1995).

7. The Duma and government agree not to initiate any new spending proposals in 1995 after the Budget Act is adopted, except under extraordinary conditions and with a supermajority (e.g. two-thirds of the Duma).

8. The rouble will be maintained a stable, market exchange rate against the dollar, based on the preceding principles, and backed by a stabilization fund provided by the IMF.

9. The government, the Central Bank, and the Duma (e.g. via the Chairman of the Budget Committee) publicly commit to cooperate in order to enforce the Agreement on points 1–8. The Chairman of the Duma Budget Committee should be invited into a special oversight panel to verify that budgetary expenditures are carried out according to the Budget Act.

Proposals like these would help to establish the minimum of clarity, credibility, law and order, transparency, etc., necessary for successful stabilization. The public would have a much better idea of what stabilization is really trying to accomplish. Most important, there would be less chance that individual ministers, or the presidential apparatus, or the Central Bank, could undermine the stabilization through new improvisation.

From a purely financial point of view, Russia is not that far from stabilization under the budgetary proposals presented by the government to the Duma in December 1994, if the budget can be adopted and actually implemented; if the government can achieve sufficient credibility with the public; and if the war in Chechnya does not destroy all of the existing financial and political assumptions. Specifically, as I have argued on many occasions, it should prove to be possible to finance a budget deficit of 7–8 per cent of GDP in a non-inflationary manner, based on:

- 2–3 per cent of GDP in net sales of domestic T-bill financing;
- 4 per cent foreign financing (approximately $12 billion);
- 1 per cent of GDP in privatization revenues (approximately $3 billion) from sales to foreign investors.

An additional key step would be the introduction of a $6 billion rouble stabilization fund to allow the rouble to serve as a nominal anchor for the entire stabilization programme, assuming that the rest of the package can also be put in place.

Conclusions

The technical conditions for stabilization are neither mysterious nor impossible to implement. This has been true from the start of Russia's reforms in 1992. Yet, each delay has brought greater political and financial risks. The souring of the public's support for reforms; the flight from the currency; the growing tax evasion; and the war in Chechnya, all add to the difficulties of stabilization in 1995. Perhaps the fragile democratic institutions will function effectively enough to achieve stabilization. Perhaps real stabilization will have to wait for another election. Or perhaps the opportunity for peaceful, democratic stabilization of the economy has been tragically squandered in the past three years.

Notes

1. Some recent estimates suggest that the credits might have been a bit smaller, perhaps 7 per cent of GDP. Even this lower estimate is, of course, enormous, and makes Russia the largest 'aid giver' in the world in 1992 as a proportion of GDP.
2. Ironically, Yeltsin goes on to attribute the stabilization shortcomings during that summer heavily to the absence of an appropriate wage freeze (p. 174), without apparently appreciating the much greater significance of monetary factors at that point.
3. Until mid-1994, the government lived off of the tight monetary policies of the end of 1993. Inflation came down to around 6 per cent per month in the summer of 1994. Then, in July–September, there was another enormous increase of Central Bank credits to the budget, to finance agricultural subsidies, the Northern regions, and many state enterprises in the military–industrial complex. The rouble collapsed in October, and inflation soared in November and December.

References

Fischer, S. (1994) 'Prospects for Russian Stabilization in the Summer of 1993', in A. Åslund (ed.) (1994) *Economic Transformation in Russia*, Pinter, London.

Sachs, J. (1993) 'Western Financial Assistance and Russia's Reforms', in S. Islam and M. Mandelbaum (eds) (1993) *Making Markets*, Council on Foreign Relations, New York.

Sachs, J. (1994a) 'Prospects for Monetary Stabilization in Russia', in A. Åslund, (ed.) (1994) *Economic Transformation in Russia*, Pinter, London.

Sachs, J. (1994b) 'Russia's Struggle with Stabilization', Annual Bank Conference on Development Economics, World Bank, Washington, DC.

Sachs, J. and Lipton D., (1993) 'Remaining Steps to a Market-Based Monetary System', in A. Åslund and R. Layard (eds) (1993) *Changing the Economic System in Russia*, Pinter, London, pp. 127–62.

Yeltsin B.N. (1994) *The Struggle for Russia*, Times Books, New York.

Part IV
Social Evaluation

10 The Conditions of Life

Andrei Illarionov, Richard Layard and Peter Orszag*

First published in 1994

Introduction

The Western media often depict the average Russian as starving and destitute. This is of course absurd. But hardship has increased since the reform for a substantial portion of the population. Average living standards have fallen and inequality has increased. How much? We begin by documenting the changes as accurately as possible, showing what is true and what is exaggerated.

In the next section, we ask why it has happened. Why have real wages fallen and why has wage dispersion increased? We find that economic forces explain much of the story. And how have pensions and family benefits adjusted? The social safety net, though well-organized, has left many large families poor. The problem of poor children is much more serious than the problem of poor pensioners.

The following section looks at unemployment – tomorrow's economic and social problem. We note how inflation has eroded the value of unemployment benefits and also outline an appropriate employment policy framework to cope with the unemployment problem as it unfolds.

Finally, we look at the rise in regional inequality, which will be an increasingly important feature of the Russian scene.

What Has Happened to Living Standards?

Average Income and Consumption

In January 1992, Russia liberalized its prices and they rose immediately by 3.5 times. During the rest of 1992, prices rose again by 7.5 times. How did living standards respond? The shock of the initial price rise was substantial,

Table 10.1 Indices of real income, consumers' expenditure, wages and pensions (1991=100)

	Income	Consumers' expenditure	Average wage	Average pension	'Minimum pension'
1985	74.5	88.5	87.3	63.1	69.5
1990	101.0	109.4	111.4	74.3	84.2
1991	100.0	100.0	100.0	100.0	100.0
1992	48.7	43.3	67.7	36.6	42.4
1992 Q1	42.5	42.1	59.8	32.2	44.3
Q2	41.7	38.2	63.3	36.6	42.1
Q3	53.3	43.5	70.7	36.6	42.9
Q4	57.0	49.2	76.8	41.0	40.3
1993 Q1	45.5	43.8	64.8		35.4

Note: The table depicts the relevant nominal figure deflated by the Soviet Union retail price index for 1985–90 and the Russian consumer price index for 1991 onwards. The quarterly figures are given on annual basis.

but from then on incomes adjusted surprisingly well to the ongoing inflation (with some improvement in standards of living over the year). Our discussion therefore focuses on the average standard of living in the year 1992, though we give details on each quarter in the tables.

We begin with the standard figures on real income and real consumption, which give a very distorted impression. We then go on to explain why they exaggerate the problem. On the standard measures (shown in Table 10.1), real income fell by one-half compared to the previous year and by one-third compared with 1985.[1] The corresponding falls in consumption were 57 and 51 per cent.

As the figures in Table 10.1 imply, the savings rate differed dramatically in these years.[2] In 1985, it was 5.7 per cent; in 1991, 20.8 per cent; and in 1992, 31.3 per cent. In 1985 savings were forced up since produce markets did not clear due to price controls. But in 1991 and 1992 savings were forced up by inflation, which made it necessary to save in order to maintain the real value of bank balances. In fact, savings were not high enough in either year to avert a fall in the real value of household financial assets.[3]

Clearly consumption is a better measure of welfare than income. In evaluating the consumers' expenditure figures, however, several important offsetting features must be noted. First, even consumers' expenditure is a misleading guide to the level of welfare because many key services — the most prominent of which is housing — are still heavily subsidized. Thus if money outlays fall by one-half relative to the prices of purchased goods and services, it does not follow that welfare falls by the same proportion. Somewhat more formally, suppose that utility is given by $X_1^\alpha X_2^{1-\alpha}$, where the price of X_2 is approximately zero. Then if the quantity of purchased goods falls by one-half, utility only falls by roughly $\alpha/2$.[4] Since, in Russia, housing is almost free, as is domestic heating, electricity, gas, telephone, and public transport, α may be

Table 10.2 Indices of real consumers' expenditure: measured vs. survey data
(1991=100)

	Measured consumers' expenditure	Survey data consumers' expenditure
1991	100.0	100.0
1992 Q1	42.1	51.8
Q2	38.2	52.8
Q3	43.4	74.2
Q4	49.2	70.4

Note: The table presents indices of the relevant nominal figures deflated by the consumer price index. The survey data figures apply only to workers' households.

as low as 2/3. The fall in welfare has therefore been substantially less than the fall in measured real purchases.

Second, queues have largely disappeared. The value of this change is difficult to measure. Suppose the average adult woman spent 15 hours per week queuing when she would have otherwise been at work (if employed) or at home (if a pensioner). Suppose further that the comparative disutility of queuing were equal on average to one-fifth the average wage.[5] Then the personal utility cost of queuing was at least 5 per cent of total income and at least 6 per cent of consumers' expenditure in 1985. It is perhaps equally important that people no longer experience constant frustration in searching for goods.

Third, there has been a visible improvement in the quality of services and, in some cases, in the quality of goods.

Fourth, the official statistics fail to reflect unmeasured expenditure. Since expenditure is measured as income minus taxes minus the increase in asset holdings, measured expenditure excludes the impact of unmeasured income – a growing proportion of total income. This is partly offset by the fact that unmeasured asset holdings (e.g. dollars) have also risen. But the overall effect of the measurement problems is probably to bias downward the change in consumers' expenditure. This bias is evident in Goskomstat's survey data on consumers' expenditure (obtained from regular surveys of 49,000 households). This is compared with the measured consumers' expenditure data in Table 10.2. The survey-based consumers' expenditure has fallen significantly less than measured consumers' expenditure. Moreover, by end-1992 the survey figure appeared to exceed the measured figure by some 50 per cent.[6]

Finally, consumption of self-produced food, especially potatoes, has increased during the economic reform process. These five considerations strongly suggest that real consumption has fallen less than suggested in Table 10.1.

Structure of Consumption

However, there has certainly been some fall in real consumption. A standard indicator of living standards is the share of expenditure spent on food: the poor spend a higher proportion of their income on food than the rich. This is of course a rather crude indicator since it is bound to reflect relative prices as well as real income. However, in the Russian case continuing subsidies to the agro-industry have tended to reduce the relative price of food since the beginning of the reform process (see Figure 10.1). Other things being equal, we would therefore have expected the share of food expenditure to fall.[7] In fact, according to the Goskomstat household budget survey, it rose significantly (see Table 10.3). This seems to confirm a fall in living standards.

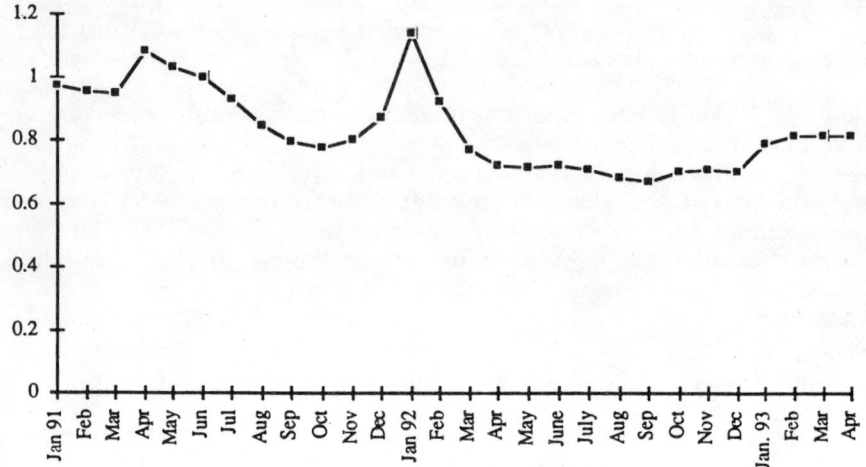

Figure 10.1 The relative price of food (CPI for foodstuffs/CPI for non-foodstuffs, Dec. 1990 = 1)
Note: The consumer price indices in 1992 (Q4) with 1991=1.0 were as follows: 29.5 (CPI), 24.5 (food), 31.5 (non-food), 23.9 (alcohol), 35.5 (paid services).

Table 10.3 Expenditure shares

		Total	Foodstuffs	Non-foodstuffs	Alcohol	Services
Workers' households:						
1991		100	37	49	4	9
1991	December	100	34	54	3	9
1992	Q1	100	45	43	4	8
	Q2	100	43	44	3	10
	Q3	100	41	48	3	8
	Q4	100	44	45	3	7
Pensioners' households:						
1992	January	100	71	16	5	8
	April	100	69	7	5	19
	July	100	79	10	6	5
	October	100	78	13	4	6

Table 10.4 Indices of real expenditure (1991=100)

		Food	Non-food	Alcohol	Services	Total
Workers' households:						
1991		100	100	100	100	100
1992	Q1	60	44	66	60	52
	Q2	69	42	65	56	53
	Q3	100	68	70	50	74
	Q4	101	61	78	40	70

Table 10.5 Consumption of food and food products (kg per person)

	1991	1992	1992				1992/1991
			Q1	Q2	Q3	Q4	
Bread products	101	104	26	26	27	26	1.03
Potatoes	98	106	28	26	23	29	1.09
Vegetables and melons	87	78	17	15	25	20	0.90
Fruits and berries	35	29	7	4	9	9	0.85
Sugar	29	26	6	6	6	8	0.91
Meat and meat products	65	58	15	14	13	16	0.89
Milk and milk products (litres)	349	294	62	75	82	75	0.84
Fish products	14	12	3	3	3	3	0.81
Eggs (number)	229	243	54	72	65	52	1.06
Vegetable oils and other fats	6	7	2	2	2	2	1.10

The striking thing in the household survey data is that, by the second half of last year, real expenditure on food had recovered to its average 1991 level (see Table 10.4). The real declines were in the consumption of non-food items like clothing and footwear, which were nearly halved, and in expenditures on services like cultural activities and holidays.

This pattern, by type of consumption, is confirmed if we look in more detail at the consumption of individual goods. Table 10.5 presents the household survey data on food consumption, including consumption of self-produced food and payment in kind. As is clear from the table, the consumption of basic carbohydrates like bread and potatoes did not fall between 1991 and 1992. Even for meat and milk products, the decline in consumption was quite small. The fall in food purchases during the first half of 1992 (see Table 10.4) was significantly offset by consumption of home-produced potatoes and by drawing on other accumulated stocks of food.

By comparison, there have been significant falls in purchases of textiles and footwear. these are shown in Table 10.6.

Table 10.6 Purchases of non-food commodities (per person)

	1991	1992	1992/1991
Textile material (metres)	9	6	0.67
Knitted underclothes	7	5	0.66
Socks and stockings (pairs)	15	10	0.70
Footwear (pairs)	8	6	0.70
Soap (kg)	4	2	0.55

Table 10.7 Income inequality (individual data, monthly per capita income)

	Upper decile*	Median*	Lower decile*	Upper ductile/ median	Lower ductile/ median	Upper decile/ lower ductile	Gini coefficient
1991	333.5	183.5	96.3	1.82	0.52	3.46	0.26
1992							
January	154.7	88.8	49.7	1.74	0.56	3.11	0.24
February	138.2	86.1	49.1	1.61	0.57	2.82	
March	146.2	87.2	49.2	1.68	0.56	2.97	0.28
August	155.3	83.8	38.6	1.85	0.46	4.03	0.30
November	146.9	82.6	39.1	1.78	0.47	3.76	
December	243.9	117.5	53.8	2.08	0.46	4.53	0.33
1993							
March	147.6	78.4	36.8	1.88	0.47	4.02	0.32
April	122.8	67.4	29.8	1.82	0.44	4.12	0.32

Note: *Roubles, December 1990 prices.

Inequality

Not only has real income fallen; it has also become more unequal. Table 10.7 shows the distribution of individuals according to the per capita income of their family (a 'family' is defined as any group of relatives sharing a common budget). The most striking change has been the fall in the income of the poor relative to the average. The lower decile income (i.e., the tenth percentile) is now only 44 per cent of the median, compared with 52 per cent in 1991.

At the upper decile, we find no substantial increase in inequality relative to the median. However, there has almost certainly been a significant increase in inequality at the very top of the income distribution, which is not analysed in detail in the published statistics. One should also note that the budget survey, though it covers 49,000 families, tends to under-represent people working in the most rapidly developing parts of the economy (including many of the *nouveaux riches*) as well as people on the margin of society (including those whose incomes have suffered most).[8]

The figures in Table 10.7 represent the distribution of nominal income; three other considerations should in principle be taken into account. First,

Table 10.8   Distribution of per capita consumption of meat (kg per month)

	Upper decile	Median	Lower decile	Upper decile/ median	Lower decile/ median	Upper decile/ lower decile
1991	6.3	2.7	1.0	2.33	0.37	6.30
1992	6.5	2.7	0.9	2.41	0.33	7.22

Table 10.9   Income inequality in the United Kingdom and Russia (individual data, monthly per capita income)

		Upper decile/lower decile	Gini coefficient
United Kingdom	1985	3.8	0.30
Russia	December 1992	4.5	0.33
	April 1993	4.1	0.32

since relative food prices have fallen and the income elasticity of food consumption is less than one, the true increase in inequality is less than that shown in Table 10.7. Second, goods with extremely low prices (like housing and transportation) were and continue to be distributed more equally than money income, which would also imply that true inequality has grown less than measured income inequality. On the other hand, when there is rationing by queues, true inequality is less than measured inequality in income, because poor people are willing to devote more time to queuing (Polterovich, 1993). Thus the abolition of queues of itself tends to increase inequality. It is not practicable to give a quantitative evaluation of these three factors, but they may tend to cancel each other out. Many discussions of inequality in Russia point to the high proportion of people who can barely afford to purchase meat. Yet the data show that this was so even before the reform. Inequality of meat consumption increased only marginally in 1992 (see Table 10.8).

So how does inequality in Russia compare with that in the West? This is a difficult question, which was a principal focus of the book by Atkinson and Micklewright (1992) on inequality in the pre-reform period. For the United Kingdom, they give data on the distribution of individuals in 1985 by household income per capita as shown in Table 10.9.[9]

Given the point made earlier about free services, one can probably conclude that income inequality in Russia is still no greater than in the UK. This is of course substantially less than in the United States.

Who Are the Poor?

The main policy issue is the well-being of those at the bottom end of the income scale. Indeed, it is crucial for policy purposes to identify the groups which have the highest incidence of poverty. To examine this issue,

Table 10.10   Minimum subsistence level per person, 1992 (R/month)

	Average person	Older adults	'Minimum pension'* (x1.2)
February	686	468	410
April	1,016	700	650
June	1,344	926	1,080
August	1,868	1,381	1,584
September	2,147	1,561	1,584
October	2,763	1,990	1,584
November	3,450	2,464	2,700

Note: *Males over 60, females over 55.

Goskomstat is undertaking, in collaboration with the World Bank, a longitudinal study of some 7,000 households. This is intended to be a more representative sample than the household budget survey. The income of each individual is then compared with a minimum subsistence level of income established by the Ministry of Labour. The subsistence standard differs with age and starts from FAO/WHO estimates of the diet an average individual would need in order to maintain body weight at a satisfactory level of activity (which is necessarily a somewhat subjective concept). This is increased by one standard deviation of the distribution of individual differences in need. It is then augmented further to account for non-food purchases, making food account (on average) for 68 per cent of total expenditure. Table 10.10 shows the calculated subsistence level for the average person and the average pensioner.[10]

Using this standard, it is possible to address the question of poverty.[11] The proportion of people living in poverty in each group in society in July–September 1992 is shown in Table 10.11. The results are striking and

Table 10.11   Percentage of individuals living below the poverty level

		%
Total population		37
Children 0–6		46
Children 7–15		47
Young adults		36
Females 31–54		35
Males 31–60		34
Females 55+		34
Males 60+		22
Families with	3 or more children	72
	2 children	47
	1 child	34
Families	with a single parent	55
	with an unemployed member	45
	with a disabled member	45
	with an elderly person	31

somewhat surprising.[12] One half of Russia's children live in poverty. This compares with 37 per cent of all Russians. Elderly women are no more likely to be poor than the population at large, and elderly men are less likely.[13]

The most severe incidence of poverty is among families with three or more children, families with a single parent, and families with an unemployed or disabled member. Only 19 per cent of poor households are headed by an elderly person (often living on their own). This raises policy issues to which we return later.

Why the Changes?

What explains the pattern of incomes thus described? The family depends on its wage income, if any, and on the social safety net. We begin with wages.

Average Wages

The measured real wage (the average wage divided by the price level) in 1992 was one-third lower than in 1991, and nearly a quarter lower than in 1985. Why have real wages fallen so much?

We can describe real wages by the following identity:

$$\frac{W}{P} \equiv \alpha \ \left(\frac{Y}{N}\right) \ \left(\frac{P_Y}{P}\right)$$

where W is the wage per worker, P is the consumer price level, α is the share of wages in value added, Y is real value added, N is the number of workers, and P_Y is the price index of value added. Comparing 1992 with 1991, the key facts are that real wages fell by about 33 per cent. Real GDP fell by 20 per cent and employment fell by 4 per cent, so that productivity fell by about 16 per cent. Distinguishing the remaining two changes is more difficult. Using standard figures there is no change in the ratio of P_Y to P, implying that the combined impact of changes in indirect taxes minus subsidies and in relative import prices was zero. Though this is somewhat surprising, the remaining fall in real wages must be due, at least partly, to a fall in α (i.e., a rise in the profit mark-up). Though national accounts data are not accurate enough to confirm this, there is some evidence of a rise in the profit mark-up — though nothing like the scale asserted by the critics of price liberalization.

So why did productivity fall? Clearly because output fell and enterprises were unwilling to reduce employment. The fall in output was partly a continuation of the 15 per cent decline during 1991, which in turn was undoubtedly caused primarily by the break-up of the command system of allocation and its only partial replacement by the market system. But the increased rate of decline during 1992 reflects in addition the reduction in demand during the first half of the year. Production was stabilized during the second half of the year because of the high rate of credit expansion — most of which simply induced inflation but a part of which maintained production.

Table 10.12   Wage inequality across manufacturing industries, 1991 and 1992

	Standard deviation of $log(w_i)$
January–February 1991	0.14
December 1991	0.41
January–February 1992	0.46
December 1992	0.38

In this analysis, a further fall in real wages is almost inevitable as the government continues its financial squeeze in accordance with its agreement with the Central Bank.

Wage Distribution

What about the distribution of wages? They have become more unequal. We have not been able to obtain recent data on the inter-personal distribution of wages, but data on average wage levels across industries highlights the profound changes at work.[14] The distribution of wages across 37 different sectors of manufacturing has become increasingly unequal. This is shown in Table 10.12, which depicts the rise in the standard deviation of log wages across industries. The increase in inequality is particularly striking during the course of 1991 (0.14 to 0.41).

This increase in the dispersion of wages across industries is reflected in the fact that industries which paid relatively high wages in the beginning of 1991 also tended to experience relatively rapid wage growth during 1991 and 1992. In very rough terms, approximately one-half of the final wage dispersion is an amplified version of the original wage distribution and the other half is an additional random factor.[15] Many of the high-wage industries, such as energy and metals production, experienced very high subsequent wage growth. But, in addition, there were some unsystematic changes, with rapid wage growth occurring in some formerly low wage industries, like oil refining.

Why did wages grow more quickly in some industries than in others? One powerful explanation for the growth rate of wages across industries is the growth rate of employment across industries. This is a type of 'Phillips Curve' relationship, in which relatively tight labour markets generate higher wages than slack markets. A regression of the growth rate of wages against the growth rate of employment across industries shows that a 1 per cent increase in the employment rate raises wages by 2.4 per cent – a magnitude similar to that in West European countries.

Finally, in order to fully understand the increase in wage inequality, we must understand why those industries with relatively high wages in 1991 were the ones which have expanded employment relatively rapidly since then. This may be an accident of history, with the industries having the least pleasant working conditions (or requiring the most skills and training) also having the best opportunities for employment growth due to expanded access to world markets.

Table 10.13 Wage differentials across branches (as a proportion of the average wage)

	Q1 1991	Q4 1992	Jan–Feb 1993
Industry	1.08	1.16	1.19
Education	0.81	0.61	0.82
Health	0.76	0.61	0.75
Agriculture	0.81	0.77	
Transportation	1.15	1.40	
Construction	1.25	1.30	1.26
Finance and insurance	1.51	2.34	
Culture and art	0.75	0.49	0.70
Science	1.23	0.73	0.68
Coefficient of variation of wages across branches (%)	0.16	0.28	

We now take a wider view of the whole wage structure (see Table 10.13). The central policy issue has been the level of wages in the budgetary sphere, especially education and health. In the early part of the reform these wages, already below average, fell further. This, more than any other factor, contributed to a widening in the dispersion of wages across branches. (At the same time, wages in transportation as well as in finance and insurance rose sharply.) In autumn 1992, however, a new system was introduced whereby budgetary wages were systematized and indexed quarterly to the consumer price index.[16] By early 1993, there were signs that inequality from this source had been somewhat reduced.

Wages in the budgetary sphere will inevitably remain an issue. However, the new arrangement guarantees that real wages will not fall in the budgetary sector at a time when real wages and employment are likely to be falling elsewhere.[17] The budgetary sector should not therefore experience any increasing difficulty in retaining labour.

Pensions

The fall in real wages is a major reason for reduced real incomes in Russia, but what about transfer payments, especially pensions and child support? Russia has a well-developed pension system. Each person receives his or her individual minimum pension plus an earnings-related supplement (in early 1993 about 60 per cent of pensioners received such a supplement). The minimum pension for an individual equals 'the Minimum Pension' plus an additional 1 per cent for each year worked in excess of 25 (men) or 20 (women). The maximum such increase to 'the Minimum Pension' is 20 per cent. Since most women work for most of their adult lives, the minimum pension for most people is 20 per cent above 'the Minimum Pension'. Only about 100,000 old people get less than 'the Minimum Pension'.

Details on minimum and average pensions are given in Table 10.1 and

Table 10.14   Wages, incomes and pensions

	Income (R bn)	Consumers' Expenditure (R bn)	Average wage (R per month)	Average pension (R per month)	Minimum pension (R per month)
1985	245	202	201	75	50
1986	254	207	207	77	50
1987	264	213	216	80	60
1988	287	228	235	83	60
1989	325	250	259	87	60
1990	385	290	297	102	70
1991	733	510	516	266	161
1992	6,243	3,772	6,011	1,667	1,102
1992					
January	119		1,438	438	342
February	174		2,004	638	542
March	226		2,726	638	542
April	276		3,024	738	642
May	274		3,672	1,383	900
June	369		5,067	1,383	900
July	511	259	5,452	1,383	900
August	539	305	5,870	1,803	1,320
September	624	386	7,379	1,803	1,320
October	758	469	8,853	1,803	1,320
November	907	558	10,576	4,000	2,250
December	1,466	851	16,071	4,000	2,250

Table 10.14, which shows that the average pension is now about one and a half times 120 per cent of 'the Minimum Pension'. This is roughly the same as in the 1980s. But the real value of the average pension has dropped substantially. In 1992 it averaged one-third of its 1991 level (though it was improving throughout the year). The pension in 1991, however, was exceptionally high by historical standards, and the real value of the average pension in 1992 was down by only about 40 per cent relative to its 1985 level. In the first quarter of 1993, the individual minimum pension for the 60 per cent of pensioners for whom the pension was the only source of income equalled 25 per cent of the average net wage (this compares, for example, with 29 per cent for the United Kingdom in 1991).[18]

How has the fall in the real pension affected the degree of inequality? It has certainly increased inequality as measured by income per head. For, even in 1991, the average monthly pension was less than the average income per head (R 266 compared with R 407). Even though some 20 per cent of pensioners also have jobs, it is likely that the average pensioner lives in a household with below average income per head. Therefore, the sharp decline in the pension relative to average income helps to explain the increase in inequality of per capita income shown in Table 10.7.

The policy implications of these developments are, however, somewhat ambiguous. For, as Table 10.11 showed, pensioners are no more likely to be poor than the population at large (after taking account of different subsistence requirements). Rather, the most severe poverty problems are associated with large families.

The pension is now indexed quarterly to the CPI. This means that under high inflation, the real pension falls substantially in between upratings. But once inflation has been controlled, the average real pension (taken over a quarter) will rise by almost 15 per cent. There seems no obvious need for any further steps to boost pensions, except for special local assistance to needy individuals.

In the longer term, there is a strong case for raising the pension age to the more reasonable level of 65. This could be done by raising, each year, the retirement age by half a year. Without some such step, the dependency ratio will become undesirably large.[19]

Child Benefits

This brings us to the problem of children. Despite a fairly extensive system of child benefits, costing roughly 3 per cent of GDP, child poverty is a serious problem – especially in large families and families headed by single mothers. Benefits in April 1993 were as shown in Table 10.15. There are also clothes allowances, adding something like 10 per cent to these benefits.

The value of children's benefits is loosely tied to the minimum wage, though occasionally child benefits have been raised when the minimum wage has not. One reason why inequality has risen in Russia is therefore the fact that the minimum wage (and with it child allowances) has not risen as fast as the average wage (see Table 10.16).

Child benefits, though expensive, often fail to prevent poverty because they are non-targeted. What is needed is a larger benefit for poor families with the benefit declining to zero for richer families. Even if the means-testing is not precise, it is clearly necessary.

Table 10.15   Child benefits in April 1993

	Ages 0–1.5	Ages 1.5–6	Ages 6–16	Additional payment for child of single mother
R per month	2375	1900	950	2137
% of average wage	7.7	6.2	3.1	7.0

Table 10.16   The minimum wage

		Real minimum wage (1985=100)	Minimum wage as % of average wage
1985		100	35
1990		87	24
1991		83	25
1992		32	15
1992	Q1	35	17
	Q2	37	18
	Q3	34	14
	Q4	20	8
1993	Q1	26	12

Unemployment: Tomorrow's Problem

The Unemployment Rate

Families affected by unemployment are among the poorest in Russia. Unemployment is still relatively low but it will inevitably rise. We begin by discussing the current situation and end with some remarks about the future.

The official statistics of unemployment are based on employment office data. Those recorded as 'out of employment' are registered job-seekers who are out of work and available for work. This definition approximates the OECD/ILO definitions of unemployment, but it excludes job-seekers who do not use the employment exchanges.

In February 1993, 1.5 per cent of the labour force was 'out of employment'. At the same time, only 0.6 per cent of the labour force received unemployment benefits. This is because laid-off workers continue to be paid during the first three months of unemployment by their former employer,[20] and because benefit recipients cannot refuse reasonable job offers.

Since only about one-third of vacancies are registered at the job centres, many unemployed workers would not register if it were not a condition for receiving benefits.[21] But even the benefit requirement is not sufficient to ensure that all unemployed people register. The World Bank/Goskomstat household survey shows an unemployment rate of 3 per cent.

In this survey, the unemployment rates are roughly the same for both men and women. But among the 'registered unemployed' (a category in between 'out of employment' and 'benefit-recipients'), three-quarters are female. An unemployment rate of 3 per cent is low by international standards, though we should note that an additional 9 per cent of the industrial labour force was estimated in December 1992 to be working reduced hours (often involuntarily).

Income while Unemployed

Laid-off workers receive the following percentage of their previous nominal wage:

Period	Percentage
First three months	100 (from employer)
Next three months	75 (benefit)
four months	60 (benefit)
five months	45 (benefit)

The minimum benefit is equal to the minimum wage, which is indexed quarterly to the consumer price index and in spring 1993 was about 14 per cent of the average wage.[22] In addition, all new labour force entrants who are unemployed get the minimum wage. In a period of high inflation, the minimum becomes binding for the vast majority of unemployed people – which is why the average unemployment benefit payment has typically been close to the minimum wage.[23]

If inflation continues at its current rate and unemployment rises, unemployment benefits will surely become an issue, and the real value of the minimum benefit may have to be raised. A better policy would be to control inflation.

Employment Policy

The future of employment will become a central social and economic issue in the reform. One argument against lay-offs is that enterprises provide many crucial social services to their employees. The typical Russian enterprise spends 35–40 per cent of its wage bill on social services. But some of this, such as housing, would undoubtedly continue to be provided even after workers are disemployed. A transfer of responsibility for social benefits to the oblasts is urgent, but this should not be allowed to impede the adjustment process. A constructive framework for employment policies would have the following elements:

1. Unproductive workers should not be retained when output contracts. To contain inflation, unemployment must rise towards West European levels. In this process, it is important to ensure the maximum productivity for any particular level of employment. Thus employment must decline with output. In Russia, manufacturing output fell by 20 per cent in 1992 and employment only fell by 4 per cent. In the future, when output contracts, workers must be released for more productive employment in new spheres of activity.
2. Unemployed workers should be offered all possible help in becoming employable in new fields. A major national programme of training is needed for unemployed people as well as for workers. Most of this training should focus on commercial skills, which are still relatively scarce in

Russia. The training should be of a quality appropriate for the high educational level of the unemployed.[24]
3. Unemployment benefits should continue to be payable only for a limited duration. Beyond that time, income maintenance should be conditional on participation in training or public works programme. If this is not done, West European experience suggests that it will be impossible to prevent the build-up of long-term unemployment, which demoralizes the unemployed and does little to contain inflation. The proposed Restructuring Fund should expect to devote substantial resources to training and works programmes, organized in conjunction with the oblasts. Many of these capacities cannot be developed effectively through the enterprises themselves.
4. In company towns, a different approach is needed, since the local enterprises will have to be helped to sustain their employment. But this should be the exception, not the rule.

Regional Differences

A major new source of inequality in Russia will be regional differences in income and employment. Under Communism, inequality between regions was mitigated by the administrative transfer of resources from the rich to the poor regions. But during the reform, such automatic transfers had to be reduced in order to cut public expenditure and to increase incentives. This has already altered the distribution of real income between regions.

We look first at the simple inequality of money incomes across regions (Table 10.17). For a long time, the Far East and the North had the highest incomes, while the North Caucasus, Central Chernozem, and Volgo–Vyatka were the poorest. But since the first month of the reform (January 1992), incomes have grown well above average in the North and the Far East, as well as in Siberia — areas rich in natural resources. At the same time, money incomes have grown much more slowly in the Central region (which includes Moscow) and the North West (which includes St Petersburg), due to the loss of privileges associated with the old administrative system.

However, before any firm conclusions can be drawn, we need to allow for differential inflation across the regions. Data only exist for food prices; these are shown in Table 10.18. The highest prices are in the Far East, North, North West, and Central regions. The lowest are in North Caucasus, Central Chernozem, and the Povolozhsky. There is thus some positive correlation between the levels of prices and incomes (0.5).

There is also a positive correlation (0.5) between the change in prices and incomes, but even so there is some change in the distribution of real income. In Table 10.19, we show comparative levels of real income obtained by dividing money income by food prices. This shows that most of the area which had real incomes above the national average also experienced higher than average growth rates. The striking exception is the Central region.

As Table 10.20 shows, the purchasing power of rouble incomes has declined sharply in the North West and Central regions since the first month

Table 10.17 Regional income differences: nominal income per capita (as percentage of average)

	Jan 92	Apr 92	Jul 92	Oct 92	Jan 93	Mar 93
Russia	100.0	100.0	100.0	100.0	100.0	100.0
North	117.3	137.2	129.1	127.4	137.3	146.3
North-west	111.6	88.5	73.2	74.8	72.3	75.1
Central	118.5	112.0	94.4	98.8	90.0	85.3
Volgo–Vyatka	84.7	80.9	82.5	76.2	79.6	76.4
Central–Chernozem	80.3	71.4	69.3	81.9	79.5	76.0
Povolzhsky	89.3	88.5	82.7	92.1	98.4	91.4
North Caucasus	68.5	61.7	57.2	73.1	65.9	75.1
Urals	97.0	89.3	104.1	99.6	102.0	101.7
West Siberia	103.7	127.9	138.4	130.8	142.4	144.6
East Siberia	103.8	124.5	125.2	117.4	119.0	120.7
Far East	124.6	139.5	193.1	152.2	150.4	155.4
Average CR/month	783	1872	3553	5240	8269	14470
Coefficient of variation	0.18	0.27	0.38	0.26	0.29	0.30

Table 10.18 Regional income differences: food price index (as percentage of average)

	Jan 92	Apr 92	Jul 92	Oct 92	Jan 93	Mar 93
Russia	100.0	100.0	100.0	100.0	100.0	100.0
North	91.1	116.4	108.2	119.5	110.6	114.2
North-west	123.2	120.2	113.4	102.7	101.6	117.4
Central	107.1	94.5	105.0	105.7	117.9	112.9
Volgo–Vyatka	95.0	98.0	94.5	86.8	87.2	91.3
Central–Chernozem	95.0	76.7	78.8	81.5	74.1	75.3
Povolzhsky	82.9	79.6	78.8	78.5	71.6	72.4
North Caucasus	92.3	89.6	82.5	89.4	87.6	87.3
Urals	99.0	102.0	104.7	107.8	94.1	90.1
West Siberia	84.5	106.3	93.0	95.8	96.4	92.9
East Siberia	97.3	121.8	107.4	95.5	102.6	100.2
Far East	110.7	123.9	134.1	144.7	138.1	137.6
Coefficient of variation	0.12	0.16	0.17	0.19	0.20	0.20

Table 10.19 Regional income differences: real per capita income (money income/food price index) (as percentage of average)

	Jan 92	Apr 92	Jul 92	Oct 92	Jan 93	Mar 93
Russia	100.0	100.0	100.0	100.0	100.0	100.0
North	128.8	117.9	119.3	106.6	124.1	128.1
North-west	90.6	73.6	64.6	72.8	71.2	64.0
Central	110.6	118.5	89.9	93.5	76.3	75.6
Volgo–Vyatka	89.2	82.6	87.3	87.8	91.3	83.7
Central–Chernozem	84.5	93.1	87.9	100.5	107.3	100.9
Povolzhsky	107.7	111.2	104.9	117.3	137.5	126.3
North Caucasus	74.2	68.9	69.3	81.8	75.2	86.0
Urals	98.0	87.5	99.4	92.4	108.4	112.9
West Siberia	112.7	120.3	148.8	136.5	147.7	155.7
East Siberia	106.7	102.2	116.6	122.9	116.0	120.5
Far East	112.6	112.6	144.0	105.2	108.9	112.9
Coefficient of variation	0.16	0.19	0.27	0.18	0.24	0.25

Table 10.20 Changes in income, food prices and real income, January 1992–March 1993 (Jan. 1992 = 1.0)

	Nominal income per capita	Food prices	Real income per capita
Russia	18.49	15.31	1.21
North	23.05	19.20	1.20
North-west	12.44	14.60	0.85
Central	13.31	16.15	0.83
Volgo–Vyatka	16.66	14.71	1.13
Central–Chernozem	17.50	12.13	1.44
Povolzhsky	18.93	13.36	1.42
North Caucasus	20.52	14.49	1.42
Urals	19.38	13.92	1.39
West Siberia	25.78	16.83	1.53
East Siberia	21.49	15.76	1.36
Far East	23.05	19.03	1.21
Coefficient of variation	0.21	0.14	0.19

of the reform (we should note, however, that we have no data on hard currency earnings). In most other regions, the so-called 'provinces', real income has risen — especially in Siberia and the Urals. The slowest growth has occurred in the Volgo–Vyatka region which had a highly militarized economy.

Clearly these changes are primarily the result of economic forces, which will operate with increasing force. It seems unlikely that the political process will undertake sufficient redistribution to offset them.

Interestingly, with the exception of the North, unemployment rates are also highest in those areas where incomes have risen least — the North West,

Table 10.21   Out of employment by region, February 1993

	'Out of employment' (thousands)	Unemployment rate (percentage)
North	78.2	2.6
North-west	84.7	2.1
Central	235.3	1.6
Volgo–Vyatka	88.4	2.1
Central–Chernozem	42.4	1.1
Povolzhshy	96.9	1.2
North Caucasus	95.2	1.2
Urals	134.1	1.3
West Siberia	103.1	1.4
Eastern Siberia	50.1	1.1
Far East	53.6	1.4

Central and Volgo–Vyatka regions (see Table 10.21). The correlation is 0.43. Thus there is a kind of regional Phillips Curve.

Conclusion

We draw seven main conclusions about the record to date:

1. Average consumption (properly measured) fell in 1992 to perhaps 80 per cent of its 1991 level. At the same time, the reduction of queuing has been a major welfare gain. The fall in consumption is due primarily to the ongoing fall in output caused by the breakdown of the old command system.
2. Food consumption has fallen little; the main falls in consumption have been in other goods and in services. Relative food prices have been kept low by subsidies and credits to the agricultural sector.
3. Inequality has risen, especially at the bottom end of the income distribution. Measured real income at the lower decile in March–April 1993 was only one-third of its level in 1991 and consumption at that level may have fallen by one-half.
4. The rise in inequality is mainly due to a rise in wage dispersion and the fall in the ratio of children's benefits to the average wage.
5. The incidence of poverty is highest in large families and families headed by single parents, while the distribution of well-being among pensioners is similar to the population at large.
6. The families of the unemployed, though small in number, are also highly prone to poverty. This is largely due to the effect of inflation in eroding the value of earnings-related benefits.
7. Regional inequality has risen due to the impact of economic forces and diminished political will for redistributive programmes.

Looking to the future, there are four main points to be made:

1. Financial stabilization will inevitably lead to further temporary falls in output and living standards.
2. Wage dispersion will continue to widen, aggravating the poverty problem.
3. The main problem with the social safety net is children's benefits, which should be increased in real terms for poor families and reduced for others by means-testing. Some savings on pensions would be possible if the retirement age is gradually raised.
4. Unemployment is bound to rise. The effects of this secular rise could be extremely serious unless major training programmes are implemented, especially in market-orientated skills. Before the reform began, many observers forecast a social catastrophe. It has not occurred, though there are major problems — many of which will get worse. But Russia has the means to overcome them.

Notes

*   The views expressed in this chapter are those of the authors alone, and do not necessarily represent the views of either the Russian or US governments or any agencies thereof. The authors would like to thank Eugene Gontmacher, Timothy King, and Barry Popkin for several extremely beneficial discussions. All data are from Goskomstat (the Russian State Statistical Committee) unless otherwise noted. Further details can be obtained from *Russian Economic Trends* (see references).

1.   In these statistics, household income is measured at the point of payment, so that income is the sum of *recorded* wage payments, pension payments, and so on. Of this household income, some is devoted to increased holdings of roubles (currency and deposits), some to taxes, and the remainder is recorded as consumers' expenditure. Real values of income and expenditure are then calculated by deflating the consumer price index (CPI).

2.   The savings rate is defined as savings divided by disposable income (income minus direct taxes). The other difference between income and consumption is direct taxes.

3.   The inflation tax paid by households (assets × inflation rate) equalled over 100 per cent of household income in 1991 and (ignoring the January 1992 price jump) 40 per cent of household income in 1992.

4.   More precisely, the new level of utility is equal to $(1/2)\alpha$ times the old level of utility, assuming that $X/2$ consumption is unchanged.

5.   Any loss of money income due to queuing has already been incorporated into our measure of income. Here we only include the losses due to the disutility of queuing relative to the alternative activity.

6.   For example, in November 1992, the survey data indicate that expenditure per capita for families with one or more workers was R 6455, and for families with pensioners, R 2809, (see Table 10.22).

Table 10.22 Real measured consumers' expenditure and retail sales (1985=100)

	Measured consumers' expenditures	Retail sales
1985	100.0	100.0
1991	113.0	109.0
1992	48.9	50.3

Note: The table depicts the relevant nominal figure deflated by the Soviet Union retail price index for 1985–1990 and the Russian consumer price index for 1991 onwards.

Multiplying the worker figure by 120 million and the pensioner figure by 30 million, we obtain an estimate of aggregate consumers' expenditure of R 859 bn. In the same month, measured consumers' expenditure was R 558 bn. The legitimacy of this calculation is, however, somewhat uncertain.

Retail sales figures throw a little further light on the issue. Officially measured retail sales fell slightly less during 1992 than measured consumption (see below). Retail sales are based on data for sales of goods through standard retail outlets, whether privatized or not. They do include the vast majority of sales, including goods re-sold on the street, but exclude goods entering the retail market through the new cooperatives, 'commercial shops', kolkhoz and street markets. The share of these informal sales has surely risen, implying a larger downward bias in the measured retail sales figure.

7. The elasticity of substitution between food and other goods is less than one.
8. The survey sample was originally selected from a sample of enterprises and households in the 1950s, and replacements are made as extant participants disappear.
9. Atkinson and Micklewright (1992), p. 137. UK data are from the Family Expenditure Survey using 'normal earnings'. Russian data relate to income within the month.
10. See Popkin, Mozhina, and Baturin (1992). The income needed for different age groups were the following proportions of the average in November 1992: children ages 0–6, 0.78; children 7–17, 1.16; adult males, 1.26; adult females, 1.05; and pensioner adults, 0.71. The share of food for each of the groups is (%): 74, 74, 62, 62, and 83.
11. One problem with this methodology is that it assumes an individual can continually spend his entire disposable income. But if individuals wish to maintain some level of real balances, the inflation tax must be subtracted from disposable income before obtaining a measure of potential consumption. For extremely poor people, this may not be a particularly important caveat.
12. The table is based on preliminary analysis of data on 5,000 families.
13. The minimum individual pension was around R 1300 per month in the third quarter of 1992 (after allowing for the 20 per cent tenure supplement discussed), while the subsistence requirement for older people averaged over R 1400. It follows that pensioners can only have been below the poverty threshold if they lived in large families or if their job tenure was unusually short.
14. We do have data for the wage distribution across workers in September 1991, which yield the following statistics: lower decile/media=0.48, top decile/median=2.11. The standard deviation of log wages is 0.53. it is interesting to note that in medium-sized firms in 1991 Q3, wages across job categories were in the following ratios:

Unskilled	1.0
Skilled	2.7
Professional	2.9
Vice director	4.3

There was not change over the subsequent year in firms of all sizes except that wages of managers in large firms grew more rapidly than average. Of all firms in the sample, 25 per cent reported an increased spread of wages and 17 per cent a decreased spread.

15. The regression of log w_2 on log w_1 yields: log w_2 = 1.68 log w_1 − 0.78, with a standard error of 0.29 and an R_2 of 0.53. Thus var(log w_2) = 1.68^2var (log w_1 + 0.29^2 = 2.82var(log w_1) + 0.089 = 2.82 (.035) + 0.08 = 0.18.

16. In April 1993, the minimum wage in the budgetary sphere was raised to R 8125 (equal to the minimum pension). This was 34 per cent of the average wage (R 23559) at the beginning of April, but a declining proportion over the subsequent three months (since the minimum wage is uprated only once per quarter). All other budgetary wages are fixed multiples of the minimum budgetary wage.

17. If the rate of inflation falls, and indexation remains quarterly, the average real wage over the quarter will rise.

18. For the purposes of this comparison, housing costs are excluded from the incomes of pensioners and workers in the United Kingdom.

19. The share of national income spent on state pensions is slightly more than 6 per cent; in the UK it is 6 per cent.

20. The first two months' pay is essentially severance pay since it is paid whether or not the person is unemployed.

21. Income maintenance from the third month onwards requires registration during the first two weeks of unemployment.

22. The minimum wage was raised to R 4275 per month on 1 April − 18 per cent of the average wage.

23. The minimum wage actually exceeded the average unemployment benefit during several months in late 1992 and early 1993. There seems to have been delays in adjusting the payment of benefits to changes in the minimum wage.

24. The registered unemployed have obtained the following educational levels, see Table 10.23.

Table 10.23   Educational levels of the registered unemployed

Educational level	% of registered unemployed
Higher education	18
Specialized secondary education	27
General secondary education	38
Incomplete secondary education	17

References

Atkinson, A. and Micklewright, J. (1992) *Economic Transformation in Eastern Europe and the Distribution of Income*, Cambridge University Press, Cambridge.

Government of the Russian Federation, *Russian Economic Trends*, Whurr Publishers, London.

Polterovich, V. (1993) 'Rationing, Queues, and Black Markets', *Econometrica*, vol. 61, no. 1, 1−28.

Popkin, B., Mozhina, M. and Baturin, A. (1992) 'The Development of a Subsistence Income Level in the Russian Federation', mimeo.

World Bank, (1992) *Russian Economic Reform: Crossing the Threshold of Structural Change*.

11 Labour Market Adjustment: The Russian Way

Richard Layard and Andrea Richter

First published in 1995

Introduction and Summary[1]

In restructuring an economy one of the biggest challenges is how to transfer people from old jobs to new ones with the minimum of social distress. It is a permanent problem in any economy, and an even greater one in post-Communist countries cutting back on military production and heavy industry. So it is not surprising that in most East European countries unemployment has risen above the Western European average of 10 per cent.[2] Most people expected the same by now in Russia. Why has it not happened so far?

Russia has in effect had much more real wage flexibility than many other countries, due to more factors than solely high inflation. In Britain an employer faced with a fall in demand for his product can only expect a small real wage response from his workers. By contrast, a Russian firm facing loss of revenue is under far less pressure to maintain the real wage of its workforce. This means that it need not lay off as many workers as it would if wages were more rigid. Thus few Russians have been pushed out of jobs compared with Britons.

There are basically two ways in which people can be transferred from old to new jobs (see Figure 11.1).

1. They can be directly *pulled* from the old job into the new. This is the way in which most professional people change jobs: they discover a new position that is more attractive than the present one.
2. They can be *pushed* out of the old job with no immediate prospect of a new one. In this case they enter unemployment. Only after a period without work do they find their way into a new job.

159

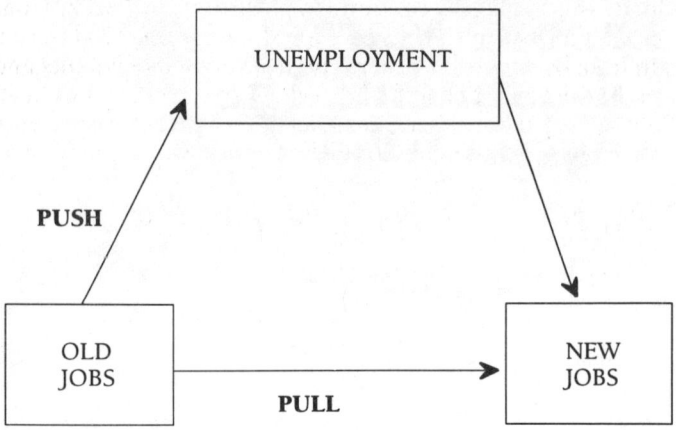

Figure 11.1   Two routes for reallocating labour

In most Western countries the 'push' route predominates, especially for manual workers. Russia so far has been quite different. In 1993 about 1.5 per cent of the labour force were made redundant.[3] Yet there was substantial reallocation of labour, with 21 per cent of workers moving between jobs.

Wage rigidity is not only a Western phenomenon. In Poland, for example, where unions are much more powerful than in Russia, relative wages have proved more rigid than in Russia. This is one reason why unemployment in Russia has risen so slowly. On international definitions Russian unemployment rose from 4.8 per cent of the workforce in 1992 to 5.9 per cent in early 1994. Of the unemployed only 2 per cent had taken the trouble to register at the Employment Office. In addition to the unemployed many other workers were involved in short periods of involuntary leave, often unpaid. The typical period of leave was a month and at any one time in early 1994 some 2 per cent of workers were on leave. A further 4.5 per cent were working short-time and 1 per cent had left the labour force.

Thus there has been an implicit contract between workers and managers. Workers accept highly flexible wages and hours, and managers may in return offer a high degree of job security. Most labour force adjustments are achieved through voluntary quitting.

Why has this come about? From the workers' side there are three main reasons. First, the enterprise provides many other benefits to its workers as well as wages (particularly in welfare and housing, but also access to the enterprise's tools, which can be used in secondary jobs). Second, membership of a firm provides a source of social identity. Third, unemployment benefits are very low in real terms, and will continue to be low as long as inflation erodes their real value. So workers are unwilling either to become unemployed or to force the firm into financial crisis. Another reason for industrial peace is that managers have traditionally had great authority, which was eroded little when Communism collapsed.

But why do the managers continue to pay for more workers than they need to produce existing output? There are a number of financial reasons why they would gain little by sacking workers (high severance payments and the excess wages tax). But many managers also feel a strong sense of obligation to their workers, either for paternalistic reasons or because in many enterprises the workers are now majority shareholders. Yet other managers have unrealistic hopes of a recovery in demand for their product.

The situation will surely become much more difficult as tight budget constraints become more general, and as the Federal Bankruptcy Agency goes into action. Unemployment is bound to rise. In this situation, it is important to have some clear policy priorities in mind.

Policy Proposals

Unemployment can be a bad experience in any country and a horror in Russia, where benefit is so low in real terms. Surveys in Britain show that while rich people are happier than poor people (other things being equal), the difference in happiness is much smaller than the difference between those who are employed and those who are unemployed (Oswald and Blanchflower, 1995). So some efficiency loss in the enterprise could be accepted in order to reduce unemployment. But how much efficiency loss does overmanning involve in any case?

The experience of Western Europe shows the extraordinary inefficiency of long-term unemployment, which, in addition to weighing heavily on the nation's budget, does almost nothing to control inflation and erodes the nation's human capital. In Russia this has so far been avoided, by a mixture of devices including overmanning. This could clearly have bad effects if the surplus workers kept on in enterprises continued to work on the shop floor and thus delayed restructuring. But some form of surplus labour may be acceptable. An example is when workers are kept *off* the shop floor through involuntary periods of leave. In such cases it is essential that their spare time is used well – especially in well-organized training supported by Federal Employment Service funds. The search for better work is also crucial, and poorly paid workers in insecure jobs do look for better jobs – and may well find the job search easier from the base of an existing job than from the demoralizing base of unemployment.

We find that four policy areas in particular are in need of further development:

1. *Unemployment benefit.* For workers the present earnings-related benefit is quite inadequate since inflation erodes its purchasing power. It would, however, be quite adequate if those benefits were *indexed* to price inflation. Since a period of mass lay-offs must be approaching, such a reform is surely necessary on simple humanitarian grounds.
2. *Commercial training.* A massive retraining effort is needed – almost entirely in commercial skills. In a market economy almost a third of workers are employed in jobs for which formal commercial training makes

an enormous difference (management, marketing, accounting, financial services, retail and wholesale trade, basic accounting and self-employment). For the employed, commercial training is needed to raise productivity and to reduce the probability of entering unemployment. It is needed for the unemployed to help them back into work, and for the young so that they have the necessary qualifications to be able to start their adult lives with a job.

In many Western countries empirical evidence on the rate of return to training for unemployed people shows varied results. But in the Russian context, where commercial skills are currently so scarce, the returns could not fail to be high.

There are enormous economies of scale in such a training effort if good teaching packages are developed and waves of teacher-trainers are taught to use these packages. Very little of this has been done so far. But it should be a top priority for the nation.

3. *Public works.* It is vital to keep people from entering long-term unemployment. This problem has not yet arisen in Russia, with only 10 per cent of the unemployed out of work for more than one year. But it is vital that no-one unemployed for over a year be paid 'material assistance' for doing nothing. Support for individuals out of work for a long time should be through wages paid for working on a public works project. Plans need to be laid now for what projects are worth developing in which areas.

4. *Housing.* In some areas it will be extremely difficult to generate enough jobs even for those older employees who want work. Young people will have to move. Everything must be done to make this possible. This means the abolition of the *propiska* (the residence permit required for some major Russian cities) and of all unreasonable restrictions on the use of housing space. If possible, empty public buildings should be made available as hostels for migrant workers.

The basic objective of employment policy has to be to prevent the development of a dependency culture. Instead, people need active help to become and remain employable. However, the natural situation of a person must be to earn his own living. This has so far remained the case in Russia more than in many countries, and with care Russia can avoid many of the mistakes that have been made in the West.

This in outline is our argument. In this chapter we describe in some detail what has been happening to employment in the first section and to wages in the second section. We then analyse more fully the reasons for the wage flexibility that has occurred, before concluding with our thoughts on policy.

Labour Market Flows and Unemployment

Let us begin with flows in the labour market. These are depicted in Figure 11.2 where the arrows show what percentage of the workforce flowed in each direction in 1993. The figures in each box show the stocks in less than full employment in early 1994 (again as a percentage of the workforce).

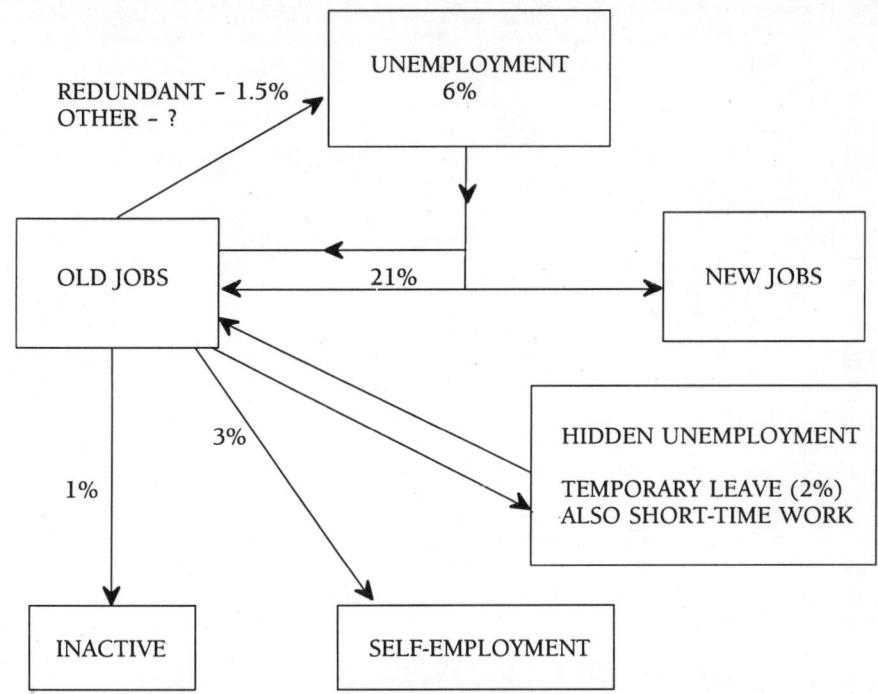

Figure 11.2 Labour force flows, as per cent of labour force, 1993

The inflow of redundant workers into unemployment in 1993 was only 1.5 per cent of the workforce. How was this low level possible? One explanation which quickly comes to mind is that nothing changed – simple stagnation. But this is wrong: there were considerable changes in the pattern of employment across sectors (see Table 11.1).[5] Employment fell by 8 per cent in industry, but rose in services. And there were even more changes at firm level. So how did these adjustments happen without mass redundancies?

Hirings

The main answer is that there was a lot of hiring – 21 per cent of the workforce in 1993. Enough new jobs opened up, which attracted mainly workers who were already employed. While the majority of firms were reducing staff, a sizeable minority were expanding (see Figure 11.3). This in turn initiated a chain of movement of workers between old jobs.

Table 11.1 Change in employment in 1993 (as per cent of employees in the sector): Employees in organizations with more than 200 workers

	Net change in employment	Hiring	Separations	of which workers made redundant	Vacancies (end of yr)
Total	−4.0	21.1	25.1	1.5	1.1
Industry	−8.7	20.1	28.8	1.8	0.6
Agriculture	−3.2	11.3	14.5	0.7	0.3
Transport	−3.1	26.5	29.6	1.1	1.5
Communications	−1.1	32.1	33.2	1.7	1.4
Construction	−5.4	38.7	44.1	1.9	0.8
Retail sales and catering	−5.0	22.7	27.7	2.9	0.5
Wholesale trade	−2.4	21.7	24.1	2.9	0.8
Accommodation services et al.	5.7	36.2	30.5	1.3	2.5
Health, sports, social safety net	0.8	18.0	17.2	0.5	2.5
Education	2.7	15.2	12.5	0.5	1.4
Culture and arts	1.8	15.7	13.9	0.8	2.7
Science and scientific services	−13.0	12.1	25.1	2.0	1.2
Finance and insurance	7.3	22.5	15.2	1.8	2.7

Source: Goskomstat (1994)

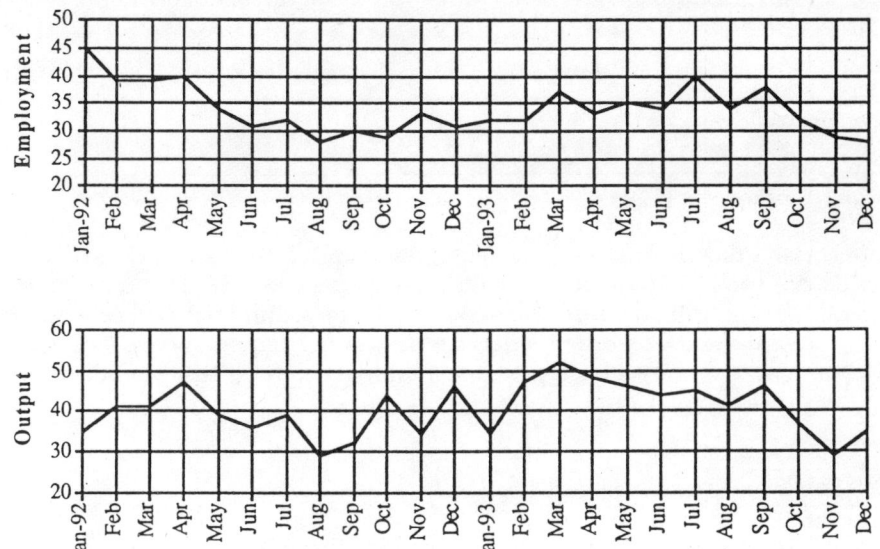

Figure 11.3 Percentage of industrial firms expanding over the previous month
Note: The data refer to a sample of around 180 medium-sized firms (employing 250–2000 employees).
Source: Russian Economic Barometer 1994.1, p. 52.

Involuntary Leave, Short-Time Working and Wage Arrears

A second reason for few redundancies was hidden unemployment within firms. One form of this is involuntary leave. It should be noted that the figures commonly used in public debate have been wildly exaggerated. This is because the raw figures show how many workers have *ever* been placed on involuntary leave during a period. For example they show that 6.5 per cent of workers experienced unpaid leave in 1993.[6] This much-quoted figure is not the number on leave at any one point in time. To find this figure we need to use data on how long the leave lasts – in the first quarter of 1994 the average was around 16 days for workers placed on involuntary leave.

In Table 11.2 we show the proportion of workers on involuntary leave at any one time – around 0.7 per cent on average in 1993 but up sharply in early 1994.[7] This increased substantially towards the end of 1993. We also show the proportion on short-time working. This is now 4.6 per cent. Unfortunately there are no data on the scale of the reduction in hours. But we do know that in 1993, taking into account both involuntary leave and short-time work, average hours per worker were only 4 per cent lower than in 1992. And in the first quarter of 1994 the average number of hours worked was 3 per cent lower than in the same period in 1993.

Another coping strategy for firms is simply to delay paying their bills – including the wages they owe (which are normally the second claim upon an

Table 11.2 Workers on involuntary leave (paid or unpaid) and short-time work (per cent of total labour force)

	1993: Q1	Q2	Q3	Q4	1994: Q1
Involuntary leave	0.6	0.5	0.7	1.2	2.2
Short-time working	1.3	1.3	1.5	2.2	4.6

Source: Goskomstat (1994).

enterprise's money after tax payments). By March 1994 total wage arrears in industry, construction and agriculture had reached 38 per cent of one month's wage bill in those sectors – up from around 20 per cent in the previous quarter. Of workers interviewed in a household survey in January, 18 per cent had not yet been paid last month's income – up from 10 per cent in the previous quarter.[8]

Self-Employment and Non-Participation

A third mechanism for averting mass redundancies has been the growth of self-employment. The net flow into self-employment in 1993 was 3 per cent of the labour force. A final form of adjustment is exit from the labour force altogether. But in 1993 labour force participation in fact fell by only 1 per cent of the workforce.

Despite these three major coping strategies – involuntary leave, short-time working and wage arrears – many firms have been forced to cut jobs. The main method has been not to replace workers who quit (some of whom quit into unemployment), and the other is redundancy.

Employment and Unemployment

We can now look at the total change in the numbers employed and unemployed. The available figures provide a fairly consistent picture – with employment falling some 2 per cent between 1992 and early 1994, and unemployment rising by about 1 percentage point.[9] Table 11.3 gives aggregate Goskomstat estimates of employment. The number of employees fell quite sharply, but two-thirds of this fall was offset by strong growth in self-employment (including partnerships).

Table 11.3 Employment (millions)

	1992	1993·	1994: Q1
Employees	67.6	64.6	
Self-employed	4.4	6.4	
Total	72.0	71.0	70.5

Source: Goskomstat (1994)

The picture of unemployment is fairly consistent, whether we use the Federal Employment Survey figures or the Labour Force Survey. The Labour Force Survey questionnaire is based on the European Labour Force Survey, and the answers make it possible to calculate the number of people unemployed on the ILO/OECD definition. On this basis people are unemployed if they:

(a)   did no work for pay or profit in the reference week;
(b)   sought any work within the last month;
(c)   are available for work.

The definition is narrow in one way since it excludes people who did any work (however short), but wide in another since it includes people seeking work of any kind (however short).[10]

Using the ILO/OECD definition the proportion of Russian workers unemployed rose from 4.8 per cent in 1992 to an estimated 5.9 per cent in early 1994 (see Table 11.4). Of these unemployed, about a fifth were students or pensioners and only a third were looking for permanent work.

The numbers registered as 'out of work' with the Employment Service were little more than a quarter of the survey figure, but the striking fact is that the Employment Service number had risen by almost exactly the same amount as the survey number — from 1.0 per cent of the workforce in 1992 to 1.7 per cent in the first quarter of 1994 (and 2.0 per cent at the end of April).

To understand unemployment in any country one must understand the system of unemployment benefit. A new benefit system, set up in 1991 and administered by the Federal Employment Service under Fyodor Propokov, works through a network of 2400 well-staffed Employment Offices. Details of benefits are set out in Appendix 2. Broadly, workers made redundant get paid by the firm for three months. But they need to register at once with the Employment Service if they are to be entitled to benefit from the fourth month onwards. This benefit is a declining proportion of their former nominal wage, subject to a minimum benefit equal to the Minimum Wage (about 8 per cent of the average wage in the economy in June 1994). In a period of high inflation the Minimum Wage soon becomes the binding constraint. All other employed workers are entitled to the Minimum Wage

Table 11.4   Stock of unemployed people (per cent of labour force)

	1992	1993	1994: Q1
Labour force survey	4.8	5.5	5.9
Registered as out of work at the FES	1.0	1.4	1.7
of which:			
Redundant	0.5*	0.5	0.4
Receiving benefits	0.2	0.6	1.1

* This figure is for November 1992.
Source: Goskomstat (1994), FES.

Table 11.5 Source of unemployment for people registering at the Federal Employment Service (per cent of total)

	December 1992	December 1993	March 1994
Redundant	41	31	25
Quit	38	47	
Other	21	22	
	100	100	100

Note: The table refers to those registered as 'out of work', not the narrower number of officially 'registered unemployed'.
Source: Federal Employment Service

Table 11.6 Unemployed people registered with the Federal Employment Service (per cent of labour force)

	All workers		Redundant workers	
	Inflow	Outflow	Inflow	Outflow
1993	2.9	2.8	0.4	0.6
1994: Q1 (annual rate)	4.5	3.5	0.9	0.7

Note: The table refers to those registered as 'out of work', not the narrower number of officially 'registered unemployed'.

(except those who were sacked for disciplinary reasons or refuse job offers, who can be refused benefit for up to three months).

So how many of the unemployed have been made redundant? In March 1994 only one-quarter of the stock of those registered as out of work had been made redundant (see Table 11.5). Of the inflow to unemployment, redundant workers formed an even smaller proportion (see Table 11.6). While in 1993 2.9 per cent of workers registered a new spell at the Employment Service, this included the 0.4 per cent of the workforce who had been made redundant.

The total number of redundant workers who registered a new spell at the FES in 1993 was around 300,000 (0.4 per cent of all workers), which compares with total redundancies of around 800,000 implied in Table 11.1. This raises the more general question of why the numbers of unemployed registered at the Employment Service are so much lower than the numbers of unemployed reported in surveys. There are a number of possible reasons.

1. Benefits are low in nominal terms, and their value is quickly eroded by inflation. Even so, it is surprising that young people at least would not claim them.
2. The Employment Service covers a fairly small percentage of placements in the economy. It is said to have on its books a third of all vacancies, but these are skewed towards manual vacancies (about 85 per cent of the total). About one-third of those who leave the Employment Service's register (of those 'out of work') go to a job obtained with the help of the

Table 11.7 Unemployment duration of the Federal Employment Service registered unemployed (per cent of those registered as unemployed at end of month)

	March 1993	March 1994
Less than 1 month	15	15
1 to 4 months	43	40
4 to 8 months	29	24
8 to 12 months	11	12
More than 1 year	2	9

Service. This flow amounts to about 1 per cent of the workforce per year — compared with a total flow of hiring (in Table 11.2) of around 20 per cent.
3. The Employment Service has so far provided very little retraining for unemployed workers. In March the numbers in training reached 58,000 — only 4 per cent of the number of unemployed on the books of the Federal Employment Service.
4. Some people do not like to claim money except for work done.
5. Parts of the population are out of reach of the Employment Service.
6. More of the survey unemployed are lying; in fact they have undeclared earnings.

Those who believe that unemployment in Russia is already high will tend to stress reasons 1 to 5. Others will tend to stress reason 6. The truth is that some people who are in desperate trouble (but doing some petty work) may be excluded from both Survey and FES figures, while even the FES figures may include some people who are not in serious trouble.

We have no data on the duration of unemployment except for those registered at the Employment Service. As can be seen in Table 11.7, the percentage of individuals registered as unemployed with the FES for more than one year had grown to nearly 10 per cent in March 1994, from only 2 per cent one year earlier.

To conclude our discussion of unemployment, let us give some basic data on the survey of unemployed (Table 11.8). Unemployment rates decrease with education, but not very sharply. Unemployment rates are especially high for young people, but it is surprising that young people have not so far had more trouble in the labour market. Survey unemployment rates are similar for men and women. They are higher for blue-collar workers — not surprising when about a quarter of white-collar workers who got jobs through the Employment Service in 1992 got blue-collar jobs.

Real Wage Flexibility

We turn now to the evidence on real wage flexibility, before attempting to explain it in the next section. We begin with the real average wage before looking at the more important disaggregated picture. As can be seen from Figure 11.4, when real aggregate demand fell from 1991 to 1992 the real

Table 11.8   Unemployment rates (survey-based), 1993

	Unemployment rate	% of the unemployed	(% of FES unemployed)	
			Jan. 94	Jan. 93
By education				
Higher education	3.1	10	21	18
Special secondary school	5.2	32	41	27
General secondary school	5.8	37	25	38
Uncompleted secondary school or less	6.0	21	13	17
	5.5	100	100	100
By age				
15–19 (up to 18)		15	5	5
20–24 (18–22)		15	13	13
25–29 (22–29)		11	18	20
30–49		45		
50–54		6	57	54
55–59		5		
60–72 (pensioners)*		3	7	8
By sex				
Male		51	32	28
Female		49	68	72
By occupation				
White collar			29	
Blue collar			71	

Note: *These categories are relevant for FES data

consumption wage dropped by a third. There has been significant recovery in real wages since January 1992, but by April 1994 the average real wage was still only 72 per cent of its level in 1985.

More striking is the fact that, as between industries, the fall in real wages was greater, the bigger the contraction of demand (as reflected in the fall in employment). In fact for each extra percentage fall in employment between January–February 1991 and December 1992, industry wages fell by 2.4 per cent.[11]

How does this compare with flexibility in other countries? We have only limited evidence. A similar analysis was done for Poland in relation to changes in employment and wages in 20 industries during 1990. In the Polish case a 1 per cent change in employment induced a 1.7 per cent change in relative wages (Jackman, Layard and Scott, 1992). This analysis is for a shorter time interval than the one for Russia referred to above. One would expect the impact to be stronger in the short term than in the long term, since, in industries subject to a once-and-for-all relative decline in demand, relative wages would begin to recover once enough people had left. Thus if we look at changes in Russia during 1991 a 1 per cent fall in employment was associated with a 5.8 per cent fall in relative wages.[12]

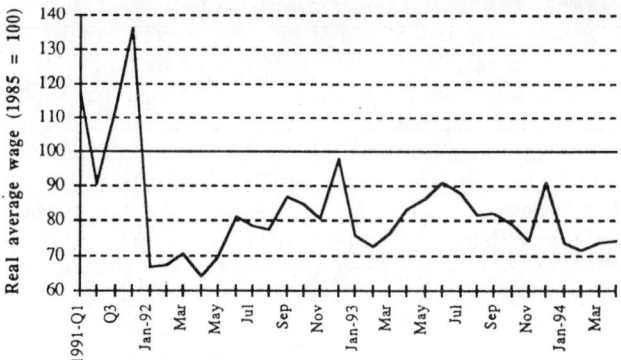

Figure 11.4 The real average wage

These numbers from post-Communist countries can be compared with typical Western numbers. In Britain for changes in wages and employment in the 2-year period 1982–84 the coefficient was 0.2 (t-statistic = 3.5) compared with 2.0 for Russia (and for the period 1983–85 in Britain it was only 0.04 with t-statistic = 2.0).[13]

Other comparisons are more difficult. There are many analyses of the impact of regional and national unemployment on wage behaviour. As Oswald and Blanchflower (1995) have shown, there is a strong tendency to find that, if unemployment rises by 1 per cent of the labour force, real wages fall by $10/u$ per cent (where u is the percentage unemployment rate). But the sudden fall in aggregate real wages in Russia in January 1992 cannot usefully be compared with such statistics, since the speed of this fall was mainly due to the (partly unanticipated) scale of the January 1992 price jump. Nor should the Oswald and Blanchflower statistics be compared with the shifts in relative industrial wages in Russia.

Why So Few Layoffs?

The evidence in the last two sections raises two questions:

1. What explains the remarkable real wage flexibility?
2. Why is the scale of downsizing less than can be explained by wage flexibility – i.e. why do firms continue to employ people whose marginal product is zero?

Why Real Wage Flexibility?

As John Maynard Keynes pointed out in the 1920s, it is difficult to get falls in nominal wages. Thus one might explain higher real wage flexibility in Russia by the higher-than-average inflation, in relation to other post-Communist economies, which the Russian economy has experienced since price liberalization in January 1992. But if relative wages are to change by 25 per cent per year, this can be as easily achieved with 50 per cent inflation as with 500 per cent. Thus we must find other reasons for higher real wage flexibility in Russia than in Poland.

The flexibility of wages is explained by the willingness of workers, constrained by low mobility of labour and weak labour unions, to accept pay cuts in order to preserve jobs. Russian workers appear to be much more willing than workers elsewhere to let wages fall, if this saves jobs. Why?

There are five main reasons. First, there is the social support provided by enterprises — above all health care and housing. When a worker leaves his enterprise, his family may lose access to the enterprise's hospital/clinic or to financial support for other health care. Housing is different. No one can force a worker out of his home. But, if the enterprise is in financial collapse, it cannot heat or maintain the housing. Other forms of social support are subsidized child care, meals, food and vacations — as well as social assistance in case of hardship (see Table 11.9). But many of these are on the decline.

Second, the enterprise is a source of personal identity. As in Japan, membership of an enterprise structures a person's life much more than in the West. There is therefore greater aversion to open unemployment in Russia and Japan than in the West.

Third, the alternatives to staying in the enterprise are poor. Unemployment benefit is low and its earnings-related component unindexed. By contrast, if the worker stays in his enterprise his nominal wage at least is likely to rise even if his relative wage falls. Moving home to find other work is difficult due to a rigid housing market and local *propiska* systems, so that laid-off workers cannot easily seek a better life in another city.[14]

Fourth, retaining ties to the enterprise allows workers to continue using the enterprise's tools and equipment. While a second job is generally not a major source of income, access to the enterprise's tools does allow workers to earn some additional income from petty jobs.

Fifth, workers are in generally poorly organized to oppose such cuts. Except in mining, worker organization is weak, and trade unions historically have played a minimal role in wage determination. In 1992 only 27 strike days were lost per 1000 workers. This compared with the OECD average of 110 in that year (or 340 on average for 1983–92). For Poland the 1992 figure was 230 (or 100 on average for 1990–92). In Russia the incidence of strikes has been falling: in 1993 only 4 days were lost per 1000 workers, and in the first quarter of 1994 less than 1 day per 1000 workers was lost.

The Case Against Layoffs

But even if real wage cuts have made keeping on workers cheaper, why do managers continue to pay workers whose marginal productivity is zero? There are probably six main reasons. The first is that workers actually do have some power in the enterprise, especially where they are shareholders.[15] Even if they do not strike, there is an implicit *quid pro quo* of managers

Table 11.9 Social services provided by enterprises, 1993 (share of surveyed individuals who received these services)

	April	August	December
Free or subsidized meals	14	9	9
Subsidized food and other goods	21	13	20
Retraining and education	6	4	4
Income support for hardship cases	14	12	11

Source: VCIOM 'Survey of the Working Population' (1993)

promising few redundancies to employees (made possible by low real wages), in exchange for employees–shareholders not voting the manager out of his job. A second reason is that beyond this pressure, many managers see employment as a social good and do not eliminate jobs for paternalistic reasons. They may also be under pressure from the authorities. Third, access to cheap government credit may be directly linked to the number of people earning a living through the enterprise. Fourth, many managers have been overly optimistic about the future. This is nicely demonstrated in Table 11.10.

But there are also two important financial reasons why firms may gain little (or sometimes nothing) from laying off workers. One is the excess wage tax, which is incorporated in the profits tax and works as follows.[16] In computing taxable profit, an enterprise can only include as wage-cost the wage bill that would have been paid if the average wage was six times the minimum wage. Thus average wages above six times the minimum wage are subject to a profits tax rate of around 35 per cent.[17] Thus enterprises have an incentive to reduce their average wage.

Table 11.10 Percentage of industrial enterprises experiencing changes and forecasting changes, 1993, 1994

	Increase	No change	Decrease	Total
Output				
Actual 1993: Q4	18	30	50	100
Forecast 1994: Q1	18	49	31	100
Actual 1994: Q1	8	28	61	100
Forecast 1994: Q2	17	38	40	100
Employment				
Actual 1993: Q4	11	45	40	100
Forecast 1994: Q1	6	56	35	100
Actual 1994: Q1	2	45	50	100
Forecast 1994: Q2	4	49	43	100

Source: Centre of Economic Analysis and Forecasting (1994), 1994.1.
Note: These data are from the quarterly *Business Survey* conducted by the Centre for Economic Analysis and Forecasting. It involves 1,400 firms in the majority of manufacturing sectors.

This in turn affects the relative advantage of dismissing a worker, instead of keeping him on but cutting his wage. If the worker is retained but his wage is cut, this reduces the average wage, so that the savings in excess wage tax may well exceed the wage cost of retaining the worker rather than firing him.[18]

The other financial consideration is the substantial cost of severance. If the firm has to pay the worker for another three months anyway (albeit without any wage increase), its immediate gain from a lay-off is small.

Policy Conclusions

If this is how Russia's employment problems have been handled so far, how should they be handled in the future? We know that the problem will become increasingly difficult. Many enterprises will be simply unable to maintain the paternalistic policy adopted so far. Others, under aggressive outside owners, will be unwilling to do so, even if they could afford it. But how should public policy attempt to influence events?

We begin from the position that open unemployment is a real evil. Its costs exceed any loss of output involved. For, as Oswald and Blanchflower 1995 have shown, unemployment is one of the main sources of human misery: the difference in reported happiness between an unemployed person and the average person in work (*ceteris paribus*) far exceeds the difference in happiness between rich and poor. In Russia the psychological effect of open unemployment could be even more devastating, especially when one considers the social stigma which has historically been attached to being unemployed.[19] It should therefore be a major policy goal to restructure the economy with as little open unemployment as possible.

Foreign Experience

There is in fact a wide zone of experience. In the West countries differ greatly in their average unemployment rates over the last ten years – from under 5 per cent (Austria, Japan) to over 15 per cent (Spain, Ireland). The evidence suggests that two sets of factors (above all) influence the outcome.[20]

The first is how the unemployed are treated. Unemployment is higher where high benefits are available for a long period with few conditions and little active help (like training or temporary work) provided to unemployed people. Such arrangements tend to induce the completely useless phenomenon of long-term unemployment.

The second set of factors relates to wage bargaining. Because unemployment has to be high enough to control wage pressure, unemployment is higher where there is no other method of controlling such pressure. By contrast, unemployment is lower in countries which have some coordinated procedures for discouraging a high average level of wage increases.

Implications

This foreign experience, combined with Russia's experience so far, suggests the following main policy conclusions for Russia.

1. *Retraining.* Since economic reform requires a massive shift into commercially based jobs, there should be a major campaign to provide training in such jobs at all levels (from basic bookkeeping to management). Such training should be available for unemployed people and anyone else wanting commercial education.
2. *Public works.* No-one who has been unemployed for over a year should receive income support for doing nothing. Support for people in this position should be provided through temporary public work.
3. *Unemployment benefits.* Unemployment benefits for people made redundant must be adequate for them to support themselves. If inflation was under control, the present provision would be adequate. For other unemployed people, such as young people entering the labour market and those returning to the labour force, countries like Italy have until recently had minimal provision. This may be a sensible model for Russia. At present in Russia the work ethic is in this respect quite well developed, due perhaps to the socialist principle 'From each according to his ability, to each according to his work.' It would be a pity to erode these feelings and encourage welfare dependency.
4. *Excess wage tax.* Like all tax-based incomes policy, this has the objective of increasing the level of employment consistent with stable inflation.[21] It does this in two ways: by encouraging general wage restraint and, implicitly, subsidizing the employment of low-wage labour. Russia's present tax is doing the job well and should be continued. It provides quite sufficient flexibility for changes in relative wages.
5. *Housing policy.* It is essential that labour can move. This requires complete deregulation of the housing market. In particular, enterprises need to be encouraged to sell of their housing stock in order to revitalize the private housing market. Also, the state should make empty public buildings available as hostels for migrant workers.
6. *Support for work sharing.* Perhaps the most difficult issue is how far firms should be assisted in keeping on their workers. There are advantages and disadvantages of trying to ensure that people only leave at the rate at which other jobs become available — thus avoiding open unemployment. The advantage is that people do not lose contact with the labour market. (Search on the job may be more effective than search from unemployment.) If there is no work for people to do in the enterprise, they at least have access to equipment which they can use to do petty jobs outside. And their spirit is not broken. In addition, social peace is preserved — as long as workers actually get paid.

On the other side, the pressure of too many people on the books of an enterprise impedes restructuring. Though in principle half the workers could be made jobless *within* the firm, while the productivity of the other half doubles, this is much less likely to happen than if half the workers are dismissed.

In practice the balance of the agreement must depend on the external labour market situation. How does existing policy stack against this? The Federal Employment Service is instructed to supplement the wages for workers on unpaid or part-paid leave for up to three months, if it has the resources. This is a sensible power, but only in a really collapsed labour market. Similarly the Federal Employment Service can lend an enterprise money to finance an investment that will save jobs. This power is more dangerous, and should probably be exercised by some broadly based local development agency, analogous to the successful Scottish Development Agency.

To conclude, Russia's labour market adjustment has been quite successful so far. There has been much re-deployment, with few people openly unemployed. The tough phase is coming now. The chief secret of success is a massive effort to enable people to retrain for the commercial opportunities which are clearly there or soon will be.

Appendix 1: Supplementary Tables

Table 11A:1   Numbers employed, including self-employed (millions)

	1980	1985	1990	1991	1992	1993
TOTAL	73.3	74.9	75.3	73.8	72.0	71.0
Industry	23.8	24.2	22.8	22.4	21.5	20.8
Agriculture	11.0	10.7	10.0	10.0	9.5	9.6
Transport and						
Communication	7.0	7.3	5.8	5.8	5.7	5.2
Construction	7.0	7.1	9.0	8.5	8.3	8.0
Trade and Catering	6.1	6.2	5.9	5.6	5.7	
Services				3.2	3.1	3.2
Health, Sport, Social Security				4.3	4.3	4.4
Education, Culture, Art				7.3	7.5	7.7
Science and scientific services				3.1	2.6	2.4
Finance and Insurance				0.4	0.7	
Public Administration				2.0	2.2	2.4

Source: Goskomstat *1992 Yearbook* (1993) and Goskomstat Monthly Reports (various)

Table 11A:2   Unpaid leave and delayed wage payment: VCIOM survey results, January 1994 (per cent of sample)

	All	Moscow and St Petersburg	Other large cities	Medium and small cities	Rural areas
Did you have to take any unpaid leave in the last 3 months? If so, for how long?					
No	80	87	77	78	85
Yes, less than one week	6	3	8	6	5
Yes, between one week and one month	8	5	9	10	6
Yes, more than one month	5	3	6	6	3
No answer	1	2	0	0	1
Was last month's income paid on time and completely?					
Yes	41	64	45	37	32
Fully but delayed	29	19	27	30	34
On time but not fully	4	4	4	2	8
Delayed and not fully	8	4	9	9	9
Have not been paid yet	18	7	15	22	17
No answer	0	2	0	0	0

Source: The Russian Centre for Public Opinion Research (VCIOM), 'Survey of the Working Population' (January 1994), in *Bulletin of Information: Economic and Social Change* (March/April 1994).

Appendix 2: The Unemployment Benefit System

Scale of Benefit

1. A worker made redundant and remaining out of work gets:

First 3 months	His last monthly wage, *unindexed* (paid by the employer).
Next 3 months	75 per cent of last wage (average of last 2 months, *unindexed*).
Next 4 months	60 per cent of his last wage (as above).
Next 5 months	45 per cent of his last wage (as above).
Thereafter	'Material assistance': up to the minimum wage plus occasional lump sum payments.

2. Other unemployed workers receive the minimum wage for 12 months and 'material assistance' thereafter.
3. Dependants: Benefit is increased by 10 per cent for each dependant but dependants may also receive 'material assistance'.

Conditions

1. Active job search reported when individual signs on (at least twice a month).
2. Those who refuse 2 appropriate job offers or who were dismissed from their last job for personal reasons may lose benefit for up to 3 months.
3. To get benefit, a redundant worker must register within 2 weeks of losing his job (i.e. at the beginning of the 'first 3 months').
4. No age limit.

Appendix 3: Excess Wage Tax and Employment Incentives

Suppose that an enterprise worker i earns W_i and the other $(n - 1)$ workers earn an average of W. Let t_π be the profit tax rate, N the permitted (tax-free) average wage and t_L the employer's rate of social security taxation.

If worker i is sacked, the firm pays a total tax (including excess wages tax and social security tax) of

$$t_\pi(W - N)(n - 1) + t_L(n - 1)\, W$$

If worker i is kept on at a lower wage (equal to $W_i - \Delta$), the total tax plus the wage of worker i is

$$t_\pi \left[\frac{W_i - \Delta + (n - 1)W}{n} - N \right] n + t_L\, [W_i - \Delta + W(n - 1)] + (W_i - \Delta)$$

It is cheaper to keep the worker on if

$$(t_\pi + t_L)[W_i - \Delta + (n-1)W] - t_\pi nN + (W_i - \Delta) < (t_\pi + t_L)(n-1)W - t_\pi N(n-1)$$

This condition reduces to

$$\frac{W_i - \Delta}{N} < \frac{t_\pi}{t_\pi + t_L + 1}$$

Currently in Russia the profit tax rate is 35 per cent and the social security tax 39 per cent. The deductible wage bill is based on six times the minimum wage – the average wage in April 1994 was roughly 12 times the minimum wage. Using these figures as an example, and assuming that W_i originally equals the average wage (171,500 roubles in April 1994), it is financially advantageous for the enterprise to reduce worker i's wage to roughly 1.2 times the minimum wage (17,200 roubles) rather than to sack him. Thus the excess wages tax provides an incentive for retaining low-paid labour, and thus reduces open unemployment, since the norm is 6 times the minimum and the average is 12 times the minimum. Hence it is financially advantageous for the firm to keep a worker provided the worker is willing to accept a low wage.

Notes

1. We gratefully acknowledge comments and suggestions provided by Liam Halligan and Peter Boone, and by participants of the Stockholm Institute of East European Economics Conference 'Russian Economic Reform in Jeopardy' (June 1994). For further details on many topics in this paper see *Russian Economic Trends*, Whurr Publishers, London.
2. In 1993, unemployment in Poland was 15 per cent, in Hungary 12 per cent, in the Czech Republic 3 per cent and in Slovakia 14 per cent (*Financial Times*, 29 July, 1994, p. 11).
3. Not all these entered unemployment: 0.4 per cent registered at the Employment Office.
4. We gratefully acknowledge the provision of data and comments by T.L. Gorbacheva of Goskomstat.
5. More details data are in Appendix 1, which include the self-employed as well as the employed.
6. The data on involuntary leave and short-time work include only those in industry, construction, transport, communications, personal services and science. But these represent the majority of workers on involuntary leave and short-time work. In Table 11.3 these numbers are therefore expressed as a proportion of the total workforce.
7. For survey-based data on involuntary leave see Appendix 1, Table 11A:2.
8. VCIOM 'Survey of the General Population'. See Appendix 1, Table 11A:2 for details.
9. This casts doubt on the idea that employers increasingly over-record employment.
10. In the US it is found that expanding the work definitions in both criteria (a) and

(b) increase the total number of unemployed by about one-third.

11. Ellam and Layard (1993), *Russian Economic Trends*, vol. 2, no. 2, p. 65.

12. See Ellam and Layard (1993). Perhaps the best way to analyse these phenomena is the basic model of Chapter 2 of Layard, Nickell and Jackman (1991). In this model wages are set to maximize a function that includes both profits and the welfare of the average worker. Workers' welfare depends in turn on wages and the incomes from the existing employer plus the chances of lay-off and the level of outside opportunities. In such a model an anticipated fall in relative demand in the industry will induce a fall in expected employment and in relative wages. But eventually, if relative demand stopped changing, relative wages would gradually revert to their former level, once enough workers had left the industry.

In the model just described managers set employment to maximize profit, after wages have been set and the level of demand has been revealed. In an alternative model, wages and employment would be jointly determined, but in such a model it would be difficult to explain the scale of positive hiring.

13. For three-year changes we have, as we expect, small effects: for 1982–85, a coefficient of 0.13 and for 1983–86, a coefficient of 0.02. The analysis above was kindly conducted by Steve Nickell and covers 59 manufacturing firms, using CBI wage settlement data.

14. A *propiska* (or residence permit) is needed to be able to live in most major Russian cities.

15. During the voucher programme of industrial privatization in Russia (December 1992–June 1994) the most frequently chosen mechanism of privatization involved 51 per cent of the enterprise's shares going to the enterprise's employees.

16. For a detailed exposition of the workings of the excess wages tax see Roxburgh and Shapiro (1994).

17. In 1993 the tax operated on average wages above four times the minimum wage. The tax rate was 32 per cent on excess wages between four and eight times the minimum wages and 50 per cent on the part of excess wages above eight times the minimum wage.

18. Appendix 2 shows the necessary condition.

19. In the Soviet Union until at least the late 1980s, being unemployed for more than a certain period of time was a punishable offence.

20. See Layard, Nickell and Jackman (1991).

21. See for example R. Layard (1982).

References

Aukutsionek, S. and Kapelyushnikov, R. (1994) 'The Labor Market in 1993', *Russian Economic Barometer* 1994, no. 1.

Ellam, M. and Layard, R. (1993) 'Prices, Income and Hardship', in A. Åslund and R. Layard (eds) *Changing the Economic System in Russia*, Pinter, London, pp. 39–61.

Feldstein, M.S. (1975) 'The Importance of Temporary Layoffs', *Brookings Papers on Economic Activity* 3, pp. 725–44.

Goskomstat (1994) 'The Russian Federation Labour Market in 1993', mimeo, Moscow.

Government of the Russian Federation (1993, 1994) *Russian Economic Trends*, Whurr Publishers, London.

Jackman, R., Layard, R. and Scott, A. (1992) 'Unemployment in Eastern Europe', mimeo, London School of Economics, London.

Layard, R. (1982) 'Is incomes policy the answer to unemployment?', *Economica* 49, August, pp. 219–39.

Layard, R., Nickell, S. and Jackman, R. (1991) *Unemployment*, Oxford University Press, Oxford.

Layard, R., Nickell, S. and Jackman, R. (1994) *The Unemployment Crisis*, Oxford University Press, Oxford.

Oswald, A. and Blanchflower, D. (1995) 'An introduction to the wage curve', *Journal of Economic Perspectives* 9(3), pp. 153–67.

Roxburgh, I.W. and Shapiro, J.C. (1994), 'Excess Wages Tax', *Socio-Economic Survey*, no. 17, Moscow.

The Russian Centre for Public Opinion Research (VCIOM) 'Survey of the General Population' (1993 and 1994, various months) and 'Survey of the Working Population' (1993, various months), in *Bulletin of Information: Economic and Social Change*, Aspect Press, Moscow.

Russian Economic Barometer (1994) various issues.

Epilogue
Anders Åslund

Five years have passed since the reform team led by Yegor T. Gaidar bravely launched Russia's leap to a market economy. At the time, neither the reform ministers nor their multiple opponents thought they would last for long. Indeed, the reform ministers called themselves a kamikaze cabinet, which did not enhance their credibility, though it did reflect reality.

Half a decade is a sufficiently long period for an evaluation. The Russian economic transformation can be assessed from many perspectives. First, what is the current state of affairs? Second, what was the main problem? Third, what could have been done to improve the performance or solve the main problem earlier? Fourth, what can we learn from the experiences of other post-Communist countries? Fifth, where is Russia going today? Finally, I would like to add a personal note on what happened to the people who undertook the reform.

An Economic Overview

The task of the reformers was to build capitalism — a market economy with a stable currency based on private ownership and the rule of law. The ultimate outcome of these measures should be to build economic welfare — economic growth and a growing standard of living. In addition, a certain degree of equity is desirable, even if socialist egalitarianism is nothing to aspire to.

A substantial liberalization did occur at the beginning of 1992, but two-thirds of exports remained regulated, and the distortions of the still-controlled prices were enormous. In the spring, the state price of oil was only 1 per cent of the world market price. Energy, agriculture and trade in general have been subject to persistent regulations, as detailed in Marek Dabrowski's chapter. The regulations, in turn, have given rise to plenty of arbitrage between state-controlled and free prices as well as corruption. Yet, deregulation has continued, which appears to have been reflected in the crime rate — it doubled from 1988 till 1992, but it has stagnated since 1993.

The most apparent problem with the Russian transition from a collapsed socialist economy to a market economy has been the persistent high inflation.

182

Table 12.1 Results of Russia's economic transformation, 1992–96
(Annual change in per cent, if nothing else is indicated)

	1992	1993	1994	1995	1996
Inflation (CPI)*	2510	840	215	131	22
GDP	−15	−9	−13	−4	−6
Export	−17	11	14	20	9
Trade balance (bn $)	5.4	11.5	16.2	21.9	28
Consumption	−39	8	8	−6	−1
Unemployment**	4.8	5.7	7.5	8.8	9.3
Gini coefficient**	0.33	0.398	0.409	0.381	0.375

Sources: Russian Economic Trends, vol. 5, no. 2, pp. 96, 105, 146, 153, 164–5; vol. 6,
no. 1, pp. 6, 76, 93, 112, 124; Maleva (1996), p. 48.
Notes: * December over December.
  ** End of year.

Inflation peaked at 2500 per cent in 1992, and it has finally been brought under control only in 1996 – to slightly over 20 per cent a year (see Table 12.1).

Statistics on privatization tend to be approximate or partial. However, the official claim is that about 70 per cent of the Russian economy, both in terms of GDP and labour force, pertains to the private sector. Trade and consumer services have been almost completely privatized, as well as the vast majority of large industrial enterprises. Curiously, infrastructure appears to have been more privatized than agriculture, because agriculture has been a fortress of Communist resistance against market economic reforms, contrary to what many had anticipated.

Institutional change is difficult to measure, but quite a lot has been accomplished. Russia has become a democracy, which has held two democratic presidential elections and two democratic parliamentary elections. In December 1993, a new constitution was adopted through a referendum. Russia has free and analytical media. Freedom of association has taken hold. Plenty of new legislation has been adopted, including a substantial Civic Code and a company law. From the beginning of 1995, Russian enterprises have tended to utilise the economic courts to settle their claims.

However, the accomplishments in the real economy are not very impressive to date. Output and the standard of living have fallen substantially. Russia is a telling illustration of how harmful high inflation is to output. Throughout the post-Communist world, economic growth has only returned after inflation has been brought below 40 per cent a year – usually one year later (Fischer, *et al.*, 1996). Even in 1996, Russian output is slumping by about 5 per cent. Thus, the total decline in GDP has been about 39 per cent in the five years 1992–96 (see Table 12.1). Originally, the statistics showed an even greater decrease in GDP, and presumably statistical revisions will further reduce the measured fall in output, but the fact remains that the decline has been substantial.

How have conditions of life evolved after Andrei Illarionov, Richard Layard and Peter Orszag wrote their article? Consumption and the standard of living plummeted in 1992, but recovered in 1993 and 1994, and official consumption has fallen much less than output. Yet, in 1995 as financial stabilization started biting, there was a renewed though less marked drop in the standard of living.

The much touted problem with high and rising income differentials does not look all that bad in the official statistics. In fact, income differentiation actually shrunk in 1995 (see Table 12.1). World Bank statistics, based on household surveys, suggest higher income differentials, but only what is ordinary for middle-income countries, such as Russia (World Bank, 1996, p. 68).

Unemployment has gradually risen, but the current rate of about 9.5 per cent of the labour force remains slightly below the West European level, and the conclusions drawn by Richard Layard and Andrea Richter in their chapter in this volume appear to hold true. Also in other regards, 1995 and 1996 appear to reflect a certain social stabilization.

Yet, the economy has not only contracted, it has been fundamentally restructured. Starkly, the service sector has expanded as a share of GDP, while industry has shrunk as it should, since the USSR was heavily over-industrialized, and it produced plenty of military hardware that was really a form of waste. One reflection of this restructuring is the development of exports. Russian exports halved from 1990 to 1992, but they have risen sharply since 1993, and they are continuing to surge in double digits (see Table 12.1). Imports have not increased correspondingly, and Russia has developed a trade surplus which is very substantial. As Russia has a great need for investment, such a large trade surplus appears somewhat misplaced, but it is a reflection of a certain economic strength.

Essentially, Russia has undertaken the transition to a market economy, though it is a rather messy one, as it is still subject to much more state intervention that the economies of East–Central Europe. However, the transformation has been pretty slow, which has led to relatively high social costs.

Rent-Seeking Was the Fundamental Problem

Why have the social costs been relatively high in Russia? In hindsight, it is obvious that the dominant problem of the transition in Russia was rent-seeking, implying that certain people used the state to their benefits, either reaping monopoly rents thanks to state intervention, or receiving subsidies from the government.

The rent-seeking took primarily three forms: subsidized credits, export rents and import subsidies. In 1992, most credits were issued by the Central Bank of Russia at an interest rate of 10 or 25 per cent per annum, while inflation was 2500 per cent that year. The subsidized credits boosted inflation. The export rents occurred as people with access to raw materials at very low state-controlled prices – often as little as 1 per cent of the world market price – exported them on their own account and took the difference for themselves. Imports of essential foods were subsidized by 99 per cent in 1992. Altogether, these three forms of rents that went to the rich and well-connected amounted to no less than 75 per cent of GDP in 1992 (Åslund, 1996).

The voucher privatization is usually blamed for excessive enrichment by managers, but by comparison it offered managers a tiny flow of resources. In the spring of 1996, the total market capitalization of the 200 most important Russian companies was about 5 per cent of GDP (*Russian Economic Trends*, vol. 5, no. 2, p. 114). The rest of the about 16,000 voucher-privatized large and medium-sized enterprises cannot have been worth more than an additional third. Thus, the total value of the voucher-privatized enterprises, including Gazprom and all the oil companies, was only about 7 per cent of GDP. Of those shares, managers held about 20 per cent according to World Bank surveys. Hence, by 1996 the managers had received less than 2 per cent of GDP from voucher privatization, and that is a total amount, while the financial flows detailed above are given only for the peak year 1992.

Capitalism is undoubtedly about enrichment, and nobody could have expected the transition to be just, so these are not our concerns. The prime problem is rather that rent-seeking encouraged managers to continue living off the state instead of restructuring their enterprises. A rent-seeker does not care about output or enterprises profits, as they tend to be irrelevant to his rent. Therefore, it is not surprising that output fell so sharply as long as rent-seeking through inflationary means remained the preoccupation of managers. Privatization, on the contrary, is by definition a transfer of a finite resource – an enterprise. After that enterprise has been transferred to new owners, they have a palpable incentive to restructure the enterprise and boost its profits and value. This should result in a return to economic growth in due time.

The numbers above run counter to the current myth that the voucher privatization made Russian managers rich. The cause of this pervasive myth appears to be that the voucher privatization was a comparatively open and transparent process, and people tend to exaggerate the value of smoke-stacks and understate the value of invisible financial flows. The problem in Russia was not the early privatization, but the limited liberalization and late stabilization, which caused a prolonged decline in output and the standard of living as well as an extraordinary enrichment of the rent-seekers.

Could the Reforms Have Been More Successful?

With the advantage of hindsight, it is obvious how the economic policy should have been amended. Essentially, four measures were needed to eliminate these forms of rent. An early deregulation of exports and the freeing of domestic prices of export goods (primarily, oil, gas, metals, chemicals and timber) would have led to the instant elimination of export rents. A unification of the exchange rate would have led to the immediate abolition of import rents. An early introduction of positive real interest rates would have annulled the subsidization of credits, which would also have helped sorting out the problems with the rouble zone. These were four simple measures that could have been imposed with the stroke of the pen by the government and the Central Bank. Technically and economically, they harboured no mysteries, and the radical reformers in the Russian government aspired to undertake these very measures.

But was it politically possible to undertake them? It would have been, if the West had been prepared to support the Russian transformation with a standard IMF programme in early 1992. Most of the standard ingredients of a successful economic reform were in place. First, Russia had a strong popularly elected political leader in President Yeltsin, who supported radical reform. Second, he had appointed a very competent reform team under Yegor Gaidar. Third, in his big speech to Parliament on 28 October 1991, President Yeltsin had presented a comprehensive radical reform programme. Fourth, the later so troublesome Russian Parliament had approved this reform speech and extraordinary powers for the President with overwhelming majority.

The important element that was missing was international financial support provided on IMF conditionality. The West did offer commodity credits, but they went straight to the rent-seeking food importers and were positively harmful, as they led to the maintenance of import subsidies. If a standard IMF programme with ordinary financing had been offered, it would have been possible for Yegor Gaidar to undertake all the four measures suggested above from the beginning of January 1992. It was no real problem that Russia was not a member of the IMF as yet. A shadow programme with bilateral financing could have been arranged, if the West has shown the political will. When the IMF finally acted in early 1995 and concluded an ordinary stand-by agreement with Russia with a financing of about $6.8 billion, Russia's finances did stabilize. This could have been done in early 1992, and the problem was that the West did not believe in Russia, President Yeltsin or Yegor Gaidar. This is the line Jeffrey Sachs argued so forcefully in late 1991 and he repeats it in his chapter in this volume.

All the solutions presented here pertain to radical reform or what its adversaries prefer to call 'shock therapy'. However, a broad range of people argue that the problem with Russia is that the radical reformers went too fast. What they concretely suggest is usually:

1. that prices should have been liberalized even more slowly;
2. that the budget deficit should have been even larger;
3. that Russia should have been more protectionist;
4. that privatization should have been slower – or at least different.

From today's perspective, it is easy to evaluate these proposals by posing the question: would such measures have increased or decreased rent-seeking? A slower price deregulation or foreign trade liberalization would have caused even larger import and export rents. A slower fiscal adjustment would have provided more subsidies to the rent-seekers. In addition, it would have caused higher inflation, which would have brought about an even greater fall in output and consumption. A slower privatization would have further delayed enterprise restructuring and thus the recovery of output. The gradualists should face up to reality and acknowledge that their proposals would have led to negative consequences in all regards. Tellingly, their programme was heralded by the rent-seekers. The relevant criticism of the Russian reform program is provided by Marek Dabrowski in his chapter in this volume.

A bizarre gradualist illusion is that the post-Communist state in transition should give additional state resources to the poor. The underlying assumption was that the state was good and strong. All evidence from the former Soviet Union shows, on the contrary, that the state was extremely corrupt and weak. Consequently, it gave as much as possible to the rich and privileged but little to the poor and suffering. The way of improving the fate of the poor was not to let the state divert more resources but less. In short, the issue was to minimize the state so that it did not harm society. Any discretionary state action of such a weak state was likely to help the wrong people.

Russia's Place in an International Comparison

There is a tradition both among Russians and foreign specialists on Russia to treat the country as an incomprehensible mystery that cannot be understood by any laws of social science. One favourite quote of the proponents that Russia is exceptional is the nineteenth-century Russian poet Fedor Tiutchev's line: 'You cannot understand Russia with your intellect'. Another is Winston Churchill's words: 'Russia is a riddle wrapped in a mystery inside an enigma.' However, a nice quote or two are no good substitutes for hard analysis.

Today, there is ample evidence from 27 other countries that formerly belonged to the Soviet bloc. Their experiences are well studied, and the lessons from post-Communist transformation are striking.[1] There is a strong positive correlation between all important reform measures: liberalization, financial stabilization, privatization, private enterprise development and institutional development. The idea that there is choice between doing one radical measure or another is simply wrong. There is no trade-off but, on the contrary, complementarity.

Moreover, the more radical a reform has been in these terms, the smaller the fall in total output, the earlier the rise in output, the smaller the decline in standard of living, and the more even the income distribution. Only the rent-seekers benefit from slow reform, while there are definitely no socially beneficial effects arising.

We can be more specific and compare Russia with the most similar country, namely Ukraine. In 1990, Ukraine's GDP per capita was officially 10 per cent per capita higher than Russia's, but today the Ukrainian average dollar wage is about half of the Russian wage measured in dollars, and it is evident to the bare eye that Ukraine is far worse off economically. The explanation is obvious. For almost three years, Ukraine did all those things the gradualists require. As a result, Ukraine ended up as an unmitigated economic disaster – far worse than Russia by all economic standards. In 1993, its inflation was 10,155 per cent compared to 840 per cent in Russia, and its output continues to fall more than Russia's. It would be hard to find a cultural explanation why the more Western Ukraine should be more backward than Russia. The reason plainly lies in economic policy, which is determined by a few and can be implemented by few top policy-makers. Therefore, there is a great deal of choice. The government and its economic policy do matter.

Admittedly, the former Soviet Union has done collectively far worse than East–Central Europe. Much of this can be explained with the harmful persistence of the rouble zone, as discussed by Jeffrey Sachs and David Lipton as well as Brigitte Granville. However, there are no doubt additional reasons, notably that the elite has been so much less constrained in the former Soviet Union than in East–Central Europe. Thus, it could indulge all the more in rent-seeking. The environment of economic policy matters a great deal, as Sergei Vasiliev has discussed in this volume.

The conclusion, however, is hardly that the government should be less energetic in its reform efforts. Petr Aven's chapter provides a nice illustration. On the one hand, the government is more likely not to succeed in undertaking a very radical policy. On the other hand, it is all the more necessary, and eventually Russia will have to go further towards reducing the role of the state than East–Central Europe for the simple reason that the state functions so much worse in Russia. Who wants corrupt officials to reallocate your money and limit your freedom of action?

Where Is Russia Going?

Today, Russia has become a market economy, with dominant private ownership, though it is a rather distorted market economy. A widespread opinion is that it is impossible to do big business in Russia without having senior government officials as some kind of partners. Income differentials are as great as in Latin America. In fact, Russia is most reminiscent of Latin American crony capitalism most pronounced in the 1970s at the height of world leftism. The state is exploited by the privileged to their own benefit and it is enhancing – not reducing – inequality in society.

Fortunately, this state of affairs can hardly last in Russia. The government collects ever less taxes, so it can no longer afford to pamper the elites as much as before. Furthermore, Russia has not yet returned to growth, and it might not before the arbitrary tax system and the excessive regulations are amended. At the same time, Russians have learned market economics the hard way, and no longer accept unabated rent-seeking. The 'Washington consensus' on the essence of a sound market economy is steadily winning ground in the minds of the Russians. The basic rules of a market economy have been established and block much of the rent-seeking. The new capitalists and the regional pressure groups are ambiguous forces, but they basically favour decentralization and more freedom from the federal state.

Thus, there are many factors that suggest that Russia will be compelled to move as the Latin American countries in the direction of a much more liberal state and economy, but it is not obvious how fast that will happen.

There has been much talk in Russia about a German, Swedish, or East Asian model, but it can be dismissed. All those states have well-functioning governments, while the Russian administration functions like a corrupt Latin American government. Characteristically, the East Asian model is primarily advocated by red directors who want to avoid democracy and competition. West European models are suggested by them as well, but also by social democrats and people who refuse to understand the limitations of the capacity of the Russian state. Russia's real choice is between a Latin American model of the 1970s or today.

What Happened to the Russian Reformers?

The reform ministers were ousted one by one. In May 1992, the first one fell — Vladimir Lopukhin, who had antagonized the mighty energy lobby, headed then as now by Viktor Chernomyrdin. In December 1992, Yegor Gaidar, Petr Aven and Minister of Economy Andrei Nechaev were ousted under pressure from the Parliament. The entry of Boris Fedorov as Minister of Finance salvaged much of the reformist energy in the government, but by January 1994 he felt compelled to resign, as did Gaidar after a brief return. Other original reform ministers have abandoned or moderated their cause. Since then, Russia's reform efforts have been painfully concentrated in one man — Anatoly Chubais. He has accomplished a great deal. He designed and implemented Russia's mass privatization, and he carried out the financial stabilization that eventually succeeded in 1995 and 1996. But one man cannot do everything.

What happened to the reformers? Chubais and his followers, such as Maxim Boycko and Sergei Vasiliev, and a few others remain in government. Initially, many reformers became politicians, notably Yegor Gaidar and Boris Fedorov. However, their success in politics has been rather limited, and gradually many leave politics. Several of our reformers have become important bankers or investment bankers: Petr Aven, Andrei Nechaev, Vladimir Lopukhin, Andrei Kazmin and Boris Fedorov. A few stay in academia — Yegor Gaidar, Andrei Illarionov and Aleksei Ulyukaev. Nobody is really suffering. Most of the Western collaborators have continued working on Russian affairs, and several have produced substantial books on the Russian transformation.[2]

Notes

1. Åslund et al., (1996); World Bank (1996); Banarjee et al., (1995); Citrin and Lahiri (1995); EBRD (1994, 1995, 1996).
2. Apart from the four conference volumes, I would mention Åslund (1995); Boycko, Shleifer and Vishny (1995); Granville (1995); Layard and Parker (1996). The

article by Lipton and Sachs (1992) should also be noticed. Richard Layard has led the publication of *Russian Economic Trends*, which is a quarterly publication with the best current economic statistics and analysis. It has been published for the last five years.

References

Åslund, A. (1995) *How Russia Became a Market Economy*, Brookings, Washington, DC.

Åslund, A. (1996) 'Reform Vs. "Rent-Seeking" in Russia's Economic Transformation', *Transition*, 26 January, pp. 12–16.

Åslund, A., Boone, P. and Johnson, S. (1996) 'How to Stabilize: Lessons from Post-Communist Countries', *Brookings Papers on Economic Activity*, vol. 26, no. 1, pp. 217–313.

Åslund, A. and Dmitriev, M. (eds) (1996) *Sotsialnaya politika v period perekhoda k rynku: problemy i resheniya (Social Policy in the Transition to a Market Economy: Problems and Solutions)*, Carnegie Endowment for International Peace, Moscow.

Banarjee, B., Koen, V., Krueger, T., Lutz, M.S., Marrese, M. and Saavalainen, T.O. (1995) *Road Maps of the Transition: The Baltics, the Czech Republic, Hungary, and Russia*, IMF, Occasional Paper No. 127, Washington, DC.

Boycko, M., Shleifer, M. and Vishny, R. (1995) *Privatizing Russia*, MIT Press, Cambridge, Mass.

Citrin, D.A., and Lahiri, A.K. (eds) (1995) *Policy Experiences and Issues in the Baltics, Russia, and Other Countries of the Former Soviet Union*, IMF, Occasional Paper No. 133, Washington, DC.

European Bank for Reconstruction and Development (EBRD) (1994) *Transition Report*, EBRD, London, October.

European Bank for Reconstruction and Development (EBRD) (1995) *Transition Report 1995*, EBRD, London.

European Bank for Reconstruction and Development (EBRD) (1996) *Transition Report 1996*, EBRD, London.

Fischer, S., Sahay, R. and Vegh, C.A. (1996) 'Stabilization and Growth in Transition Economies: The Early Experience', IMF Working Paper, mimeo, Washington, DC, March.

Government of the Russian Federation (1992–1996) *Russian Economic Trends*, Whurr Publishers, London.

Granville, B. (1995) *The Success of Russian Economic Reforms*, The Royal Institute of International Affairs, London.

Layard, R. and Parker, J. (1996) *The Coming Russian Boom: A Guide to New Markets and Politics*, The Free Press, London.

Lipton, D., and Sachs, J. D. (1992) 'Prospects for Russia's Economic Reforms', *Brookings Papers on Economic Activity*, vol. 22, no. 2, pp. 213–65.

Maleva, T. (1996) 'Differentsiatsiya dokhodov naseleniya v usloviyakh finansovoi stabilizatsii (Differentiation of Incomes of the Population under Financial Stabilization)', in A. Åslund and M. Dmitriev, *Social Policy in the Transition to a Market Economy*, Carnegie Endowment for International Peace, Moscow, pp. 45–62.

World Bank (1996) *From Plan to Market: World Development Report 1996*, Oxford University Press, Oxford.

Index

urban development   27
Uzbekistan   103, 106, 107, 110, 111, 112

value-added tax (VAT)   50, 62, 66
Vasiliev, Sergei   189
Vegh, C. A.   183
Vishny, R.   189
Vnesheconom-bank   57
Vneshtorgbank   102
Volskii, Arkadii   22
voucher system
  in privatization process   69, 70, 73-5, 76,
    173, 180, 185

wage arrears   51, 165-6, 177
wage bargaining   175
wage distribution   146-7, 156, 157
wage flexibility   159, 160-1, 169-71, 172
wage payments   86, 87, 88, 99, 103
wage regulation   15, 47-8, 52, 53, 95, 97,
    134
wage rigidity   160
wages   15, 17, 46, 49-50, 138, 184

average   145-6, 173
excess wage tax   173, 174, 175, 178-9, 180
in independent states   152-4
minimum   15, 150, 151, 158, 167-8
real   6, 43, 137-9, 142, 156, 171
welfare *see* social welfare
Western experience
  of unemployment   174-5
Western support
  for economic reform   123-4, 127, 128,
    129-30, 131-4, 186
Williamson, J.   101, 103
work sharing   175-6
  see also labour market
workers' benefits   160, 172-3
World Bank   127, 144, 184, 185, 187

Yavlinski, Grigorii   18
Yeltsin, Boris   1, 2, 44, 45, 46, 48, 130, 131,
    134, 186
young people *see* children and young
    people
Yugoslavia   25